PENGUIN / PORTFOLIO

HUMANS ARE UNDERRATED

Geoff Colvin, *Fortune*'s senior editor at large, is one of America's most respected journalists. He lectures widely and is the regular lead moderator for the Fortune Global Forum. He appears frequently on TV and is heard daily on the CBS Radio Network, reaching seven million listeners each week. His book *Talent Is Overrated* was a national bestseller and has been translated into a dozen languages.

HUMANS ARE UNDERRATED

WHAT HIGH ACHIEVERS KNOW THAT
BRILLIANT MACHINES NEVER WILL

GEOFF COLVIN

PORTFOLIO / PENGUIN

PORTFOLIO / PENGUIN
An imprint of Penguin Random House LLC
375 Hudson Street
New York, New York 10014
penguin.com

First published in the United States of America by Portfolio / Penguin 2015
This paperback edition with a new preface by Geoff Colvin published 2016

ISBN 9781591847205 (hc.)
ISBN 9780143108375 (pbk.)

Printed in the United States of America
1   3   5   7   9   10   8   6   4   2

Set in Century MT Std
Designed by Spring Hoteling

For my sons, Cristian and Grayson

CONTENTS

CHAPTER SIX | 91
EMPATHY LESSONS FROM COMBAT
How the U.S. Military Learned to Build Human Skills
that Trump Technology, and What It Means for All of Us.

CHAPTER SEVEN | 117
WHAT REALLY MAKES TEAMS WORK
It Isn't What Team Members (Or Leaders) Usually Think.
Instead, It's Deeply Human Processes That Most Teams Ignore.

CHAPTER EIGHT | 141
THE EXTRAORDINARY POWER OF STORY
Why the Right Kind of Narrative, Told by a Person, Is Mightier Than Logic.

CHAPTER NINE | 161
THE HUMAN ESSENCE OF INNOVATION AND CREATIVITY
Computers Can Create, but People Skillfully Interacting
Solve the Most Important Human Problems.

CHAPTER TEN | 178
IS IT A WOMAN'S WORLD?
In the Most Valuable Skills of the Coming Economy,
Women Hold Strong Advantages over Men.

CHAPTER ELEVEN | 193
WINNING IN THE HUMAN DOMAIN
Some Will Love a World That Values Deep Human Interaction.
Others Won't. But Everyone Will Need to Get Better—And Can.

PREFACE

I was talking with a group of staff members at Boston Children's Hospital about the message of this book, discussing with wonder the latest developments in autonomous surgical robots. These new devices won't be like the original surgical robots, which weren't robots at all but rather power tools operated by human surgeons. These devices will perform surgical procedures all by themselves. They have eyes far sharper than any human's eyes, brains that can hold far more of the latest research than any human brain could absorb, and "hands" that are steadier, surer, more precise than any human's hands. I reported that in addition to university research on such devices, a number of medical device companies were developing them, and Google was rumored to be doing so. Autonomous robots had already begun to perform low-risk procedures such as extracting and transplanting tiny hair follicles on men's heads for cosmetic purposes—faster, more efficiently (more of the extracted follicles were usable), and with more natural results than any human surgeon could achieve. I mentioned to the group what Peter Diamandis, Silicon Valley entrepreneur and founder of the X Prize Foundation, had told me enthusiastically when we were discussing this topic a short time before: "Not only are autonomous surgical robots on the way, but patients will demand them—because they'll be better than human surgeons."

At this point, a surgeon, still in his scrubs from the morning's work, raised his hand. I braced myself for a stern lecture on the surgeon's art and how no mere machine could ever supplant this uniquely human skill that he had spent so many hard years developing. But that's not what I heard.

"This is coming," he said quietly. "I can see it. It's in the operating room already. In some places, automated anesthesiology is taking the place of human anesthesiologists right now." He was right. The technology is FDA approved, and while a human must still supervise the devices, he can monitor several surgical procedures simultaneously instead of being physically present in the operating room. "It's only a matter of time," the surgeon said. "I have gray hair. I'll be fine. But I really don't know what to tell young surgeons about the kind of career they'll have."

As technology continues to advance faster than we dare to imagine, the anxiety that prompted me to write *Humans Are Underrated* has only intensified, and all evidence suggests it will continue to do so for a long time. We've accommodated ourselves to technology taking over jobs in factories and offices, at airline check-in counters and supermarket checkout counters, but—in operating rooms? Where will it all end? And so we reach, with increasing urgency, the question that I set out to answer: In a world like that, how will we poor humans add value?

The optimistic answer proposed in this book—that we will add our greatest value through skills of deep human interaction, which are innately within us and can be built and extended by all of us—has looked stronger every day since the book appeared. In addition, as the trends identified here have continued, the issues of exactly how that answer might be applied have begun to crystalize around four big questions. As answers emerge, the way forward is becoming clearer.

Is advancing technology leading to more jobs or fewer, to better jobs or worse?

This is the great big question, getting bigger. Since the dawn of humanity, advancing technology has always eliminated some jobs, but it has always created even more jobs, and those new jobs have been, on average, better than the old ones. That's the foundation of the economic miracle of the past few centuries, with billions of people living dramatically better, healthier, longer lives. Today, the economic traditionalists argue that many people are needlessly freaking out because, as usual, we can identify perfectly the jobs that are being eliminated but cannot even imagine the new jobs that will be created; have faith, they say, and all will be well, just as it always has been. The skeptics respond that technology is now advancing so fast that the classic pattern cannot hold, and by the way, maybe you've noticed that living standards across wide swaths of the developed world have stopped improving; if technology is still working its economic miracle, it's taking its own sweet time.

Continued economic stagnation in countries where technology is most advanced has drawn adherents to the skeptics, even those who argue radically that we're headed for a future of mass unemployment, a future in which improving technology becomes almost infinitely more skilled than we are at most of the activities by which we earn a living. In that world, millions and maybe eventually

billions of us globally won't be able to support ourselves because
we won't be able to do anything better than machines. So how
would we live? Some of the skeptics have an answer. "The idea of
a Universal Basic Income is taking off," say the promoters of a
"Create-a-thon for Basic Income in the United States." The problem they can solve, they say, is that "improvements in technology
are disrupting the traditional employment model and automating/
transforming more and more existing jobs in a way that so far benefits a privileged few." Their simple solution is to give every person
an equal amount of money every month. Their aim is to "transform the accelerating loss of jobs to machines from a fear to a
goal." And before you dismiss this idea as obviously loony, note
that Finland and Ontario are experimenting with it.

Maybe we really are headed for an unimaginably different
future. It happens; life in a developed economy today would have
been unimaginable 120 years ago. Or maybe the transformation
will be subtler. Northwestern University economist Robert J. Gordon, in a monumental book titled *The Rise and Fall of American
Growth*, argues that, "The problem created by the computer age is
not mass unemployment but the gradual disappearance of good,
steady, middle-level jobs that have been lost not just to robots and
algorithms but to globalization and outsourcing to other countries,
together with the concentration of job growth in routine manual
jobs that offer relatively low wages." That explanation squares well
with the stagnation of living standards.

The all-will-be-well school points out reassuringly that as the
U.S. economy emerged from the 2008–2009 recession, the unemployment rate fell to very low levels around 5 percent. Sounds
good, but look closer. Something strange and disturbing is going
on, and it's consistent with technology taking over jobs that
humans want to do. The unemployment rate is a crude measure
that doesn't distinguish between full-time and part-time work; in

addition, it counts as unemployed only people who have taken recent steps to find work. Looking underneath that number, we find that even when the unemployment rate had fallen to 5 percent, the lowest in nine years, the number of people unemployed twenty-seven weeks or more was still higher than it had been at its worst in the twelve years before the recession. The number who wanted a job now and were available but were discouraged and had given up looking because they believed no job was available was still higher than at its worst in the previous twenty-five years, which encompassed two earlier recessions. The number who were working part-time solely for economic reasons was also higher than it had been at its worst in the twenty-five years before the 2008–2009 recession.

By those measures and others, what used to be as bad as it got for workers has begun to look like as good as it gets. Why? After reviewing changes in employment and income, economist and former Secretary of the Treasury Lawrence Summers concludes that advances in technology "increasingly take the form of capital that effectively substitutes for labor." One result, he observes, is that "wage rates fall."

As this trend persists and technology's pressure on workers builds, the key to surviving and thriving lies increasingly in the skills of deep human interaction. An extreme example illustrates. The number of people classified as bank tellers in U.S. government statistics held steady from 1980 to 2010 despite the onslaught of automated teller machines. How could that be? MIT labor economist David Autor observed in an article that it happened because tellers gave up "routine cash-handling tasks" and moved to "'relationship banking' . . . forging relationships with customers and introducing them to additional bank services. . . ." They're still called tellers in the official statistics, but they aren't tellers as most of us understand the term; their work has been entirely transformed. And note how. Instead of being human machines behind a counter, they're now sitting at desks building relationships. The required skills are completely different, and they're the skills of human interaction. For tellers and many others, these deeply human abilities are the high-value skills that are increasingly separating the economy's winners from the losers.

Will advancing technology help or hurt women?

In this book I argue that women are uniquely advantaged as skills of human interaction become more valuable. Research shows clearly that, on average, women are better than men at these skills. But do we really need the research? Don't we all know from life experience that when it comes to discerning what another person is feeling or thinking, to responding appropriately, to understanding the motivations of others, that women generally are just better? It's important to note that research supports this notion "on average." That doesn't mean that every woman is better than every man at these skills; in addition, both men and women can improve their skills. But in a world that increasingly values these skills, women on average are—for reasons of nature and nurture, as I explain— likely to play a growing role in creating economic value.

That's the good news. The bad news is that women may also be more harmed than men by advancing technology, at least in the near term. The job held by more men than any other in the United States is truck driver; at last count there were 3.5 million of them. That job is going away—not tomorrow, but eventually, as the accelerating advance of autonomous vehicles has made clear. The job held by more women than any other in the United States is office and administrative worker; there are 3.5 million of them. Many, perhaps most, of those jobs are going away too, and much sooner than truck driver jobs.

Both those trends are unstoppable. The open question is what millions of men and women will be doing in future years instead of driving trucks and working in offices. Sitting at home collecting their universal basic income? Scraping by with lower-paid jobs that are the best they can get? Or working at well-paid jobs we can't identify because they haven't been invented yet? The answer will certainly include at least some of that last category. The effect on women will depend on at least three variables: the number of such jobs that are created; whether those jobs particularly reward skills of deep human interaction, as I believe they will; and whether women capitalize on their advantages in such skills by seeking those jobs.

No one can predict those variables. My guess is that, as always in the real world, multiple trends will play out simultaneously, helping and harming women, and that, as always, the effects will be distributed unevenly. Many of the new jobs will require all of us to think of work in new ways, and some people just won't be comfortable doing that. Some of those jobs, while valuing human skills, will also require new kinds of training that some people won't want or be able to do. Nonetheless, evidence suggests that, over time and across the economy, the downsides of advancing technology will affect employment of men and women more or less equally, while women will bring their specific, increasingly valuable advantage to the new world of work, benefiting them disproportionately.

The changes may be beginning already. Here's a hint of how. USAA, the big U.S. financial services company, conducted an experiment with a sample of customers to learn how they prefer to interact with the firm. Customers mostly liked the convenience and speed of interacting online. If they wanted to talk to a representative, they could call or put in an online request and speak with whomever happened to be available. But when stock markets plunged in early 2016, the number of customers wanting to talk with someone rocketed, and the company tried something new.

When you asked online to speak with someone, you'd see the names and photos of several representatives, and you could choose the one you wanted to talk to. USAA got a big surprise: Customers chose women 95 percent of the time. The experimenters analyzed the data to see if women customers were choosing female advisers more than men were, or if there was some kind of correlation based on ethnicity or other factors. There wasn't. When customers felt the need to bypass technology and talk to a human being, they overwhelmingly wanted to talk to a woman.

Not all women will be winners as these trends advance—the world is too big and complicated for that—but I believe that women on the whole will be.

Can government policy help people adapt as advancing technology revalues skills?

Big question, short answer. Government programs to help workers acquire new skills have historically proven to be very modest successes. Two major exceptions are instructive. The first was the "high school movement" of the late nineteenth and early twentieth centuries, when a high school education in the United States was transformed from an experience for the few to an experience for the many. This transformation prepared millions for a new world of work that required higher levels of classroom-taught skills and was a major factor in the American economy's explosive growth through most of the twentieth century. The high school movement was not a federal initiative. As the name suggests, it was a realization that swept the country and was implemented individually by thousands of local governments.

The second exception to the mostly modest effectiveness of broad-scale government training efforts was the GI Bill, which sent some 2.2 million U.S. service members to colleges and universities after World War II. The program perfectly matched the moment, when the economy was ready to reward college-level skills on a large scale. The broad upgrade of America's human capital helped power the U.S. economy into the 1970s.

Today, as employers, educators, and researchers focus on the fundamentally new type of skills that work demands—deeply human skills—policymakers mostly aren't there yet. They are pulling the levers they know how to pull—adjusting unemployment benefits, subsidizing traditional education in the spirit of the GI Bill, talking about reforming the tax code without ever doing it. Their best bet may instead be heeding the lesson of the high school movement, letting answers emerge from a thousand experiments by local governments, nonprofits, and private enterprise. Frustratingly for policymakers, who like to make things happen, it may be more effective in this case to allow things to happen. That's especially true given that, at the federal level, discussion of any significant issue now usually degenerates into party-based warfare.

What about our kids?

This is the most emotionally freighted question. As I discuss the topics of this book with groups of every kind, this issue is the one that is guaranteed to come up every time, even if I don't mention it. Anxiety centers on two specific worries.

One is that, at just the time when skills of human interaction are becoming the key to people's economic value, young people are abandoning those very skills in favor of digital communication. We've all seen teenagers sitting together at a table, silently absorbed in their phones, texting furiously—and if we dare to engage them in conversation, we find that they're texting one another. In an economy that will increasingly value the most human of interactions, many people ask, how can my company prosper by hiring this generation?

The only answer is that not all young people are like that, but virtually all of them harbor, somewhere inside, a hunger for deep human connection, and that yearning is waiting to be brought out and freed. Employers will have to screen carefully for the skills they value, and as they do, the message gets back to parents and schools that employers want human skills. I describe in this book how educators from kindergarten to graduate school are starting to develop empathy and other human skills in students, and the trend is accelerating. Employers are doing the same. I've spoken with bank managers who have built simulated branches in which to train employees in human interaction, and with hotel executives who put employees at every level through intense simulations to train them in effective interaction with guests and with one another. In chapter 5, I describe the U.S. Army's pioneering work in training soldiers for "the human domain," and that work continues. The army is developing new software to train commanders in the human element of effective communication; an Army Research Laboratory manager explained to me, "We tell them there are flight simulators and truck simulators. This is a people simulator."

Yes, your company can still prosper if it responds to new requirements and a new generation with new ways of thinking.

The second concern looks further ahead. What should my elementary school or high school kids be studying? What jobs will be there for them when they graduate? Many, many parents ask me these questions, and it's hard to give a confident answer. The best I can do is begin with the classic advice that their kids should sample all disciplines and study whatever they like, and then I add that in the vast majority of fields, the high-value differentiator will be human skills. Business leaders across the economy are realizing it—software writers, doctors, lawyers, even a publication for accountants cited my book, quoting an industry leader saying that "collaboration, creativity, anticipation, empathy, and trust—these 'success skills' are increasingly the differentiators for CPAs."

While schools are making progress in teaching the "success skills," parents shouldn't count on schools to carry the burden. Much of the job will have to be done at home, especially since kids' digital immersion is weakening their skills of human interaction around the clock.

Popular culture is stoking parents' anxiety about the future. In this book I state explicitly my assumptions that people, not machines, will remain in charge of the economy and the world, and that a truly indistinguishable humanoid robot will not exist in our grandchildren's lifetimes. But Hollywood cannot resist the opposite assumptions, and the resulting movies and TV shows, which are multiplying quickly, usually envision a near future that is very dark. Could I be wrong and they be right? Absolutely. No one knows. I can't blame parents for being worried; like the surgeon, they may figure they're old enough to survive the revolution, but their kids may not be.

So let's confront the question of whether the machines will one day become just like us, only better. The best way to think about it is not by studying technology but rather by pondering a very old, extremely profound question that in Philosophy 101 was called dualism. It's about your mind, what some would call your soul or your spirit, the part of you that falls in love or laughs at a stupid joke or is seized by an inspiration to create a work of art. Does that part of you arise entirely from the chemicals and electricity in your brain? Or does it come from something separate, independent of the physical you? That is, are you most fundamentally one thing or two things?

If you believe you're one thing, that your mind arises entirely from your brain, then you probably must conclude that the indistinguishable humanoid robot is inevitable. It's only a matter of time before scientists can match the physical processes in your skull with physical processes in a box. But if you believe you're two things, something more than physics and chemistry inside your skull, then you can at least hold out the possibility that scientists will never create a complete imitation human. Your kids and all humanity will remain forever unique.

I can't tell you the answer to the question. For many people it's a matter of religion, not just reason. I believe it's important to keep thinking about this question, to discuss it with friends and family, as technology advances; an ancient philosophical issue is becoming current and practical. I also believe that regardless of your answer, it doesn't change the best advice for you and your kids when you get up tomorrow morning. Follow your passion, study it assiduously, and as you pursue it, strive in addition to become more intensely human. Doing so will improve your material well-being as the economy evolves, and it will bring you a richer, fuller life. All the evidence I see says that will be sound advice for a long time to come.

HUMANS ARE UNDERRATED

CHAPTER ONE
COMPUTERS ARE IMPROVING FASTER THAN YOU ARE

As Technology Becomes More Awesomely Able, What Will Be the High-Value Human Skills of Tomorrow?

I am standing on a stage, behind a waist-high podium with my first name on it. To my right is a woman named Vicki; she's behind an identical podium with her name on it. Between us is a third podium with no one behind it, just the name "Watson" on the front. We are about to play *Jeopardy!*

This is the National Retail Federation's mammoth annual conference at New York City's Javits Center, and in addition to doing some onstage moderating, I have insanely agreed to compete against IBM's Watson, the cognitive computing system, whose power the company wants to demonstrate to the 1,200 global retail leaders sitting in front of me. Watson's celebrated defeat of *Jeopardy!*'s two greatest champions is almost a year old, so I'm not expecting this to go well. But I'm not prepared for what hits me.

We get to a category called "Before and After at the Movies." *Jeopardy!* aficionados have seen this category many times over the years, but I have never heard of it. First clue, for $200: "Han

Solo meets up with Lando Calrissian while time traveling with Marty McFly."

Umm . . . what?

Watson has already buzzed in. "What is *The Empire Strikes Back to the Future*?" it responds correctly.

It picks the same category for $400: "James Bond fights the Soviets while trying to romance Ali MacGraw before she dies." I'm still struggling with the concept, but Watson has already buzzed in. "What is *From Russia with Love Story*?" Right again.

By the time I figure this out, Watson is on the category's last clue: "John Belushi & the boys set up their fraternity in the museum where crazy Vincent Price turns people into figurines." The correct response, as Watson instantly knows, is "What is *Animal House of Wax*?" Watson has run the category.

My humiliation is not totally unrelieved. I do get some questions right in other categories, and Watson gets some wrong. But at the end of our one round I have been shellacked. I actually don't remember the score, which must be how the psyche protects itself. I just know for sure that I have witnessed something profound.

Realize that Watson is not connected to the Internet. It's a freestanding machine just like me, relying only on what it knows. It has been loaded with the entire contents of Wikipedia, for example, and much, much more. No one types the clues into Watson; it has to hear and understand the emcee's spoken words, just as I do. In addition, Watson is intentionally slowed down by a built-in delay when buzzing in to answer a clue. We humans must use our prehistoric muscle systems to push a button that closes a circuit and sounds the buzzer. Watson could do it at light speed with an electronic signal, so the developers interposed a delay to level the playing field. Otherwise I'd never have a prayer of winning, even if we both knew the correct response. But, of course, even with the delay, I lost.

So let's confront reality: Watson is smarter than I am. In fact,

I'm surrounded by technology that's better than I am at sophisticated tasks. Google's autonomous car is a better driver than I am. The company has a whole fleet of vehicles that have driven hundreds of thousands of miles with only one accident while in autonomous mode, when one of the cars was rear-ended by a human driver at a stoplight. Computers are better than humans at screening documents for relevance in the discovery phase of litigation, an activity for which young lawyers used to bill at an impressive hourly rate. Computers are better at detecting some kinds of human emotion, despite our million years of evolution that was supposed to make us razor sharp at that skill.

One more thing. I competed against Watson in early 2012. Back then it was the size of a bedroom. As I write, it has shrunk to the size of three stacked pizza boxes, yet it's also 2,400 percent faster.

More broadly, information technology is doubling in power roughly every two years. I am not—and I'll guess that you're not either.

A NIGHTMARE FUTURE?

The mind-bending progress of information technology makes it easier every day for us to imagine a nightmare future. Computers become so capable that they're simply better at doing thousands of tasks that people now get paid to do. Sure, we'll still need people to make high-level decisions and to develop even smarter computers, but we won't need enough such workers to keep the broad mass of working-age people employed, or for their living standard to rise. And so, in the imaginary nightmare future, millions of people will lose out, unable finally to best the machine, struggling hopelessly to live the lives they thought they had earned.

In fact, as we shall see, substantial evidence suggests that

technology advances really are playing a role in increasingly stub-
born unemployment, slow wage growth, and the trend of college
graduates taking jobs that don't require a bachelor's degree. If
technology is actually a significant cause of those trends, then the
miserable outlook becomes hard to dismiss.

But that nightmare future is not inevitable. Some people have
suffered as technology has taken away their jobs, and more will do
so. But we don't need to suffer. The essential reality to grasp, larger
than we may realize, is that the very nature of work is changing,
and the skills that the economy values are changing. We've been
through these historic shifts a few times before, most famously in the
Industrial Revolution. Each time, those who didn't recognize the
shift, or refused to accept it, got left behind. But those who embraced
it gained at least the chance to lead far better lives. That's happening this time as well.

While we've seen the general phenomenon before, the way that
work changes is different every time, and this time the changes are
greater than ever. The skills that will prove most valuable are no longer the technical, classroom-taught, left-brain skills that economic
advances have demanded from workers over the past 300 years.
Those skills will remain vitally important, but important isn't the
same as valuable; they are becoming commoditized and thus a diminishing source of competitive advantage. The new high-value skills are
instead part of our deepest nature, the abilities that literally define us
as humans: sensing the thoughts and feelings of others, working pro-
ductively in groups, building relationships, solving problems together,
expressing ourselves with greater power than logic can ever achieve.
These are fundamentally different types of skills than those the economy has valued most highly in the past. And unlike some previous
revolutions in what the economy values, this one holds the promise of
making our work lives not only rewarding financially, but also richer
and more satisfying emotionally.

Step one in reaching that future is to think about it in a new way. We shouldn't focus on beating computers at what they do. We'll lose that contest. Nor should we even follow the inviting path of trying to divine what computers inherently cannot do—because they can do more every day.

The relentless advance of computer capability is of course merely Moore's Law at work, as it has been for decades. Still, it's hard for us to appreciate all the implications of this simple trend. That's because most things in our world slow down as they get bigger and older; for evidence, just look in the mirror. It's the same with other living things, singly or in groups. From protozoa to whales, everything eventually stops growing. So do organizations. A small start-up company can easily grow 100 percent a year, but a major Fortune 500 firm may struggle to grow 5 percent.

Technology isn't constrained that way. It just keeps getting more powerful. Sony's first transistor radio was advertised as pocket-sized, but it was actually too big, so the company had salesmen's shirts specially made with extra-large pockets; that radio had five transistors. Intel's latest chip, the size of your thumbnail, has five billion transistors, and its replacement will have ten billion. Today's infotech systems, having become as awesomely powerful as they are, will be 100 percent more awesomely powerful in two years. Moore's law must end eventually, but new technologies in development could be just as effective, and better algorithms are already multiplying computing power in some cases even more than hardware improvements are doing. To imagine that technology won't keep advancing at a blistering pace seems unwise.

Consider what is being doubled. It isn't just year-before-last's achievement in computing power. What gets doubled every two years is everything that has been achieved in the history of computing power up to that point. Back when that progression meant going from five transistors in a device to ten, it didn't much change the world. Now that it means going from five billion transistors on a tiny chip to ten billion to twenty billion to forty billion—that's three doublings, just six years—it means literally more than we can imagine.

That's because it's so unlike everything else in our world in ways even beyond physical growth rates. For us humans, learning, like growing, gets harder with time. When humans learn to do something, we make slow progress at first—learning how to hold the golf club or turn the steering wheel smoothly—then rapid progress as we get the hang of it, and then our advancement slows down. Pretty soon, most of us are as good as we're going to get. We can certainly keep improving through devoted practice, but each advance is typically a bit smaller than the one before.

Information technology is just the opposite. When a doubling of computing power for a given price meant going from five transistors to ten, it made a device smarter by only five transistors. Now, after many doublings, the current doubling will make a device smarter by five billion transistors, and the next one will make a device smarter by ten billion.

While people get more skilled by ever smaller increments, computers get more capable by ever larger ones.

The issue is clear and momentous. As technology becomes more capable, advancing inexorably by ever longer two-year strides and acquiring abilities that are increasingly complex and difficult, what will be the high-value human skills of tomorrow—the jobs that will pay well for us and our kids, the competencies that will distinguish winning companies, the traits of dominant nations? To put it starkly: What will people do better than computers?

CHAPTER TWO
GAUGING THE CHALLENGE

A Growing Army of Experts Wonder If Just Maybe
the Luddites Aren't Wrong Anymore.

In the movie *Desk Set*, a 1957 romantic comedy starring Katharine Hepburn and Spencer Tracy, Hepburn plays the head of the research department at a major TV network. Today a TV network's research department focuses entirely on audience research, but back then it was a general information resource for anyone at the company, and yes, networks and other companies really had such departments. Equipped with two floors of reference works and other books, its staff stood ready to supply any information that any employee might ask for—the opening lines of *Hiawatha*, the weight of the earth, the names of Santa's reindeer (all of which were queries for Hepburn's department in the movie). That is, employees could pick up the phone, call Katharine Hepburn's character, and ask in their own words for any information, and she and her staff would search a vast trove of data and return an answer far faster than the caller could ever have found it.

Hepburn's character is named Miss Watson.

All is well until one day the network boss decides to install a computer—an "electronic brain," they call it—named EMERAC (a clear reference to ENIAC and UNIVAC, the wonder machines of the era). It was invented by the Spencer Tracy character. Shortly before Miss Watson hears the news that EMERAC is coming to her department, she sees it demonstrated elsewhere, translating Russian into Chinese, among other feats. Her assessment, as expressed to her coworkers: "Frightening. Gave me the feeling that maybe, just maybe, people were a little bit outmoded."

The Tracy character, Richard Sumner, shows up to install the machine, and Miss Watson and her staff assume they'll be fired once it's up and running. In a memorable scene, he demonstrates the machine to a group of network executives and explains its advantages:

Sumner: "The purpose of this machine, of course, is to free the worker—"

Miss Watson: "You can say that again."

Sumner: "—to free the worker from the routine and repetitive tasks and liberate his time for more important work."

Miss Watson and the rest of the research staff are indeed fired, but before they can clean out their desks, EMERAC botches some requests it can't handle—a call for information on Corfu, for example, returns reams of useless data on the word "curfew," while a staffer scurries into the stacks and gets the needed answers the old-fashioned way. And then it turns out that the researchers actually should not have received termination notices after all. An EMERAC computer in the payroll department had gone haywire and fired everyone in the company. The error is corrected, the research staffers keep their jobs and learn to work with EMERAC, Miss Watson wisely decides to marry the Spencer Tracy character and not the Gig Young character (part of the mandatory romantic subplot), and once again all is well.

Desk Set is extraordinarily prescient about some future capabilities and uses of computers, and also faithful to the fearful popular sentiment about them. Of course, Miss Watson is exactly the human predecessor of today's Watson cognitive computing system. (Are the names a coincidence? The film's opening credits include this intriguing one: "The filmmakers gratefully acknowledge the cooperation and assistance of the International Business Machines Corporation." IBM's founder was Thomas J. Watson, namesake of today's Watson computing system, and his son was CEO at the time of the film.) EMERAC as explained by Sumner in the film is remarkably similar to today's Watson: All the information in all those books in the research library—encyclopedias, atlases, Shakespeare's plays—was fed into the machine, which could then respond instantly to natural-language requests (typed, not spoken) for information. Even in 1957 the idea was clear; the technology just wasn't ready.

The research staffers' fears about being replaced by a computer were also a sign of things to come. "I hear thousands of people are losing their jobs to these electronic brains," one of them says. She heard right, and the thousands would become millions. At the same time, the corporate response intended to calm those fears has remained just what Sumner said in the movie—that computers would "free the worker from the routine and repetitive tasks" so he or she could do "more important work." To this day it's striking how everyone working on advanced information technology seems to feel defensive about the implicit threat of eliminating jobs and takes pains to say that they're not trying to replace people. "We're not intending to replace humans," said Kirstin Petersen of Harvard's Wyss Institute for Biologically Inspired Engineering, in explaining the institute's development of "swarm robotics," in which large numbers of small, simple robots do construction jobs. "We're intending to work in situations where humans can't work or it's impractical for them to work." IBM

has always said that Watson is intended to supplement human decision making, not replace it—"to make people more intelligent about
what they do."

Most important, and perhaps surprising, is that even the film's
happily-ever-after ending was realistic in the large sense, at least
with regard to employment, if not romance. Viewed on the scale of
the entire economy, technology's advance indeed has not cost jobs,
despite the widespread fears. Quite the opposite. And those fears
are much more deeply rooted than most of us realize.

THE NEW SKEPTICS

The conventional view is that fear of technology arose when technology started upending the economic order in the eighteenth century, at
the start of the Industrial Revolution in Britain. But the fears were
already well entrenched, and innovators were already sounding
remarkably modern in arguing that technology was a boon, not a
bane, for workers. In the late sixteenth century, an English clergyman
named William Lee invented a machine for knitting stockings—a
wonderful advance, he believed, because it would liberate hand knit-
ters from their drudgery. When he demonstrated it to Queen Elizabeth I in 1590 or so and asked for a patent, she reportedly replied,
"Thou aimest high, Master Lee. Consider thou what the invention
could do to my poor subjects. It would assuredly bring them to ruin
by depriving them of employment, thus making them beggars." After
the royal slap down, the queen denied his patent, the hosiers' guild
campaigned against him, and he was forced to move to France, where
he died in poverty.

Some 150 years later, in the early dawn of the Industrial Revolution, an Englishman named John Kay revolutionized weaving by
inventing the flying shuttle, which doubled productivity—surely a
boon for weavers, who could now make twice as much cloth. Yet

weavers campaigned against him, manufacturers conspired to violate his patents, and he was forced to move to France, where he died in poverty just like William Lee. Dying destitute in France seemed to be an occupational hazard for innovators.

By the time the Industrial Revolution got going, the pattern was well established. People hated technology that improved productivity. Luddites, smashing power looms in the early nineteenth century, were only the most famous exemplars.

These protesters were right in the short run, but in the long run they were resoundingly wrong. New technology does destroy jobs, but it also creates new ones—jobs for people who operate the stocking frames and power looms, for example. More important, better technology creates better jobs. Workers using improved technology are more productive, so they earn more—and spend more, creating more new jobs across the economy. At the same time, the products those tech-enabled workers make cost less than before; machine-made cloth costs a fraction of what the handmade version costs. The result is that technology, over time and across economies, has raised living standards spectacularly. For centuries, the fears of Luddites past and present have been not merely unfounded but the exact opposite of reality. Advancing technology has improved the material well-being of humanity more than any other development in history, by far.

Now something has changed. The way technology benefits workers is one of the firmest orthodoxies in all of economics, but recently, for the first time, many mainstream economists and technologists have begun to question whether it will continue.

The proximate cause of their new skepticism is the sorry job-generating performance of the developed economies in the wake of the 2008–2009 financial crisis and recession. For decades, the U.S. economy regularly returned to prerecession employment levels about eighteen months after a recession started. Then, starting with the 1990–1991 recession, the lag started lengthening. After the 2008–2009 recession the recovery of employment took seventy-seven months—over six years. How come? And why did wages begin stagnating for large swaths of the U.S. workforce long before the recession began? Why is the same trend happening in other developed countries? As economists look for answers, they see factors that go far beyond the causes of the recession.

"THE DEFINING ECONOMIC FEATURE OF OUR ERA"

Lawrence H. Summers—former U.S. treasury secretary, former president of Harvard University, a star economist—is one of the new skeptics. In a significant lecture to an audience of fellow economists, he summarized in his brisk way the orthodox view of the debate over technology: "There were the stupid Luddite people, who mostly were outside of economics departments, and there were the smart progressive people. . . . The stupid people thought that automation was going to make all the jobs go away and there wasn't going to be any work to do. And the smart people understood that when more was produced, there would be more income and therefore there would be more demand. It wasn't possible that all the jobs would go away, so automation was a blessing."

Evidence overwhelmingly supported that view for decades. All you had to do was imagine the world of 1800 and compare it with the world around you. But then, quite recently, the world changed: "Until a few years ago, I didn't think this was a very complicated subject," Summers said. "The Luddites were wrong and the believers in technology and technological progress were right. I'm not so completely certain now."

Summers is far from the only expert who became doubtful. The Pew Research Center Internet Project in 2014 canvassed 1,896 experts it had identified as insightful on technology issues, and it asked them this question: Will technology displace more jobs than it creates by 2025? Half said yes, and half said no. That was an astounding result. As Summers explained, the evidence in favor of "no" was perfectly clear, or it had been. It's hard to imagine that, ten years before, as many as 10 percent of such a highly informed group would have said yes. (We don't know for sure because apparently no one thought the question even worth asking.) Now half said so. The orthodoxy was suddenly no longer orthodox.

What Summers and other economists believe has changed is, in concept, simple. The two factors of production are capital and labor, and in economists' terms they have always been regarded as complements, not just substitutes. Capital makes workers more productive. Even if it displaces some workers (substitutes for them), it also creates new, more productive jobs using that new capital so that, as Summers said, "if there's more capital, the wage has to rise" (it complements workers). But now he and others began seeing a new possibility: Capital can substitute for labor, period. Summers explained, "That is, you can take some of the stock of machines and, by designing them appropriately, you can have them do exactly what labor did before."

The key word is "exactly." A Google self-driving car doesn't complement anybody's work because nobody operates it at all. The company produced a version that doesn't have a steering wheel, brake pedal, or accelerator, and it's designed to transport even blind or other disabled people. So it doesn't make drivers, even a shrunken population of them, more productive. It does exactly what they do and thus just replaces them.

In a world like that, economic logic dictates that wage rates must fall, and the share of total income going to capital rather than labor must rise, which is indeed what has been happening. An important reason, Summers says, is "the nature of the technical changes that we have seen: Increasingly they take the form of capital that effectively substitutes for labor."

The outlook is obviously for much more capital-labor substitution as computing power gallops unflaggingly forward. That is not a happy future for many people. In fact, as Summers reasons, "It may well be that, given the possibilities for substitution, some categories of labor will not be able to earn a subsistence income."

Economists aren't the only experts who see such a trend. "Unlike previous disruptions, such as when farming machinery displaced farm workers but created factory jobs making the machines, robotics and AI [artificial intelligence] are different," Mark Nall, a NASA program manager with much real-world technology experience, told the Pew canvassers. "Due to their versatility and growing capabilities, not just a few economic sectors will be affected, but whole swaths will be. . . . The social consequence is that good-paying jobs will be increasingly scarce." Stowe Boyd, lead researcher at Gigaom Research, a technology research firm, was even more pessimistic: "An increasing proportion of the world's population will be outside the world of work—either living on the dole, or benefiting from the dramatically decreased costs of goods to eke out a subsistence lifestyle." Michael Roberts, a much respected Internet pioneer, predicted confidently that "electronic human avatars with substantial work capability are years, not decades away. . . . There is great pain down the road for everyone as new realities are addressed. The only question is how soon."

Microsoft founder Bill Gates has observed the trend also and believes it's greatly underappreciated: "Software substitution, whether it's for drivers or waiters or nurses—it's progressing," he told a Washington, D.C., audience in 2014. "Technology over time will reduce demand for jobs. . . . Twenty years from now, labor demand for lots of skill sets will be substantially lower. I don't think people have that in their mental model."

But isn't all this garment rending and teeth gnashing just the usual worry over the endless cycle of creative destruction, as new industries displace old ones? You can't earn a subsistence income with the skills of making slide rules, and that's not a problem because you can earn a better income doing something else. But the analogy isn't valid. You can't earn a living by making slide rules because nobody wants them anymore. This new argument, by contrast, holds that the economy can increasingly provide exactly the goods and services that people most want today and tomorrow, and can do it using more machines and ever fewer people.

Thus Summers's conclusion, which is significant coming from an economist of his stature: "This set of developments is going to be the defining economic feature of our era."

THE FOURTH GREAT TURNING POINT FOR WORKERS

The immediate question for most of us is obvious: Who, specifically, gets hurt, and who doesn't?

To find the answer, it helps to think of these developments as the latest chapter in a story. Technology has been changing the nature of work and the value of particular skills for well over 200 years, and the story so far comprises just three major turning points.

At first, the rise of industrial technology devalued the skills of artisans, who handcrafted their products from beginning to end: A gun maker carved the stock, cast the barrel, engraved the lock, filed the trigger, and painstakingly fitted the pieces together. But in Eli Whitney's Connecticut gun factory, separate workers did each of those jobs, or just portions of them, using water-powered machinery, and components of each type were identical. Skilled artisans were out of luck, but less skilled workers were in demand. They could easily learn to use the new machines—the workers and machines were complements—and so the workers could earn far more than before.

The second turning point arrived in the early twentieth century, when a new trend emerged. Widely available electricity enabled the building of far more sophisticated factories, requiring better educated, more highly skilled workers to operate the more complicated machines; companies also grew much larger, requiring a larger corps of educated managers. Now the unskilled were out of luck, and educated workers were in demand—but that was okay, because the unskilled could get educated. The trend intensified through most of the twentieth century. Advancing technology continually required better educated workers, and Americans responded by educating themselves with unprecedented ambition. The high school graduation rate rocketed from 4 percent in 1890 to 77 percent in 1970, a national intellectual upgrade such as the world had never seen. As long as workers could keep up with the increasing demands of technology, the two remained complements. The result was an economic miracle of fast-rising living standards.

But then the third major turning point arrived, starting in the 1980s. Information technology had developed to a point where it could take over many medium-skilled jobs—bookkeeping, back-office jobs, repetitive factory work. The number of jobs in those categories diminished, and wages stagnated for the shrinking group of workers who still did them. Yet the trend was limited. At both ends of the skill spectrum, people in high-skill jobs and low-skill service jobs did much better. The number of jobs in those categories increased, and pay went up. Economists called it the polarization of the labor market, and they observed it in the United States and many other developed countries. At the top end of the market, infotech still wasn't good enough to take over the problem-solving, judging, and coordinating tasks of high-skill workers like managers, lawyers, consultants, and financiers; in fact, it made those workers more productive by giving them more information at lower cost. At the bottom end, infotech didn't threaten low-skill service workers because computers were terrible at skills of physical dexterity; a computer could defeat a grand master chess champion but couldn't pick up a pencil from a tabletop. Home health aides, gardeners, cooks, and others could breathe easy.

That was the story into the 2000s. In the nonstop valuing and devaluing of skills through economic history, infotech was crushing medium-skill workers, but workers at the two ends of the skill spectrum were safe or prospering. Now we are at a fourth turning point. Infotech is advancing steadily into both ends of the spectrum, threatening workers who thought they didn't have to worry.

MAYBE EVEN LAWYERS CAN'T OUTSMART COMPUTERS

At the top end, what's happening to lawyers is a model for any occupation involving analysis, subtle interpretation, strategizing, and persuasion. The computer incursion into the legal discovery process is well known. In cases around the world computers are reading millions of documents and sorting them for relevance without ever getting tired or distracted. The cost savings are extraordinary. One e-discovery vendor, Symantec's Clearwell, claimed it could cut costs up to 98 percent. That may seem outlandish, but it's in line with the claims of an executive at another vendor, Autonomy, who told the *New York Times* that e-discovery would enable one lawyer to do the work of 500 or more. In addition, software does the job much, much better than people. It can detect patterns in thousands or millions of documents that no human could spot—unusual editing of a document, for example, or spikes in communication between certain people, or even changes in e-mail style that may signal hidden motives.

But that's just the beginning. Computers then started moving up the ladder of value, becoming highly skilled at searching the legal literature for appropriate precedents in a given case, and doing it far more widely and thoroughly than people can do. Humans still have to identify the legal issues involved, but, as Northwestern University law professor John O. McGinnis has written, "search engines will eventually do this by themselves, and then go on to suggest the case law that is likely to prove relevant to the matter."

Advancing even higher into the realm of lawyerly skill, computers can already predict Supreme Court decisions better than legal experts can. As such analytical power expands in scope, computers will move nearer the heart of what lawyers do by advising better than lawyers can on whether to sue or settle or go to trial before any court and in any type of case. Companies such as Lex Machina and Huron Legal already offer such analytic services, which are improving by the day. These firms' computers have read all the documents in hundreds of thousands of cases and can tell you, for example, which companies are more likely to settle than to litigate a patent case, or how particular judges tend to rule in particular types of cases, or which lawyers have the best records in front of specified judges. As more potential litigants, both plaintiffs and defendants, can see better analysis of vastly more data, odds are strong they'll be able to resolve disputes far more efficiently. One possible result: fewer lawsuits.

None of this means that lawyers will disappear, but it suggests that the world will need fewer of them. It's already happening. "The rise of machine intelligence is probably partly to blame for the current crisis of law schools"—shrinking enrollments, falling tuitions—"and will certainly worsen that crisis," McGinnis has observed.

With infotech thoroughly disrupting even a field so advanced that it requires three years of post-graduate education and can pay extremely well, other high-skill workers—analysts, managers—can't help but wonder about their own futures. What's happening in law is the application of Watson-like technology to a specific industry, but it can be applied far more widely. The breakthrough of this technology is that it understands natural language, so when you ask it a question, it doesn't just search for keywords from the question you asked. It tries to figure out the context of your question and thus understand what you really mean. So, for example, if your question includes the phrase "two plus two," that might mean "four," or, if you're in the car business, it might mean "a car with two front seats and two back seats," or if you're a psychologist, it might mean "a family with two parents and two children." Cognitive computing systems derive the context and then come up with possible answers to your question and estimate which one is most likely correct. A system's answers aren't especially good when it first delves into a field, but with experience it keeps getting better. That's why the Internet entrepreneur Terry Jones, who founded Travelocity, has said that "Watson is the only computer that's worth more used than new."

Watson-like technology works best when it has a really big body of written material to read and work with. For *Jeopardy!* Watson downloaded not only the entire contents of Wikipedia but also thousands of previous *Jeopardy!* clues and responses. Law is obviously an excellent field for this technology. Medicine is another. Memorial Sloan Kettering Cancer Center in New York City uses Watson to extract answers from the vast oncology literature, a task which no physician could ever keep up with. Financial advice looks like a fat target for this technology because it involves a vast and growing corpus of research plus huge volumes of data that change every day. Several financial institutions are therefore using Watson, initially as a tool for their financial advisers. But look just a bit down the road: Corporate Insight, a research firm that focuses on the financial services industry, asks, "Once consumers have a personal Watson in their pocket . . . why would an experienced investor need a financial adviser?"

WRITERS WHO NEVER GET BLOCKED, TIRED, OR DRUNK

Combine an understanding of natural language with high-torque analytic power and you get a nonfiction writer, or at least a species of one. A company called Narrative Science makes software that writes articles that would not strike most people as computer-written. It focused first on events embodying lots of data: ball games and corporate earnings announcements. The software became increasingly sophisticated at going beyond the facts and figures—for example, figuring out the most important play in a game or identifying the best angle for the article: a come-from-behind win, say, or a hero player. Then the developers taught the software different writing styles, which customers could choose from a menu. Next, it learned to understand more than just numerical data, reading relevant material to create context for the article. A number of media companies, including Yahoo and Forbes, publish articles from Narrative Science, though some of the company's customers don't want to be identified and don't tell readers which articles are computer-written. In mid-2014, the Associated Press assigned computers to write all its articles about corporate earnings announcements.

Then Narrative Science realized that maybe the real money wasn't in producing journalism at all (they could have asked any journalist about that) but in generating the writing that companies use internally, the countless reports and analyses that influence business decisions. So it arranged its technology to gather broad classes of data, including unstructured data like social media posts, on any given topic or problem, and to analyze it deeply, looking for trends, correlations, unusual events, and more. The software uses that data to "make judgments and draw conclusions," the company says; it can also make recommendations. The software writes it all up at a reading level and in a tone that the customer chooses, also supplying helpful charts and graphs.

This is starting to sound less like writing and more like management.

But are the writing and the analysis any good? That, at least, is for humans to decide. Except that increasingly it need not be. Schools from the elementary level through college are using software to judge writing and analysis in the form of student essays. The software isn't perfect—it doesn't yet evaluate such subtleties as voice and tone—but human graders aren't perfect either. Jeff Pence, a middle-school teacher in Canton, Georgia, who used the software to help grade papers from his 140 students, acknowledged that it doesn't grade with perfect accuracy, but, he told *Education Week*, "When I reach that 67th essay, I'm not real accurate." Similar software is being used at much higher levels. EdX, the enterprise started by Harvard and MIT to offer online courses, has begun using it to grade student papers. The Hewlett Foundation offered two $100,000 prizes for developing such software, and edX hired one of the winners to work on its version, which is available to developers everywhere as open-source code so it can be improved.

Of course, this evaluation software must itself be evaluated by humans, measuring it against the performance of humans. So researchers had a group of human teachers grade a large set of essays. Then they gave those same essays to a separate group of human graders and to the software. They compared the grades assigned by Human Group Two to those assigned by Human Group One, and they also compared the grades assigned by the software to those assigned by Human Group One. All three sets of grades were different, but the software's grades were no more different from Human Group One's grades than Human Group Two's grades were different from Human Group One's. So while software doesn't assign the same grades as people, neither do people assign the same grades as other people. And if you look at a large group of grades assigned to the same work by people and by software , you can't tell which is which.

Two points to draw from this:

One, the software is getting rapidly better. The people are not.

Two, education as currently conceived is becoming really weird. After all, the report-writing software developed by Narrative

Science and other companies is easily adapted to other markets, such as students' papers. So we now have essay-grading software and essay-writing software, both of which are improving. What happens next is obvious. The writing software gets optimized to please the grading software. Every essay gets an A, and neither the student nor the teacher has anything to do with it. But not much education is necessarily going on, which poses problems for both student and teacher.

A ROBOT'S TOUCH

The rapid progress of infotech in taking over tasks at the high-skill end of the job spectrum—lawyers, doctors, managers, professors—is startling, but it isn't especially surprising. If we thought such jobs were by their nature immune to computer competition, we shouldn't have, because these jobs are highly cognitive. Much of the work is brain work, and that's just what computers do best; they needed only time to accumulate the required computing power. The greater surprise shows up at the opposite end of the job spectrum, in the low-skill, low-pay world where the work is less cognitive and more physical. This is the kind of work that computers for decades could hardly do at all. An example illustrates the gap in abilities: In 1997 a computer could beat the world's greatest chess player yet could not physically move the pieces on the board. But again the technology needed only time, a few more doublings of power. The skills of physical work are also not immune to the advance of infotech.

Google's autonomous cars are an obvious and significant example—significant because the number one job among American men is truck driver. Many more examples are appearing. You can train a Baxter robot (from Rethink Robotics) to do all kinds of things—pack or unpack boxes, take items to or from a conveyor belt, fold a T-shirt, carry things around, count them, inspect them—just by moving its arms and hands ("end-effectors") in the desired way. Many previous industrial robots had to be surrounded by safety cages because they could do just one thing in one way, over and over, and that's all they knew; if you got between a welding robot and the piece it was welding, you were in deep trouble. But Baxter doesn't hurt anyone as it hums about the shop floor; it adapts its movements to its environment by sensing everything around it, including people.

Many similar kinds of robots operate in different environments— for example, buzzing through hospital hallways delivering medicines, hauling laundry, or picking up infectious waste. Security robots can hang out around public buildings, watching, listening, reading license plates, and sending information to law enforcement as the robot deems appropriate. Robots went into the wreckage of Japan's ruined Fukushima Daiichi nuclear power plant long before people did.

The advantage robots hold in doing dangerous work is a big reason the U.S. military is a major user of them and a major funder of research into them. By 2008 about 12,000 combat robots were working in Iraq. Some, barely larger than a shoebox, run on miniature tank treads and can carry a camera and other sensors; they gather intelligence and do surveillance and reconnaissance. Larger ones dispose of bombs or carry heavy loads into and out of dangerous places. A few robots armed with guns were sent to Iraq but reportedly were never used. Nonetheless, General Robert Cone announced in 2014 that the army was considering shrinking the standard brigade combat team from 4,000 soldiers to 3,000, making up the difference with robots and drones.

So far virtually none of those robots are autonomous; a person controls each one. But the army realized this model was inefficient, so the U.S. Army Research Laboratory developed a more sophisticated robot called RoboLeader that, in the words of project chief Jessie Chen, "interprets current situations in terms of an operator's objective"—it looks, listens, senses, and determines how best to carry out its orders—"and issues detailed command signals to a team of lower capability robots." The great advantage, as Chen explains, is that "instead of directly managing each individual robot, the human operator only deals with a single entity—RoboLeader."

Ladies and gentlemen, we have invented robotic middle management.

Robot physical skills are fast advancing on other dimensions as well. Consider a robotic hand developed by a team from Harvard, Yale, and iRobot, maker of the Roomba vacuum cleaner and many other mobile robots, including many used by the military. So fine are the robotic hand's motor skills that it can pick up a credit card from a tabletop, put a drill bit in a drill, and turn a key, all of which were previously beyond robotic abilities. "A disabled person could say to a robot with hands, 'Go to the kitchen and put my dinner in the microwave,'" one of the researchers, Harvard professor Robert Howe, told *Harvard* magazine. "Robotic hands are the real frontier, and that's where we've been pushing."

It seems that everywhere we look, computers are suddenly capable of doing things that they couldn't do and that some people thought they never would do. The less exalted skills, physical ones like folding a T-shirt, turned out to be the more challenging, but at last even they are succumbing to the combination of relentlessly increasing computing power and algorithmic skill. The number of people who wrongly believed they could never be replaced by a computer keeps growing—not slower, but faster.

THE COMPUTER KNOWS YOU'RE LYING

And yet, isn't there one last redoubt of human uniqueness, some ultimate zone of pulsing, organic personhood into which computers can never enter? Everything we've examined so far has involved abilities that originate in the left brain—logical, linear, flowchartable, computer-like. But what about the other side, the right side, and its specialty—emotion? It's irrational, mysterious, and we all understand it, even though we can't explain how. In addition, emotion is often the real secret sauce of success in many jobs, high-skill and low. Executives must read and respond to the emotions of customers, employees, regulators, and everyone else they deal with. A good waiter responds differently to customers who are cranky, tired, cheerful, confused, or tipsy, all without quite knowing how. Surely this is forever ours alone.

The founders of companies like Emotient and Affectiva might disagree, however. They're researchers in the field of affective computing, in which computers understand human emotion. As their work advances, our expert ability to navigate the flesh-and-blood, analog world of human feelings is looking a lot less special every day.

We express emotions in many ways—words, tone of voice, body language—but for anyone wanting to read a person's emotions continually and remotely (that is, without attaching sensors), the most useful indicator is facial expression. We aren't always speaking or moving when we feel an emotion, but we can almost always change the expression on our face. In fact, a researcher named Paul Ekman discovered decades ago that when we're feeling an emotion, it's almost impossible for us not to evince it through facial expression, even if we're trying hard to suppress it. The expression appears fleetingly, perhaps for only a fraction of a second, despite our best efforts not to betray our true feelings. Ekman became famous for his discovery of these so-called microexpressions, particularly for his work on spotting them as a way to detect lies. A TV series called *Lie to Me* was based on his work and centered on a character modeled on him.

But Ekman, one of the most cited psychologists of the twentieth century, did much more than figure out how to spot lies. He conducted the deepest analysis ever performed of all the things the human face could reveal. Your face contains about 40 muscles.

Ekman determined how each muscle could move and then figured out all the possible combinations. The total is over 10,000, meaning we can make over 10,000 facial expressions, at least in theory. In real life, about 3,000 of them have something to do with emotion. Ekman then figured out which emotion is expressed by each one of those facial muscle movement combinations. The result, which took many years to compile, was his Facial Action Coding System. For any possible combination of muscle movements in a person's face, and no matter how fleetingly the combination was visible, Ekman could tell you what that person was feeling.

Ekman built a successful business training people in law enforcement, commerce, and other fields to use his system to detect emotions. But as computer technology improved, other researchers were figuring out how to make computers do the same thing. You've noticed that even the camera in your phone can detect faces and put little boxes around them. More advanced software can examine those faces and spot the muscle movements from Ekman's system. The possibilities of such technology prompted six PhDs at the University of California at San Diego to form Emotient and to recruit Ekman to their advisory board.

Point a video camera at any person's face, and the company's Sentiment Analysis software can tell you that person's overall sentiment (positive, negative, neutral) plus display a continually updating bar chart showing levels of seven primary emotions—joy, surprise, sadness, fear, disgust, contempt, anger—and two advanced emotions, frustration and confusion (advanced because they're combinations of other emotions). Point the camera at a group of people and it analyzes all their emotions and gives you a composite readout. Incorporate the software into Google Glass, as the company has done, and the emotion readouts for anyone you're looking at appear before your eyes (and yes, several people quickly noted that the emotion you may very well detect is contempt for you because you're wearing Google Glass).

Emotient's initial target market for selling the Sentiment Analysis system was retailers, but the possibilities are obviously much broader.

Affectiva, a spin-off from MIT's Media Lab, also uses Ekman's research to analyze facial expressions, selling its software to marketers and advertisers so they can conduct consumer research online using webcams. No need to get your research subjects into a focus group and guess what they're thinking; just have them talk to you online and let their faces tell the story. A separate project within the Media Lab measures another feeling—stress in drivers—through biosensors in the steering wheel, detecting grip pressure, skin conductance, and palm sweat, and by analyzing the driver's voice as he or she speaks.

So this mysterious human ability to read another person's emotions turns out not to be all that mysterious. Computers can do it too. Technology has reached the point where doing it isn't even very hard.

That would be remarkable enough, but this supposedly unique human ability is less special still. Not only can computers detect emotion; they do it much better than we do.

Researchers led by Dr. Marian Bartlett, one of Emotient's founders, video recorded the faces of volunteers who were experiencing pain (induced by holding an arm in a bucket of ice water) or were faking the experience of pain. The videos were then shown to research subjects who were asked: Is this person really in pain or just faking it? They got it right 50 percent of the time. That is, they had no clue; they could have flipped a coin and done just as well. After the research subjects were given some training in distinguishing fake pain from real, they improved to 55 percent. But when software developed by Bartlett and her team analyzed the videos, it made the right call 85 percent of the time. The contest was not close. And nothing in this or other research suggests that pain is especially easy to fake or otherwise fundamentally unlike other feelings. It's reasonable to infer that software would be superior at detecting other feelings as well.

Despite our deep sense that emotion is somehow uniquely ours to understand, we shouldn't be surprised that a computer can do it better. It can look at each one of those 40 muscles in the human face, and it can remember all 3,000 combinations. A video camera shoots thirty frames per second, and a computer can analyze each frame; that's just what the computer did in the detecting-fake-pain study. Even an Ekman-trained expert can occasionally miss a microexpression, but a computer never will.

Having read human emotions better than humans can, computers can then do more with that information than we can. For example, computers analyzed the faces of college students who were being trained in an uncomplicated but demanding task, a game of finding certain groups of three cards among nine cards on an iPad screen (it's harder than it sounds). The students took a test, then received training during which they were observed by humans and computers separately gauging each student's level of engagement. Then they took another test to see how much they had improved.

It turned out that the best way to predict how well the students would do on the second test was to ask the computer—based on its analysis of their facial expressions—how engaged they had been during the training. That was a better predictor than a student's performance on the first test, and it was as good as or better than the humans' judgment of engagement. And much more could be done with the computer's readings. As the researchers point out, the computer, measuring engagement moment by moment, could continually adjust the instruction to keep a student engaged and could do it individually for an unlimited number of students. Educators could mine vast troves of engagement data to learn in fine detail what grips students and what bores them. Individual teachers, academic departments, and whole schools could monitor overall levels of student engagement.

MIT's stress-monitoring car applies the same principles in different ways. If it senses that a driver is highly stressed, it can suggest relaxing music and give the GPS guidance a more soothing tone of voice. If the driver is spacing out, it could jar him back to attention by making the steering wheel vibrate. Most intriguingly (or hilariously), the researchers even used special thermochromatic paint to make a car change its external color based on the driver's emotional state, as a signal to other drivers. Whether this technology has time to be commercialized before the arrival of autonomous vehicles makes it irrelevant is a separate question.

The power of computers to sense human emotions means, inevitably, that a machine can outdo us even in detecting our own emotions. It's surely tempting to suppose that I possess a sense of my own emotional state that no entity standing outside of me, human or electronic, could ever reach. Yet of course it isn't true. We've all had the experience of asking someone why they're in a bad mood and having that person, eyes flaming, roar, "I'm not in a bad mood!" Or more likely, we've been that person. A computer can see the obvious reality to which we're blinded. More broadly, people are notoriously awful at realizing they're stressed, depressed, angry, or in the grip of other emotions. That's why technology that warns us when we're stressed, for example, is valuable. Our supposed inner knowledge of ourselves is so frequently thwarted by inner denial that a computer is much better suited to give us a more accurate reading.

But if it's not surprising that computers can know our own emotions better than we know them ourselves, it is certainly sobering. We make life-altering decisions based on our imaginary knowledge of our own feelings. In business, love, and much else, we ask our emotions to guide us even though we're often ignorant of those emotions. Realizing this, we sometimes ask friends or relatives for their perspective on our feelings. Life has been that way forever. What's new is that for the first time, technology can read those feeling better than people do, in themselves and in others.

The overwhelming message seems to be that, in trying to out-perform technology, almost no one is safe for long. While millions of people doing a wide range of jobs are not immediately threat-ened, it's getting easier by the day to see how they might be. In work that is high-skill or low-skill, intensely cognitive or heavily physical, left-brain analytical or right-brain emotional, infotech is rapidly reaching a point—and in many cases has already reached a point—where it outperforms the best humans.

The conventional counterargument is that people needn't worry because the most productive use of computers is having them work with people, not replace people; humans and computers working together are even more effective than computers alone. But the cases in which this is true are always temporary; the computer alone proves superior eventually. A person working with a calculator could solve math problems infinitely faster than a calculator alone, which couldn't do a thing unless a person punched in the numbers. But today whole factories and warehouses are operated by computers alone doing complex math all by themselves; scanners and sensors supply the numbers. For a long time you and your highly computer-ized car could drive better than the car alone, but no more.

The favorite example to support the counterargument is chess: While IBM's Deep Blue beat world champion Garry Kasparov in 1997, by 2008 or so a person and a computer working together could beat a computer alone. You still hear this example cited as proof that people add an ineffable something that computers just can't supply. The trouble is that the argument is getting shakier by the moment. The example became famous after economist Tyler Cowen cited it in his excellent 2013 book, *Average Is Over*. But he also noted in the book that as computers improved, the day might come when humans could no longer add any value to the computer's play, and by late 2013 he was able to post a blog entry citing evidence that the day may have arrived. At this writing, human-computer teams still beat computers some of the time, but in a domain where the world's software powerhouses like IBM and Google aren't competing. Human-computer teams can't beat computers alone at checkers, and with chess, it's only a matter of time, a few more doublings of power.

The trend holds "implications for more traditional labor markets," Cowen notes:

> You might train to help a computer program read medical scans, and for thirteen years add real value with your intuition and your ability to revise the computer's mistakes or at least to get the doctor to take a closer look. But it takes more and more time for you to improve on the computer each year. And then one day . . . poof! ZMP for you.

"ZMP" means "zero marginal product"—the economists' term for when you add no value at all.

Making the trend all the more disorienting, as we keep having to remind ourselves, is that it's speeding up, not slowing down. All the technologies and developments that I've described are gee-whiz stuff as I write about them. They're probably ho-hum by the time you read this. The transition from breathtaking to boring takes only months, and that fact illustrates a crucial point. As we struggle to understand the meaning of these developments for our lives, we must force ourselves to envision larger, faster changes than the mind-blowing ones we've seen so far.

With that challenge in mind, I wanted to know what Nicholas Negroponte thought of these trends. Famous as the founder of the MIT Media Lab, he predicted decades ahead of the reality that telephones would be transformed from wired to wireless, that TV would switch from wireless to wired, and that by now we'd all be getting our news on small digital devices. That is, he has largely gotten it right.

So I e-mailed him this query: "In five or ten years, what will people do better than computers?"

His response: "Very little, other than 'enjoy.'"

"Do we really want a world without work?"

In truth, a world that's literally without work is highly unlikely for the fundamental reason that human desires are infinite. No matter how much that technology may do for us, we will always find something to want. As Milton Friedman famously observed, you could reach a point where you pay a personal psychiatrist to follow you around. (When Henry Ford—or in some tellings, John D. Rockefeller—undertook the cruel challenge of learning golf as an adult, he reportedly paid a boy to follow him around the course and remind him to keep his head down.) We'll always find some kind of work to do. The great question as we round the fourth major turning point in the history of work is what kind of work we will find: high-value or low, the work of the psychiatrist or of the boy on the golf course.

There is a clear answer, and the strange thing about it is that to see it, we must look more closely not at computers, but at ourselves.

CHAPTER THREE

THE SURPRISING VALUE IN OUR DEEPEST NATURE

Why Being a Great Performer Is Becoming Less About What
We Know and More About What We're Like.

The case in Arizona Superior Court concerned James Stone, who had
been convicted twice of sexually violent crimes involving children.
His prison sentence was nearing its end, and the question before the
jury was whether he should be confined in a psychiatric hospital after
his release—what's called civil confinement. It may seem surprising
that someone could be locked up for a further, indeterminate period
of time after having served his court-imposed sentence, but many
states have such civil-confinement laws specifically for SVPs, or sexually violent predators or persons. The central question in a civil-
confinement case is the likelihood of the person committing future
acts of sexual violence, and the key testimony comes from mental
health experts. A great deal is riding on how jurors respond to that
testimony, because in reaching their decision they have little else to
go on beyond the basic facts of the felon's crime, which may have
occurred many years previously. Will these jurors release Stone into
the community or lock him up in a hospital?

The court appointed a psychologist named Brent to evaluate

Stone, which he did by reviewing the facts of the case and interviewing Stone for over two hours. At trial, the state's attorney put Brent on the witness stand and asked him to describe his procedure, then went to the critical issue: "Now, based upon your interview and judgment, did you form a judgment of his likelihood of reoffense?"

"Yes, I did."

"And what was that?"

"His background and my experience suggest that he has a high risk of recidivating."

The state's attorney asked Brent what particularly about the interview was significant. Brent answered, "He acknowledged the behaviors in question even prior to his first conviction while he was on probation, the behavior leading to his second conviction, and even the continued problems that he really needed to continue to deal with, treatment-wise."

On cross-examination, Stone's lawyer pushed Brent hard, asking whether two to three hours was really enough time in which to make "an accurate assessment of Mr. Stone's likelihood to reoffend," and Brent insisted it was. "And all this is just based upon your opinion?" Stone's attorney asked. Brent replied, "Yes, it is based upon my opinion as a licensed psychologist."

There was more testimony, but this was the heart of it. If you had been on that jury, what would you have decided—to release Stone or to confine him?

Now consider what you would have done if the key testimony had been a bit different. Suppose that Brent had reached the same conclusion without interviewing Stone at all; that, instead of basing his conclusion on a personal interview and his own judgment, he simply plugged various bits of data—Stone's age at release from prison, his victims' gender, his relationship to his victims, and much else—into two models created by other psychologists for assessing the risks posed by sexual offenders. Suppose that Stone's scores on those actuarial instruments led Brent to testify he believed "to a reasonable psychological certainty that he [Stone] has a likelihood to recidivate."

Suppose also that on cross-examination, Stone's lawyer had asked Brent whether anyone at all, including "somebody who is not a professional," could have plugged the same data into the same models and produced the same answer, and Brent had acknowledged it was true. What if Stone's lawyer then asked Brent, "Is there some question within the industry as to whether actuarial instruments should be used in this manner?" to which Brent responded, "Yes."

If that had been the critical testimony in the case, what would you have decided?

As you might have guessed, the confinement trial of James Stone was not a real trial, exactly. It was a notably realistic reenactment of an actual Arizona SVP confinement trial; the prosecutor was portrayed by a former Arizona prosecutor, the defense lawyer by a real Arizona defense lawyer, and the psychologist by a licensed Arizona psychologist with much experience as an expert witness. Researchers produced two one-hour videos of the trial that varied only in the critical testimony; all other dialogue was taken from the actual trial transcript. They then showed one or the other of the videos to 156 people who had been called for jury duty but had not been put on a jury; like most such people, they hadn't been rejected but rather had just sat there all day and been sent home.

The results were striking. These potential jurors were swayed far more by the expert's testimony when it was based on his judgment than when it was based on data. The trouble is that they shouldn't have been. Because so many states have civil confinement laws that can lock someone up based largely on an expert's prediction of future behavior, much research has been done on how best to make those predictions. Most of the research agrees that judgment isn't nearly as good as plug-in-the-numbers models.

The jurors in this study didn't know that. They just knew what they liked, and they liked an expert who had actually seen and heard the subject in person and who could then balance his impressions, the unquantifiable human reality, with the case's other evidence in forming a judgment. In fact, the jurors loved that. As the study's authors concluded, "A fundamental disconnect in juror decision-making appears to exist in this context—jurors are more confident in their verdicts when presented with less accurate expert testimony."

It's the same in many court cases. People don't evaluate experts on their expertise. Jeremy Rose, a trial consultant with the National Jury Project, has written that "Experts who win the war of credentials with the opposing side's expert usually win on the basis of how much hands-on experience they have with the topic in question. For example, jurors find treating doctors more persuasive than expert doctors." In some cases it may be, as we've seen, that you don't even need to meet subjects in order to reach the most accurate conclusions. But people don't care. In a situation as important as a jury trial, they don't want conclusions from a bunch of data. They want to see and hear a living, feeling, judging human being.

That reality holds a powerful clue to how people will be valuable as the economy transforms. Jurors place extremely high value on seeing and hearing, in person, human experts who make human judgments about people they have in turn been able to see, hear, touch, and respond to.

The larger lesson is that human interaction rules our lives. It's even more valuable than we may realize. In a surprising number of ways, it holds the key to our value.

WHAT OUR BRAINS ARE REALLY FOR

We cannot begin to understand the changing nature of high-value skills without appreciating the hardwired power and importance of human interaction in our lives. "Natural selection mandated us to be in groups in order to survive," the eminent neuroscientist and psychologist Michael S. Gazzaniga has written. "Once there, we construct our . . . social relationships, with our interpretive minds ever busy dealing with the stuff around us, most of which involves our fellow humans. . . . Those human social relationships become central to our mental life, indeed become the raison d'être of our lives. . . . We now think about others all the time because that is how we are built. Without all those others, without our alliances and coalitions, we die. It was true . . . for early humans. It is still true for us."

That is, we are hardwired to connect social interaction with survival. No connection can be more powerful. We can easily forget—living and working in highly developed economies, doing linear, logical, rational thinking all the livelong day—that such activity is not in our deep nature. But whether we recognize our true nature or overlook it, it's there inside us, driving us. "We are social to the core," says Gazzaniga. "There is no way around the fact. Our big brains are there primarily to deal with social matters, not to . . . cogitate about the second law of thermodynamics."

Understand what he's saying. Psychologists have long puzzled over a question that definitely does not occur to most of us as we go through our day, which is why people are as smart as they are. What possible evolutionary advantage could humans have gained by developing a brain that could invent calculus or particle physics—or learn how to do algebra or drive a car? We humans flourished and developed our modern brains while living a subsistence life for millennia, so where did the ability to perform those advanced feats come from?

The answer seems to be that, out on the savanna, we did have to solve incredibly complex problems, and they were the problems of social interaction. We gained benefits from living in social groups, and doing so required us to understand how our own actions would affect the actions of others—while knowing that others were thinking the same way about us—and whether the results would benefit or harm us or our kin, realizing that we could never be sure of exactly when, how, or why others would act, but sensing changing signals. This is like chess only much harder, and the stakes are higher. "The intellectual faculties required are of the highest order," said the English psychologist N. K. Humphrey, who advanced this line of thought in the 1970s as an answer to why human brains are so highly developed.

That is: Social interaction is what our brains are for.

We mustn't be confused about this. For many years the reigning view in the social sciences was just the opposite—a newborn human was, the thinking went, a tabula rasa, a blank slate, and everything that we would ever think or feel or become arose from what was written on that slate by our experiences. "Man has no nature; what he has is history," wrote the Spanish philosopher José Ortega y Gasset. This model of human beings grew out of many impulses in the early twentieth century, and some of the motivations were noble. In particular, at a time when some people asserted that various groups—Africans, Jews, Gypsies, homosexuals, women—were inherently inferior, an effective counterargument was that they couldn't be inherently inferior because nobody is inherently anything. Whatever any of us might be, it had been inscribed on the slate by culture, which meant that it might have been something different, and in any case it could be changed.

The blank-slate view also held out hope for a better world, particularly a less war-filled world, which was powerfully appealing in the era of the two World Wars. War was not an unavoidable curse, as people through all of history had believed, this view argued, because we are not inherently warlike. New research appeared to support this view. Margaret Mead famously wrote about the nonviolent Samoans, and New Guineans who had never heard of war. Elizabeth Marshall Thomas, in her book *The Harmless People*, described the pacifist !Kung San of the Kalahari. If those cultures thrived without war, so could ours.

Unfortunately, the research was simply wrong. Other anthropologists investigated and found that the Samoans, New Guineans, and !Kung San were as bloodcurdlingly violent as any culture you've ever heard of. Years of research by psychologists, anthropologists, neuroscientists, and others has pretty well sunk the blank-slate view. The full scope of the argument is beyond our needs here (it is elucidated brilliantly in the Harvard psychologist Steven Pinker's *The Blank Slate: The Modern Denial of Human Nature*), but it's worth our while to examine a list of "human universals" compiled by the anthropologist Donald E. Brown and published in 1991. These are, Brown said, "features of culture, society, language, behavior, and psyche for which there are no known exceptions." They show up in every culture on earth. Some are highly relevant to our subject:

Empathy is universal.

People everywhere admire generosity and disapprove of stinginess.

We all cry, and we all make jokes.

All cultures create music with melody. Everyone dances. All societies have aesthetics and create decorative art.

We all have a concept of fairness, and we all understand reciprocity.

We all have pride.

We all tell stories.

Every society has leaders.

The fact that these features are universal in humanity does not mean they are necessarily innate, baked in the cake when we're born, though it seems highly likely. What matters for us is that they all involve human interaction and all apparently apply to everyone on earth. We really do carry certain deep-seated tendencies. Understanding them will help us figure out how we can best serve each other in a world where technology fulfills ever more of our wants.

DON'T ASK WHAT COMPUTERS CAN'T DO

In finding our value as technology advances, looking at ourselves is much more useful than the conventional approach, which is to ask what kind of work a computer will never be able to do. While it seems like common sense that the skills computers can't acquire will be valuable, the lesson of history is that it's dangerous to claim there are any skills that computers cannot eventually acquire. The trail of embarrassing predictions goes way back. Early researchers in computer translation of languages were highly pessimistic that the field could ever progress beyond its nearly useless state as of the mid-1960s; now Google translates written language for free, and Skype translates spoken language in real time, for free. Hubert Dreyfus of MIT, in a 1972 book called *What Computers Can't Do*, saw little hope that computers could make significant further progress in playing chess beyond the mediocre level then achieved; but a computer beat the world champion, Garry Kasparov, in 1997. Economists Frank Levy and Richard J. Murnane, in an excellent 2004 book called *The New Division of Labor*, explain how driving a vehicle involves such a mass of sensory inputs and requires such complex split-second judgments that it would be extremely difficult for a computer ever to handle the job; yet Google introduced its autonomous car six years later. Steven Pinker observed in 2007 that "assessing the layout of the world and guiding a body through it are staggeringly complex engineering tasks, as we see by the absence of dishwashers that can empty themselves or vacuum cleaners that can climb stairs." Yet iRobot soon thereafter was making vacuum cleaners and floor scrubbers that find their way around the house without harming furniture, pets, or children, and was also making other robots that climb stairs; it could obviously make machines that do both if it believed demand was sufficient. The self-emptying dishwasher is likewise just a question of when advancing technology and market demand might intersect.

The pattern is clear. Extremely smart people note the overwhelming complexity of various tasks— including some, like driving a car, that people handle almost effortlessly—and conclude that computers will find mastering them terribly tough. Yet over and over it's just a matter of time, often less time than anyone expects. We just can't get our heads around the power of doubling every two years. At that rate, computing power increases by a factor of a million in forty years. The computing visionary Bill Joy likes to point out that jet travel is faster than walking by a factor of one hundred, and it changed the world. Nothing in our experience prepares us to grasp a factor of a million. At the same time, increasingly sophisticated algorithms let computers handle complex tasks using less computing power. So year after year, we reliably commit the same blunder of underestimating what computers will do.

A BETTER STRATEGY

We should know by now that figuring out what computers will never do is an exceedingly perilous route to determining how humans can remain valuable. We'll venture down that road just a little ways, cautiously and conservatively. But a better strategy is to ask: What are the activities that we humans, driven by our deepest nature or by the realities of daily life, will simply insist be performed by other humans, regardless of what computers can do?

This strategy requires us to make two important assumptions. They sound a little strange, or maybe obvious, but they must be said explicitly:

- We assume that humans are in charge. The economy—the world—will continue to be run ultimately by and for humans. People start humming the *Twilight Zone* theme music if you mention this, and some may recall that a war between machines and humans is the basic conflict in the *Terminator* movies. And yet, in 2014, when I asked Dominic Barton, global managing director of the McKinsey consulting firm, about the effect of computers on business managers, he replied, "I think there still is a very important role obviously for leaders. We're not going to be run by machines." Obviously. Yet he felt he had to say it. We'll assume he's right.
- We assume that a perfect mechanical imitation of a human being does not exist in our or our grandchildren's lifetimes. The indistinguishable cyborg was another theme of the *Terminator* movies. And really, who knows? But we're not going to worry about it. If that's a mistake, then the issues we'll face are unimaginable now.

On that basis, what activities will we continue to insist be done by humans? A large category of them comprises roles for which we demand that a specific person or persons be accountable. A useful example is making decisions in courts of law, for which we will require human judges for quite a long time to come. It's an example in which the human-versus-computer question is not hypothetical.

Judges make parole decisions in some countries, such as Israel, where researchers investigated how those decisions are influenced by the critical human issue of lunch. Over the course of a day, the judges approve about 35 percent of prisoners' applications for parole. But the approval rate declines steadily in the two hours before lunch, almost to zero just before the lunch break. Immediately after lunch, it spikes to 65 percent and then again declines steadily. If you're a prisoner, the number of years you spend in prison could be affected significantly by whether your parole application happens to be the last one on the judge's stack before lunch or the first one after. In light of the findings on predicting recidivism by SVPs and other prisoners, it's virtually certain that computer analysis could judge parole applications more effectively, and certainly less capriciously, than human judges do. Yet how would you rate the chances of that job getting reassigned from judges to machines? It isn't a matter of computer abilities; it's a matter of the social necessity that individuals be accountable for important decisions. Similarly, it seems a safe bet that those in other accountability roles—CEOs, generals, government leaders at every level—will remain in those roles for the same reason.

In addition, there are problems that humans rather than computers will have to solve for purely practical reasons. It isn't because computers couldn't eventually solve them. It's because in real life, and especially in organizational life, we keep changing our conception of what the problem is and what our goals are. These are issues that people must work out for themselves, and, critically, they must do it in groups, partly because organizations include many constituencies that must be represented in problem solving, and partly because groups can solve problems far better than any individual can. The evidence is clear (and we'll see plenty of it) that the most effective groups are those whose members possess most strongly the basic, deeply human skills.

Another important category of people-only work comprises the tasks that we require from other humans, not machines, simply because our most essential human nature demands it, for reasons too deep even to be articulated. We want to hear our diagnosis from a doctor, even if a computer supplied it, because we want to talk to the doctor about it—perhaps just to talk and know we're being heard by a human being. We want to work with other people in solving problems, tell them stories and hear stories from them, create new ideas with them. We want to follow human leaders, even if a computer could say all the right words, which is not an implausible prospect. We want to negotiate important agreements with a person, hearing every quaver in his voice, noting when he crosses his arms, looking into his eyes.

To look into someone's eyes—that turns out to be, metaphorically and quite often literally, the key to high-value work in the coming economy, as we shall see.

IT ISN'T JUST THEORY

Changes in the nature of work of exactly this type are happening on a significant scale. Ask employers which skills they'll need most in the next five to ten years, as the Towers Watson consulting firm and the Oxford Economics research firm did, and the answers that come back do not include business acumen, analysis, or P&L management—left-brain thinking skills. Instead, employers' top priorities include relationship building, teaming, co-creativity, brainstorming, cultural sensitivity, and ability to manage diverse employees—right-brain skills of social interaction. Those responses fit well with big-picture data on how Americans work today versus how they worked in the 1970s. The biggest increases by far have been in education and health services, which have more than doubled as a percent of total jobs; professional and business services, up about 80 percent; and leisure and hospitality, up about 50 percent. The statistics don't give much detail on specific tasks being performed within those big categories, so we must draw conclusions cautiously, but the overall trend is a giant employment increase in industries based on personal interaction.

Other research supports that impression. The McKinsey Global Institute found that from 2001 to 2009, transaction jobs (bank teller, checkout clerk) decreased by 700,000 in the United States, and production jobs decreased by 2.7 million. But jobs of human interaction—doctors and teachers, for example—increased by 4.8 million. The institute reported that "interaction jobs" have become "the fastest growing category of employment in advanced economies."

No one should be surprised. Harvard professor William H. Bossert, a legendary figure at the school with wide-ranging interests in math and biology, taught a pioneering computer science course for undergraduates in the early 1970s, the first such course ever offered at Harvard. He devoted his final lecture to the future of computing and its likely effects. Intel had just produced its first chip, and people were worried about computers eliminating jobs. Bossert's emphatic response was that computers would indeed eliminate jobs, and we should be grateful because we could then focus on the essence of being human, doing what we were meant to do. That observation led him to a memorable conclusion: "If you're afraid that you might be replaced by a computer, then you probably can be—and should be."

It has taken a while, but the large-scale takeover of many thinking tasks by computers, leaving people with the deeply human tasks of social interaction, is becoming a broad phenomenon.

HOW MUCH IS THINKING REALLY WORTH?

It's one thing to argue that skills of social interaction are becoming more valuable, but it's quite another to suggest, as this analysis also seems to do, that left-brain thinking skills might actually be losing value. If computers are taking over those skills, then it stands to reason that fewer people would be required to do them. That's the theory. Could it really be happening?

The economic story of the twentieth century is largely a story of people acquiring those thinking skills through education, and how that trend expanded economies worldwide and improved living standards for billions of people. The phenomenon has been explained most persuasively and exhaustively by Harvard's Claudia Goldin and Lawrence F. Katz, who have devoted decades to assembling the data and showing what they mean. The reason America attained the world's highest living standard of any major economy by 1900 and maintained it for over a century is pretty simple, they show. "Rapid technological advance, measured in various ways, has characterized the twentieth century," they've written. "Because the American people were the most educated in the world, they were in the best position to invent, be entrepreneurial, and produce goods and services using advanced technologies." Formal education, the more the better, has been the path to prosperity, and it's been that way for the entire lives of everyone in advanced economies.

It's therefore striking that even Goldin and Katz believe that this hundred-year recipe for better living standards may not work anymore. "College is no longer the automatic ticket to success," they have asserted, remarkably. "We saw that over the course of the twentieth century new technologies rewarded general skills, such as those concerning math, science, knowledge of grammar, and ability to read and interpret blueprints," they say. Now, they say, that's about to change because there's ever more low-cost competition for high-skill jobs. The competition can come from humans in developing economies, and, in addition, "skills for which a computer program can substitute are also in danger."

So what's the way forward in this new world? "Skills for non-

routine employments and jobs with in-person skills are less sus-
ceptible" to low-cost competition, they point out. Employers are
expressing "increased demand for those who provide skilled in-person services. . . . Interpersonal skills . . . also matter a lot." Their
bottom line, announcing the end of an epoch: "No longer does having a high school or a college degree make you indispensable."
Skills of interaction are becoming the key to success.

The idea that general cognitive skills might be losing rather than
gaining economic value strikes most people as strange. None of us
have ever known a world in which that happens. But evidence in
addition to that advanced by Goldin and Katz suggests that it may
be happening now. Researchers at the University of British Columbia and York University even believe they've pinpointed the moment:
"In about the year 2000, the demand for skill (or, more specifically,
the demand for cognitive tasks that are often associated with high
educational skill) underwent a reversal," they wrote. As evidence,
the researchers show that the employment rate among the most
skilled and educated U.S. workers, which had been rising for decades,
peaked around 2000 and has been declining ever since. This wasn't
just an effect of the recession that began in 2008; the decline was
very pronounced well before it. Reinforcing the findings, separate
statistics show that inflation-adjusted wages for U.S. college graduates have stagnated since 2000. The researchers also checked an
index of the "cognitive task level" of various occupations, developed
by other economists, and how it matched up with the jobs that college graduates were doing. In other words: How much brainpower
was actually required by the jobs that college graduates held? They
found that this also peaked around 2000 and has been falling since;
by 2012 it was slightly lower than it had been in 1980. College graduates were still getting jobs—we'll always find work to do—but
those jobs have been requiring less brain work since about 2000.

These seemingly bizarre findings become less strange when we consider large economic developments. U.S. job growth was extremely slow after the recession, slower than ever before in the country's history, and wages increased hardly at all. How come? A drop in demand for general brainpower works well as part of the explanation. The researchers show what every young job seeker of recent years already knows, that "in response to this demand reversal, high-skilled workers have moved down the occupational ladder and have begun to perform jobs traditionally performed by lower-skilled workers"—thus the widely noted upsurge in file clerks and receptionists with bachelor's degrees, for example. The next step: "This de-skilling process, in turn, results in high-skilled workers pushing low-skilled workers even further down the occupational ladder and, to some degree, out of the labor force altogether." That finding not only makes intuitive sense, it also helps explain America's unusually low overall employment rate and the stagnation of wages.

FROM KNOWLEDGE WORKERS TO RELATIONSHIP WORKERS

It sounds as if smart, highly educated people will be scorned in the coming economy—but that is not necessarily the case. To see why not, consider again the situation of lawyers, whose work is increasingly being taken over by infotech. Average lawyers "face a bleak future," believes Professor McGinnis of Northwestern. Their best chance of prospering may well lie in using interpersonal abilities, "by persuading angry and irrational clients to act in their self-interest," he explains. "Machines won't be able to create the necessary emotional bonds to perform this important service." In addition, a few "superstars" will do well by using technology to cut their costs—they won't need many associates—and to turbocharge their "uniquely human judgment" in highly complex cases.

　　Smart lawyers can still do great, in other words, but not just because they're smart. The key to differentiation lies entirely in the most deeply human realms of social interaction: understanding an irrational client, forming the emotional bonds needed to persuade that client to act rationally, rendering the sensing, feeling judgments that clients insist on getting from a human being.

The emerging picture of the future casts conventional career advice in a new light. Most notably, recommendations that students study STEM subjects—science, technology, engineering, math—need fine tuning. It has been excellent advice for quite a while; eight of the ten highest-paying college majors were in engineering as of 2014, and those skills will remain critically important. But important isn't the same as high value or well paid. As infotech continues its advance into higher skills, value will continue to move elsewhere. Engineers will stay in demand, it's safe to say, but tomorrow's most valuable engineers will not be geniuses in cubicles; rather, they'll be those who can build relationships, brainstorm, collaborate, and lead.

Peter Drucker coined the term "knowledge worker" in the late 1950s to describe the most valuable workers as economies became increasingly information based. We can see that the term is no longer quite right. More people than ever will be working with knowledge, but knowledge won't be the source of their greatest value. We need a new term: The most valuable people are increasingly relationship workers.

THE MILITARY DISCOVERS "THE HUMAN DOMAIN"

The growing importance of social interaction as the critical factor in effectiveness and value is far more than a business phenomenon. It's becoming apparent across society. The U.S. military has found it to be particularly significant. As we shall see, the military has a long and impressive history of striving to understand human interactions. For a long time it focused on interactions of service members with one another and with the enemy, and it developed innovative methods of training from which business leaders can learn much. More recently, during more than a decade of war in Iraq and Afghanistan, the military came to understand the power and importance of its social interaction with civilians. Its experience in many ways mirrors the new realities that companies and workers are facing.

"At the beginning of Iraq and Afghanistan we went in believing it could be solved by integration of fire and maneuver," Marine Corps Lieutenant General George Flynn told me. Flynn retired in 2013 after a long career in which he had been in charge of training and development and had served as a commander in Iraq. "Fire and maneuver" is a basic tactic in which two units coordinate their assault on an enemy position; one unit fires on the position, enabling the other unit to move toward it more safely. In other words, the U.S. commanders were basing their strategy in a conventional way on technology and knowledge, and who could blame them? The United States possessed enormously superior technology in weapons and everything else, plus a lot more of it, and it had superior knowledge, in part through technologies such as satellites and drones.

The trouble was that the strategy wasn't working. There were the inevitable problems of unanticipated enemy innovations, such as IEDs, but more important, even when U.S. forces took control of an urban neighborhood, they found they'd accomplished little if the civilians were hostile or distrustful. "We found we had to have a detailed understanding of the problem we were trying to solve," Flynn says. "That led to an understanding of the environment"— and suddenly, "we were talking about all things human."

Commanders realized that individual, moment-by-moment social interactions between U.S. forces and Iraqi and Afghan civilians were the critical element that was getting insufficient attention. A jarring alert came in 2004 when, as General George Casey later recalled, "a young Marine made a wrong turn and drove too close to a militia leader's house in the key city of Najaf, home to the Imam Ali Mosque, the third holiest site in Shia Islam." The result was a nationwide uprising.

Yet just weeks earlier, a starkly different scene had played out in Najaf. Lieutenant Colonel Chris Hughes was leading a small unit through a street when, as *New Yorker* writer Dan Baum later described the scene, "hundreds of Iraqis poured out of the buildings on either side. . . . The Iraqis were shrieking, frantic with rage." As the Iraqi civilians closed in on the U.S. soldiers, the situation was an instant from disaster. Then Hughes ordered his men to "take a knee." As Baum recalled, "they knelt before the boiling crowd and pointed their guns at the ground. The Iraqis fell silent, and their anger subsided. The officer ordered his men to withdraw." Disaster averted, by body language.

Soldiers in Iraq and Afghanistan reported countless such experiences. "Well, I did this [holding up an index finger] to the minister [of a governmental branch] to say, 'Wait,' and he flipped out because you are supposed to cup your hand like this and say 'Hold on,'" a lieutenant reported to army consultant Leonard Wong. "You do this [holding up an index finger] to dogs, I think." As Wong notes, this "seemingly simple misunderstanding of cultural hand gestures could have led to strategic consequences."

The more that commanders thought about it, the more they appreciated that regard for deep human factors was transforming the very nature of what they did. Modern warfare is conducted in five domains—land, sea, air, space, and cyberspace—but now, Flynn recalls, "some people even wanted to create a separate domain called the human domain."

It has happened, unofficially. The human domain still isn't a formal part of army doctrine, but generals speak as if it were. "Planning for success in the Army 'involves the intersection of land power and the human domain,' [Lt. Gen. Keith] Walker said," reported the military news site military.com in 2013. Walker was then head of the army's "futures center," responsible for adapting the army to tomorrow's world. The number one factor, he realized, was social. "'The rising velocity of human interaction' through the Internet and social media 'makes influencing human behavior the centerpiece of military strategy,'" military.com reported. Success will come through "recognizing the physical, cognitive, and social influences on a civilian population targeted by an insurgency."

Generals didn't used to talk that way. They now realize that in their world, as in the world generally, technology and knowledge are wonderful advantages but no longer the decisive advantages. "I hope we never have to fight our enemies, but if we do, I want to do it fast—in a matter of days or weeks, not months," Ashton Carter told me not long before he became U.S. secretary of defense in 2015. "What will winning mean? Not maximum destruction. World War II was the apogee of the destructive war, where you won by destroying the enemy's productive capacity and in the process large parts of his society. In future wars, winning will mean having a victory that is widely accepted, including by the defeated. So you won't win by mowing down millions of people. You'll win by having people at the front edge who have human skills."

When a U.S. soldier meets a village elder, does the soldier take off his sunglasses or leave them on? Does he look the elder in the eye or gaze past him, hold up an index finger or cup his hands? Such decisions are now critical to whether a mission succeeds, and, as we shall see, the military now trains soldiers in exactly those decisions and many similar ones.

This is what military leaders mean when they emphasize the importance of nonkinetic operations, nicely defined by retired navy officer and military consultant Ralph Chatham as "everything that a soldier did not join up to do: dealing not with bombs, bullets, tanks and major battles, but with human and social interactions in a foreign culture." That means acting as, among other things, "all-source

intelligence collectors, politicians, power brokers, lawyers, negotiators, social workers, psychologists, diplomats." That is, it means
being expert at the many roles of social interaction. The emerging
high-value skills turn out to be just the same in the military as they
are in business.

THE NEW MEANING OF GREAT PERFORMANCE

In trying to identify the new high-value skills, we've found that
the conventional approach—figuring out what computers can't
do—isn't very helpful. History, plus infotech's galloping advances,
show that we'd be crazy to think we could ever predict with confidence what is beyond a computer's abilities. Rather than ask what
computers can't do, it's much more useful to ask what people are
compelled to do—those things that a million years of evolution
cause us to value and seek from other humans, maybe for a good
reason, maybe for no reason, but it's the way we are. An ability to
supply something that humans most want from other humans has
high value, and those wants won't be changing anytime soon.

One of the most important traits of the things we want is that
they aren't always rational. We want the human expert witness's
judgment rather than a purely data-driven prediction, even though
the data-driven prediction may be as good or better. Let's embrace
the reality that rationality is not our strong suit. We can do it well,
but we'll never do it better than a computer. Our deep human
approach to desires and solutions—and understanding where it
drives us and how to respond—thus shapes our future and becomes
one of the keys to our success.

It seems ironic that since the dawn of the Industrial Revolution—
the machine age—a lot of human success has derived from our being
machinelike. For decades, most of the physical work in factories and
the mental work in offices was repetitive and routine. It was designed

to be that way; that's why Henry Ford complained, "Why is it every time I ask for a pair of hands, they come with a brain attached?" It was the kind of work for machines to do, only the machines of the era couldn't do it. They improved, slowly at first, then rapidly, driven by the ever quickening pace of infotech improvement. Now machines can actually do most of the machine work of our world.

As a result, the meaning of great performance has changed. It used to be that you had to be good at being machinelike. Now, increasingly, you have to be good at being a person. Great performance requires us to be intensely human beings.

To put it another way: Being a great performer is becoming less about what we know and more about what we're like.

We've seen many reasons why that's so. There's one more. At just the time when interpersonal abilities are becoming the key to creating value, those abilities are atrophying in many people. It's worth examining why.

CHAPTER FOUR
WHY THE SKILLS WE NEED ARE WITHERING

Technology Is Changing More Than Just Work.
It's Also Changing Us, Mostly in the Wrong Ways.

For five springtime days in Southern California, a group of fifty-one sixth graders voluntarily put themselves through hell. They went in 2012 to a camp in the beautiful San Bernardino Mountains where they slept in cabins, went on hikes, identified birds, navigated by compass, practiced archery—and spent the entire time without digital devices of any kind. No phones, tablets, computers, music players, game players, or even TVs. Nothing with a screen. And these were kids who were accustomed to spending about four and a half hours a day outside of school texting, watching TV, and playing video games.

A group of psychologists wondered how this experience of five screen-free days would affect these students on one particular dimension: their ability to recognize nonverbal emotional cues from other people. We saw in chapter 1 that computers can recognize some facial expressions better than people can, on average, so why should we care any longer how well people can do it? Because it turns out that recognizing an expression or other nonverbal cue is only step one in a complex human interaction. Nonverbal cues are more numerous than we might realize—not just a person's facial expressions and tone of voice but also eye contact, posture, distance, and more—and we generally recognize them automatically, instantly, without thinking about it or even realizing we're doing it, and then the other person responds similarly. A retailer may benefit from a computer's reading of customers' emotions, but in a social interaction, reading a computer's assessment of someone else's emotions, and then using that information to fashion a response, would take far too long. The ability to spot such cues the way we spot them naturally—quickly—is crucial to our functioning in the world, enabling us to respond appropriately to others. Being good at it improves our whole lives; people who are especially adept at spotting these cues tend to do better in school, be less socially anxious, and have better relationships with peers.

So the researchers were investigating something important, and they had good reason to wonder whether five days of being unplugged would affect it. We learn how to read nonverbal emotional cues by doing it. Decades of research have established that children figure out how to do this through in-person interaction with parents, siblings, and peers. But those four and a half hours of daily screen time significantly cut the time available for in-person interaction with anyone; and while some of that screen time involves interaction, mainly texting, it obviously includes no facial expressions, eye contact, tone of voice, or body language—no learning of nonverbal emotional cues.

The psychologists measured the campers before and after their interlude in the mountains using two well-established tests. One asked them to infer emotions from photos of people's faces; in the other, the students were shown videos of actors performing various scenes with the sound of the spoken words obscured, and were then asked about the emotional states of the characters. You've surely guessed the outcome. After five days of only in-person interaction, the students were far more emotionally insightful than they were before. The results withstood every test of statistical significance.

To find that these kids could improve so much in only five days is quite amazing. It's as if that emotional savvy was inside them just waiting for a chance to get out. But an unusual intervention was required for it to happen. When was the last time you, or any kids you know, went entirely screen-free for even five days? It's almost unheard of in advanced economies and rapidly becoming so everywhere. In today's world, the opportunity to develop a crucially important emotional ability rarely comes.

FOR SOCIAL SKILLS, A SHRINKING SUPPLY AND RISING DEMAND

In our quest to identify the high-value skills of the coming economy, the story of those sixth graders holds an important clue. It's evidence—and far from the only evidence—of another side of advancing technology. It's doing much more than changing the nature of work. It's also changing us.

Those effects—simultaneously changing our work and changing us—are combining to shape a new world in which the role of people will be unlike anything we're familiar with. In economic terms, the supply of certain basic human abilities appears to be diminishing—for example, the ability to see another person's face and know, instantly and without thinking, what that person is feeling. At the same time, the demand for many of those abilities is actually increasing. That's partly because the fundamental wiring of our brains is the same as it was 100,000 years ago, so that it's in our deep nature to value getting various experiences—empathy, companionship, being heard, acting in groups—from other humans if only we can find other humans to supply them. From the dawn of human history until today, finding those experiences wasn't a problem; today it is, and will likely become more so. It's nice that those kids were able to recover some of their emotional sensing abilities in just five days of screen-free living, but we can be confident that they returned quickly to their usual media habits as soon as they got down off the mountain, in which case those abilities presumably reverted to their weakened state. Nor can we assume that the kids will build those abilities as they grow up; on the contrary, screen-time is increasing steadily among adults as well, while in-person interaction is decreasing, and evidence suggests that adults also are beginning to lose some of the basic skills of human interaction. Yet these skills are essential elements of experiences that we are hardwired to crave. As we encounter them less often, we will value them more highly.

An additional effect of technology is that it forces organizations to change much more quickly than ever before. Basic business models used to last for decades, sometimes many decades; the newspaper business model lasted for 200 years. Now technology is outmoding long-standing models in almost every industry—media, retailing, autos, energy, professional services, health care—and the new models, whatever they are, won't last nearly as long as the old ones. We humans evolved to survive amid the gradual, predictable changes of the natural world, but now our livelihoods are threatened by abrupt, unpredictable changes. Getting organizations to switch direction quickly and ever more frequently isn't easy, and doing so requires a command of the skills that can reach deep into people's brains, the skills that are in growing danger of fading.

OUR COGNITIVE, VIRTUAL LIVES

The large trend that accounts for these changes is that our lives are still largely cognitive and increasingly virtual, starving elements of our essential nature. We shouldn't expect the trend to reverse. It's a by-product of advancing technology, the benefits of which are so great that we could not and should not give them up. Those of us in advanced economies may complain about being tethered to our devices, but today's technology is a key factor in economic progress worldwide that's lifting billions of people out of appalling poverty, a blessing that was truly unimaginable until recent years. We're not going back.

But we do have to confront the way our ancient brains are affected by today's technology environment, especially the effects of two powerful factors:

- Our lives are still largely cognitive. Even as evidence of declining demand for cognitive skills accumulates, our information-based economy still requires many people to stare into screens all day and think. These are primarily the "symbolic analyst" jobs that the economist Robert Reich first described, predicting accurately that they would be at the heart of the economy. They're characterized by the use of words, numbers, and images—symbols—and by analyzing their meaning. That is, they're still mostly cognitive.

They paid well for a long time, and many still do. The broad shift to such jobs is necessary in the development of a modern economy. But as workers, we became cartoon brainiacs—great big heads and little else. Something important—our connections to our senses and our other brain functions—was diminished. For a marked contrast, consider touch, arguably the least cognitive sense we possess. It's the first sense to develop and is intimately connected to our emotional and social lives, even more than we realize. For example, in an experiment, randomly chosen subjects read a brief and deliberately vague description of a meeting between two people; whether they were friends, and whether their encounter was friendly, was hard to say. Then the subjects answered a few questions about the story. But before reading, half the subjects had assembled a puzzle consisting of five smooth pieces, and half had assembled the same puzzle with pieces covered in sandpaper. The subjects who handled the rough puzzle pieces saw a much "rougher" social encounter, rating it more adversarial, competitive, and argumentative than did those who had handled the smooth pieces. It gets weirder. People who look at a job candidate's résumé on a heavy clipboard rate the candidate as more serious—weightier—and better overall than do people reading the same résumé on a light clipboard. People sitting in a hard chair drive harder bargains than do people in a soft chair.

So we shouldn't be surprised that a much more socially direct touch experience, a handshake, affects us strongly, again even more than we would suspect. Job applicants who shake hands get rated more highly by evaluators than those who don't, even when everything else about them is the same. We judge people who shake hands to be more trustworthy and even more competent than those who don't. In experiments on negotiation conducted by Harvard's Francesca Gino and colleagues, negotiators who shook hands first were more open and honest than those who didn't, and reached better outcomes, even with all else held constant. Shaking hands affects us deeply. It is literally an electric experience: Brain imaging shows that we energize the region associated with reward sensitivity—that is, we feel rewarded—not only by shaking hands, but simply by seeing other people shake hands.

But of course you can't shake hands with people you don't meet in person. Which brings us to the second major way technology is changing our lives and thus changing how well we develop basic human abilities.

- Our lives are increasingly virtual. We experience other people (and a great deal more) mostly through digital signals, not through physical presence. This is so obvious as to not need elaboration, though the actual numbers can still be shocking. Keeping in mind that digital media use is increasing so fast that statistics are out of date by the time they're compiled, we see that Americans aged sixteen to forty-five, who have access to at least two devices, report seven and a half hours of screen time daily. This is not a rich-country phenomenon. Indonesians spend nine hours a day looking at their screens, Filipinos just a few minutes less, and both countries have per-capita GDPs that are less than 10 percent of America's. In these countries and almost all others, the screens that people look at most are the ones on their mobile phones; note that these numbers do not include time spent talking on mobile phones, just time looking at them.

It's no illusion that teenagers are utterly consumed by their phones. Across a broad, representative sample of U.S. teens, more than three-quarters have mobile phones, and those between ages fourteen and seventeen send and receive an average of 5,400 texts a month, about 180 a day. No wonder it's so difficult to have a spoken conversation with them. Over just a few years, texting has become the dominant means of communication for teenagers. At last count, 63 percent of teens say they text every day. Only 35 percent say they socialize with friends face-to-face outside of school every day.

THE DEEP DOWNSIDE OF SOCIAL MEDIA

As fundamentally social beings that have evolved over millennia to interact in person, we are entirely unprepared for this suddenly new way of living. We've embraced the revolution because it offers so many advantages in convenience, efficiency, safety, and connectedness of a sort. But at the same time, we should not be surprised that in many ways we're not responding to it well. Among American pre-teens and teenagers (ages eight to eighteen), heavy screen users are less likely to get good grades than are moderate or light users. Heavy users are also less likely to say they get along well with their parents or are happy at school; they're more likely to say they are often bored, get into trouble a lot, and are often sad or unhappy.

Other research suggests that online social networks affect us in exactly the opposite way that in-person social networks do: They make us less happy rather than happier. Researchers at the University of Michigan studied young adults who used Facebook and had a smartphone, gauging their happiness in a well-established way—sending them a very short questionnaire five times a day at random intervals, asking "How do you feel right now?" and a few other questions. The subjects were also asked at the beginning and end of the two-week study period to rate their overall satisfaction with their lives. Those two questions have become the standard way of measuring a person's subjective well-being.

The results were clear: Facebook use predicts feeling less happy and less satisfied with one's life. If you're skeptical, you might wonder if maybe people just get on Facebook more when they're feeling bad, but the researchers tested for that, and it wasn't true. And because the researchers were questioning the subjects five times a day while also tracking their Facebook use, they could determine that happiness declined after Facebook use. Would other solitary activities like exercise or reading also predict declines in happiness? Unlikely, since research has shown that people mostly enjoy such activities. Would other Internet activities like e-mailing make people unhappy? Again unlikely, based on research that found no such effect. The researchers incidentally also tracked their subjects' "direct social network interactions," otherwise known as talking in person or on the phone, and found that this "led people to feel better over time."

It is especially important to understand our subjective well-being because it seems to influence our health and even longevity. So any factor that affects well-being broadly is highly significant for individuals and the society. "On the surface, Facebook provides an invaluable resource for fulfilling the basic human need for social connection," say the researchers in this study. But, they conclude with unusual bluntness, "rather than enhancing well-being, as frequent interactions with supportive 'offline' [i.e., in-person] social networks powerfully do, the current findings demonstrate that interacting with Facebook may predict the opposite result for young adults—it may undermine it."

Even when interacting online with real, in-person friends, as distinct from Facebook-only friends, we suffer a loss. When preexisting pairs of friends talk in person, they bond more closely than when they talk by video, which in turn yields closer bonding than talking by phone, which yields closer bonding than texting. The friends rated their bonding as weaker in each medium in that sequence. In addition, psychologists independently observed the interactions and noted "affiliation cues," the automatic, unconscious behaviors—laughing, smiling, nodding, gesturing—that indicate bonding. Their ratings confirmed what the friends reported: The further they got from in-person interaction, the less zing they were getting from the experience.

We may hope and even believe that online interactions let us maintain bonds with friends whom we no longer see much, but it isn't so. And "while it may seem obvious that the weakest bonding would occur in text-based communication," the researchers observe, "this is nonetheless a socially significant finding, given that most of young people's digital communication in the United States today is taking place through texting." As we've seen, the researchers could have dropped the word "digital." By some measures, texting is the way young people communicate most, period.

The problem with all these effects is not merely that unhappiness, emotional disconnectedness, and weak social bonds are miserable in themselves. They also threaten to do damage through second-order effects. People who use social networks, for example, seem to become less trusting than people who don't—the reason is unclear—and trust, in part a matter of chemistry between humans, is a key factor in making economies go. Adam Smith observed that fact over 200 years ago, and we saw it more recently in the financial crisis, when institutions that had long done business fluidly with one another suddenly distrusted their counterparties, and the whole system froze. Rising distrust means more sand in the economic gears.

THE SURPRISING POWER OF TALKING IN PERSON

Another example: Interacting virtually rather than in person blocks deep-seated mechanisms that make us more effective in working together. When two people talk to one another face-to-face, their brains synchronize. Brain imaging shows that the same regions light up at the same time; when we describe that wonderful feeling of being "in synch" with someone else, it's actually not a metaphor. But when two people talk to one another in person but back-to-back, rather than face-to-face, the synchronization disappears. They no longer "read" one another, and they don't take turns in the conversation as frequently and easily as they did when face-to-face. When interacting digitally, of course, the connection is even weaker. As we will see, exactly those factors—reading one another and conversational turn-taking—turn out to be extremely important in determining how well a group working together can perform a wide range of tasks. Together in person, face-to-face, we become literally smarter and more capable as a group than we ever could be when meeting virtually.

In fact, interacting in person does more than just make the two (or more) of us smarter as a unit; it can also make each of us smarter individually in important ways. Besides our basic cognitive skills like counting, calculating, and remembering, we all have another set of skills called executive functions, which are essentially the ability to manage and coordinate the more basic skills, including interpersonal abilities. Executive functions are important because they enable us to solve hard problems, find and fix mistakes, plan complex activities, make difficult decisions, and override immediate impulses (eat the funnel cake) in order to achieve beneficial, more-distant goals (lose weight, be healthier, feel better). For performing well in the real world, strongly developed executive functions are key.

So what causes those functions to develop? Here's a clue. If you put two people in a room and tell them to get to know each other— or better yet, if you give them a task that requires them to try to figure out what's going on in the mind of the other person, and have them do that for just ten minutes—their executive functions get better, as researchers at the University of Michigan, the University of California, San Diego, and the Warsaw School of Social Sciences and Humanities discovered. Note that the cause of the improvement isn't a cleverly contrived experimental situation in a laboratory. While these results were reported by psychological researchers who necessarily had to recruit subjects of the study and control their environment, what the subjects did was what people very often do naturally when they get together—try to learn about each other and understand what the other person is thinking. Simply doing this seems to make us more capable.

Why should that be? Remember how our social nature drove the development of our brains. The researchers noticed that the brainpower required by supposedly simple in-person social interactions seemed to be just like the other highest-level abilities. They observed that when people engage one another in person and try to understand another person's thoughts, "they have to maintain the goal of carrying out the interaction, represent where the interaction is and where it is heading, and guide the interaction while inhibiting certain tendencies (e.g., dominating interaction) and limiting distractions (e.g., attending to the chime of a text message)." It's all "analogous to executive functioning, which involves maintaining plans and goals in an active state while monitoring performance and inhibiting distracting stimuli." Just having an in-person conversation is such an intense, fully engaging experience that it builds our highest overall mental abilities. It's further evidence that, in explaining how we developed our amazing human brains, the answer is literally staring us in the face.

Which means, of course, that to the extent we don't have those in-person conversations, pushing them out of our schedules in favor of virtual interactions, we're not developing our brains as fully as we might, socially or in broader ways.

The business of brain games, which promise to build and maintain our mental abilities, has been surging in recent years. The main reason is clearly the aging of the baby boomers, whose crusade against old age has also fueled the cosmetic surgery and teeth whitening industries. But you have to wonder if the dwindling of in-person social interaction might also be playing a role in why so many people feel a strong need to exercise their mental functions. If so, it's ironic that the solution for many people involves subscribing to online brain boosters. There's a simpler, cheaper, time-tested, and far more enjoyable way.

WE CAN TURN THE TIDE

To see so many people disconnecting themselves from the experiences that we evolved to have, gradually to lose abilities that define us as humans, is strange yet totally familiar. It's so commonplace that we mostly think nothing of it, and we all do it to at least some extent.

MIT's Sherry Turkle, who has been studying relations between people and technology for over thirty years, notes the bizarre behaviors that we take entirely for granted: "Teenagers avoid making phone calls, fearful that they 'reveal too much.' They would rather text than talk. Adults, too, choose keyboards over the human voice. It is more efficient, they say. Things that happen in 'real time' take too much time." We can all offer seemingly good reasons for behaving this way, yet deep down, we all share a sense of giving up something profound. As Turkle writes, "Tethered to technology, we are shaken when [the] world 'unplugged' does not signify, does not satisfy. . . . Sometimes people experience no sense of having communicated after hours of connection. . . . In all of this, there is a nagging question: Does virtual intimacy degrade our experience of the other kind and, indeed, of all encounters, of any kind?" Everyone recognizes what she is describing. Yet that doesn't mean we have to give up our most essentially human experiences, to lose our most deeply human skills or let those abilities atrophy. On the contrary, it's entirely up to us. We can even choose to go beyond retaining those abilities and become extremely good at them. In fact, as we shall see, we actually know more than ever about how to become tremendously skilled at the deepest human abilities.

The people who do that will lead far richer, fuller, more fulfilled lives than those who don't. And as we pursue the question of how people will be most valuable in the coming economy, what they will do and how they will work, we will arrive at that same place. As the two large technology trends of our era combine, as technology takes over more of our work while simultaneously changing us and the way we relate to one another, the people who master the human abilities that are fading all around us will be the most valuable people in our world.

Which raises the question of what, exactly, those abilities are.

We've talked about them generally as a group so far, but which ones really matter as technology advances, and why? Where do they come from? Why are some people more skilled at them than others? All those questions have answers, and in answering them, the best place to start is with one particular ability that is clearly foundational to all the rest. That's what we must consider next.

CHAPTER FIVE
"THE CRITICAL 21ST-CENTURY SKILL"

Empathy Is the Key to Humans' Most Crucial Abilities.
It's Even More Powerful Than We Realize.

Dr. Timothy Gilligan and another doctor were in the hospital where they both worked, and they had stopped to talk with a patient about his experience there. They had never met him before. The patient, seeing a couple of doctors, wanted information. "Am I going to be okay, Doc?" he asked Gilligan's colleague.

"Yes. Yes, you are."

"How do you know?"

"Because I'm a doctor."

The reality was a bit different. Not only had the reassuring doctor never met the patient before, he had not seen the patient's chart and had no idea why he was even in the hospital, let alone what his prognosis might be. The doctor had simply heard a patient who was distressed and anxious, and he wanted to make him feel better, which he undoubtedly did.

Dr. Gilligan, a cancer specialist, held a different view. "Maybe being an oncologist leads me to expect the worst," he later recounted.

"The patient had a gauze dressing wrapped around his head and could not remember how long he had been in the hospital," and those were not good signs. Dr. Gilligan asked a nurse and learned that this patient had pancreatic cancer that had spread to his brain, from which cancerous tissue had just been surgically removed. As Gilligan carefully concluded, "Maybe he was not going to be okay."

The other doctor had heard the patient's anxiety and had given him hope, motivated entirely by kindness. But had he been empathetic?

Now consider a much different scenario. Dr. Adrienne Boissy is an eminent multiple sclerosis specialist at the Cleveland Clinic. Tough cases often get sent to her. Some of them are tough for a surprising reason. Every so often she sees an MS patient who, upon thorough examination and testing, turns out not to have MS at all. "I used to say, 'Mrs. Jones, the great news is that you don't have MS,'" Dr. Boissy told me. But frequently, "the response was not 'Oh, that's wonderful!' It was, 'Who are you? Of course I have it.'"

It turns out that sometimes patients "believe they have MS but they don't, and no one tells them they don't," she explained. The same thing happens with other diseases. "If you're invested in that diagnosis—maybe you're on disability, you've quit your job, you're a speaker for the society of that disease—it's devastating to find that you don't have it." So some neurologists and MS specialists, rather than upsetting patients emotionally, tell them they have "a touch of MS" or "mild MS" or "benign MS." And, said Dr. Boissy, "they're so happy—they hug you."

She does not follow that course. She tells them the truth. How often do such cases arise? "I saw five patients in the past two weeks with this general situation. I had to tell them they didn't have what they thought."

Dr. Boissy understands what these patients are thinking and feeling, and, like the doctor who reassured the cancer patient, she wants only to help them. Yet she chooses to upset them anyway. Is she being empathetic?

WHY EMPLOYERS ARE DESPERATE FOR EMPATHY

Empathy is the foundation of all the other abilities that increasingly make people valuable as technology advances. It's inevitable. For the past two centuries, many office workers, factory workers, and others could go through their workday, and some still can, without engaging in social relationships at all. But as machines rapidly take over the largely mechanical, nonsocial elements of work, our most valuable roles become more intensely social. We've seen that we are most fundamentally social beings—that we evolved into creatures that cannot survive or approach happiness or be productive without social relationships. Empathy is the first element of how all that happens, the basis of every significant relationship. And as the stories of the two doctors show, empathy is harder than it may seem, and it frequently doesn't seem all that easy to begin with.

The term has been defined in various ways by dozens of researchers, but we all understand it well enough. It means discerning what some other person is thinking and feeling, and responding in some appropriate way. That definition encompasses much more than we often stop to realize. It goes far beyond just feeling someone else's pain. Spotting someone's joy, anger, engagement, confusion, or any other mental state is just as important. Nor does empathy refer only to understanding someone's mental state because you care about them and want to help. Helping isn't always the appropriate response, and the ability to understand what someone else is feeling and thinking proves extraordinarily valuable regardless of whether that someone is a colleague, boss, customer, prospect, competitor, police officer, doctor, patient, an unknown counterparty in a trade, someone you want to marry, or someone who's trying to kill you.

The notion that empathy is growing more important in today's economy isn't just theory. Employers around the world are saying explicitly that they value it and want more of it. When journalist George Anders scanned an online employment board for job listings that paid over $100,000 a year and that specified candidates with empathy and closely related traits, he found over a thousand of them. They weren't primarily from philanthropic institutions; instead, they were from the likes of McKinsey, Barclays Capital, Abbott Laboratories, Raytheon, Mars, Pfizer, and other major mainstream employers. Those results reinforce the findings of an advisory group of top British educators and CEOs who were asked to recommend changes to secondary education in the United Kingdom. They concluded that "empathy and other interpersonal skills are as important as proficiency in English and mathematics in ensuring young people's employment prospects." The group urged that these skills be taught to all secondary students, "but with the process of learning these starting much earlier in school life." The competencies "should be embedded throughout the curriculum."

Even infotech employers, creators of the screen-centered world that devours ever more of our time, want more empathy. The chief technology officer of one of the United Kingdom's largest retailers says what he needs most now are "people who are empathetic and collaborative." That's because the technology they're creating is increasingly for consumers, not for internal use, and a team has to build it together, so his infotech product designers need to sense the thoughts and feelings of consumers and of each other: "I can't have a great IT architect who has to be locked in a room," he says. Charles Phillips, CEO of the enterprise software company Infor, which makes giant programs for giant organizations, told me that "empathy—understanding what the customer is really feeling—is a key skill for us" and will differentiate them in the industry. Maybe, but when Bill

McDermott, CEO of a direct competitor, SAP, published a book soon thereafter, a whole section of it was called "Empathy." And Meg Bear, a high-level executive at yet another enterprise software company, Oracle, says "Empathy is the critical 21st-century skill." She calls it the skill "I need to develop in myself, my teams, and my children" and concludes that "empathy will be the difference between good and great."

Those employers are not speculating. When Jim Bush was in charge of American Express's call centers, he told me how he took the revolutionary step of throwing out the scripts that come up on the screens of the workers who answer your phone calls, and that cause most of us to hate the experience. Instead, he had the screens display information about the customer, and the service rep could say what he or she wished—a change, he said, that "brings their personality to life and brings one-to-one connections, which are what ultimately build and sustain relationships." To make the change work, AmEx had to change the way it recruited those employees, focusing not on candidates with call-center experience but on those from top hotels and cruise lines, for example—people "who love to build relationships and are able to empathize and connect with customers." Not too surprisingly—except, apparently, to those in the industry—the change worked. Customers were far more likely to recommend American Express to a friend, profit margins rose, and employee attrition dropped by half, which in a company of that size meant millions of dollars of incremental profit. Empathy was at its heart. As Bush observed, "Customers know instantly when a service professional really cares."

In addition to what employers are seeing in their own companies, other evidence shows that empathy pays. Belinda Parmar, a U.K. technology commentator who says she wants to "transform the corporate world to ensure empathy is at the heart of all business," cites research finding that "waiters who are better at showing empathy earn nearly 20 percent more in tips" and "debt collectors with empathy skills recovered twice as much debt."

Columbia University business professor Rita McGrath has even divided the history of business management into three eras, the first two of which were the eras of execution (making the earliest large organizations work) and expertise (the development of management theory and science in the twentieth century). Now, she says, "we are in the midst of another fundamental rethinking of what organizations are and for what purpose they exist. . . . Today many are looking to organizations to create complete and meaningful experiences. I would argue that management has entered a new era of empathy."

IT ISN'T RATIONAL—BUT IT'S STRONG

Some of the most dramatic and useful insights into empathy come from the field of medicine. Much of the best research on the issue has been done there for a few reasons: Practitioners realize that the issue is significant for them; medical workers are comfortable with the idea of participating in research studies; and the stakes in financial and human terms are extremely high. The findings are relevant far beyond the health care industry.

Research shows that when caregivers are high in empathy or proxy measures (verbal communication, understanding nonverbal cues, time spent with the patient), patients are more likely to comply with instructions about medication or other matters. If we were purely rational beings, that finding would make no sense—instructions are instructions—but it's the reality of social beings. In addition, empathetic doctors learn more, so their diagnoses and prognoses are more accurate. By contrast, internal medicine residents who rate low in empathy make more medical errors.

Most important, direct evidence shows that patients have bet-

ter outcomes when their doctors are more empathetic. In two studies involving over 21,000 diabetes patients and 271 doctors, the
doctors were evaluated on a clinically developed scale of empathy.
The results were clear and statistically significant: Patients with
highly empathetic doctors showed better control of their blood
sugar and LDL cholesterol, and experienced fewer acute complications, than did patients with low-empathy doctors. Again, that
makes no sense. But it's the way we are.

You can't help noticing that every effect of higher doctor empathy results in lower costs. Doctors make more accurate diagnoses
and prognoses, and commit fewer errors; patients are more likely to
follow instructions, become healthier, and suffer fewer complications. In addition, empathy saves money in another way: It makes
patients less likely to sue. This should hardly come as a shock, but
the effect is still striking. When patients rated doctors on the quality of their communication based on "physician concern for your
questions and worries" and a few other criteria, doctors who scored
poorly were more likely to be sued for malpractice.

Separate research underscores the importance and extremely
deep nature of the empathetic connection. One study shows that even
a surgeon's tone of voice during routine visits is significantly related
to the surgeon's odds of being sued for malpractice—and this is completely independent of whatever he or she might be saying. Surgeons
whose tone conveyed "higher dominance" and "lower concern," in the
judgments of independent raters, were most likely to be sued.

The significance of these findings clearly extends beyond medicine. They show that empathy is much more than politeness. It
holds surprising power to influence our feelings and thoughts, our
actions, and even our bodies. We don't evaluate it rationally; we
feel it in myriad ways and are exquisitely tuned to sense it all the
time. Does a doctor's tone of voice really tell us whether he or she
is discerning our thoughts and feelings? Maybe or maybe not, but

hardly anyone would doubt that we feel it does. Is it rational for us to decide whether to sue a doctor based on our sense of whether he or she empathized with us? Obviously not, since that factor is irrelevant in the law. But again, no one doubts that if I had a bad outcome from my surgery and felt the SOB surgeon just didn't care about me, I'd want to sue him much more than if I felt he had really understood my problem and was truly trying to help me.

For anyone in any personal interaction—in business, war, family, medicine, law, or any other setting—empathy is a powerful force regardless of whether we want it to be or whether we even recognize it. We can't set it aside. In fact, it's even more powerful than the evidence we've seen so far might suggest. That becomes clear when we consider where it comes from.

WE EMPATHIZE TO SURVIVE

We all have the experience every day of taking on someone else's emotions. Talking with a happy person makes us happier. Hearing someone sing a sad song makes us sadder. We rarely think about why this happens, but it isn't because we learned to do it. We have, literally, always done it. When we're newborns, just hours old, hearing another newborn cry will cause us to start crying. What's interesting is what does not cause us to cry. Just hearing a loud noise won't do it. Hearing a crying baby who's several months older won't do it. Even hearing a recording of our own crying won't do it. Only when we hear the crying of a baby who is very much like us do we start crying too.

It's quite amazing that we can make these distinctions immediately upon birth and that when someone like us feels distress, we automatically feel distress also. Researchers call this phenomenon emotional contagion. The neuroscientist Michael Gazzaniga has written, "Many researchers think it is the foundation stone necessary for the more highly evolved emotion of empathy."

We're subject to emotional contagion even without realizing it. Suppose you're doing some small manual task while hearing a recording of someone you don't know reading a text that doesn't especially interest you. Then you're asked to read that same text aloud. Not a highly emotional scenario, yet when researchers put several subjects through it, the results were instructive. That dry recording had been read in three versions—sad, happy, and neutral. When the research subjects read it aloud, they mimicked the emotion of the recording they'd heard, and they reported feeling that same emotion—even though, when asked later, they had no idea what the emotion of that recording had been and could offer no explanation of why they felt the emotion they were feeling. They had "caught" the emotion without knowing it.

Other evidence reinforces how incredibly sensitive we are to the emotional states of others, even more sensitive than we may consciously realize. Research subjects were shown pictures of faces with a neutral expression, preceded for just one-thirtieth of a second by a picture of a happy, neutral, or angry face. We are not consciously aware of something we see for a thirtieth of a second, and the researchers didn't ask the subjects about the fleeting image; instead, they used electrodes to measure muscle activity in the subjects' faces. When subjects unknowingly saw a happy or angry face, their facial muscles began to make a happy or angry face in response, yet it all happened so fast that the research subjects were not conscious of any of it. Since each subject was responding to an eyeblink view of someone else's expression, it seems reasonable to guess that the someone else, had he or she been real, would have "read" the research subject's fleeting expression in just the same way. We will later see evidence that this is exactly what happens. And all this emotional interaction is happening in a fraction of a second, before we're aware of it.

You sense someone else's emotional state in another highly sophisticated way that you probably know nothing about. The size of the pupils in someone's eyes is an important clue to emotions, or at least to sadness. Small pupils makes a sad face seem even sadder, and when you see a sad face, your own pupil size probably mimics the size of the pupils you're seeing; in this way, the person you're looking at can detect that you are empathizing, though neither one of you realizes it. The researchers who discovered this fact then rated their subjects using one of the standard scales for gauging empathy; they found that those whose brains showed the most emotional response to pupil size also rated highest on the empathy scale. Thus, says the British neuroscientist Michael Trimble, "pupillary signals are continuously monitored during social interactions, and convey emotional information." Who knew? The answer is, we've always known. As Gazzaniga observes, "Some emotional face-to-face communication occurs on an unconscious level." We're responding to the emotions of others—the beginning of empathizing—without even realizing it.

But why? Other primates exhibit emotion and physical mimicry, but no other animal shows evidence of anything approaching the kind of empathy that we humans practice every day. Why did we develop this unique trait? Plenty of evidence shows that we developed it because it made us stronger in the evolutionary battle.

Its most valuable benefit, long ago and now, is that it helped make us social. "Mutual aid between and among members of a species may be the most potent force in evolution," says Johns Hopkins researcher James Harris—even more important than individual adaptations and survival of the fittest. Empathy helps bind people together, which makes them safer; groups were likelier to survive on the savanna than lone individuals were. In addition, as our ancestors moved from the treetops to the ground and became hunter-gatherers, cohesive groups were the most successful at hunting prey. Some scientists even speculate that, long before we developed language, we gained an advantage from the ability to communicate through facial expressions—the semaphores of empathy—rather than with hands, because we could then use our hands to make things and do a million other useful tasks.

Ability to discern the feelings of others also protected us in a very specific way: "Your companion takes a bite of the rotting gazelle carcass and makes the disgust face. Now you don't have to test it," Gazzaniga explains. "Obviously this has an evolutionary advantage." It seems clearly meant to protect us; we see the facial expression of disgust, sense the emotion, and actually feel disgust, all in the same little area of the brain. Yet when we see someone smell a pleasing fragrance, we don't experience that same focused response—because no one needs protecting from a nice smell. We react to pain, another experience from which we need protection, much as we do to disgust, except that we don't actually feel pain when we see a person's pained facial expression, fortunately. Otherwise we'd be debilitated whenever we saw someone get hurt.

So in many ways, our distant ancestors who developed empathy survived and thrived much more successfully than those who didn't. Michael Trimble concludes, in scientific language, that "evolutionary selection must have favored cerebral mechanisms that allowed for the rapid evaluation of the emotional state of a conspecific." In other words, we're hardwired for empathy. It isn't an option we choose. It was installed at the factory. It has been there for something like 100,000 years, and it isn't going anywhere soon.

But wait—what was that about pain and how we discern it from facial expressions? Didn't we find in chapter 2 that computers can discern a pain-filled facial expression more accurately than people can? And doesn't that open the door to computers taking over our 100,000-year-old trait and improving on it, becoming more empathetic than people?

No, it doesn't. Remember that empathy is often a two-way street. I see your face express an emotion, even fleetingly, and my face responds automatically, which you see. I see that you're sad; my pupils contract, which you see. We both know that we've connected and have formed one strand in a kind of bond that, deep down, we regard as critical to our survival. You can't get much more powerful than that. It's true that sometimes you might be faking your expression and I might be fooled, in which case our relationship will change. But even if a computer is never fooled, we can't form a powerful two-way empathetic bond with it because the version of empathy that was installed in our brains all those millennia ago wasn't empathy with computers; it was empathy with people. The incredibly sensitive two-way bond is human to human.

But isn't there still one way a computer could succeed? What if it became possible to build a robot that is perfectly indistinguishable from a human? Remember that the second of our two important assumptions is that this won't happen in our or our grandchildren's lifetimes. If it does, then even the large questions we're considering here won't be nearly large enough. And the fact that such an extreme possibility is required to get us past the intensely human nature of empathy shows just how powerful it is.

MORE VALUABLE—YET LESS AVAILABLE

One more factor increases the power and importance of empathy in today's world: Empathy seems to be declining. That fact may appear to contradict the notion that empathy is an innate human characteristic, never to be extinguished, but of course it doesn't. Our bodies evolved to be physically active, but people in developed economies are far less active than people were 200 years ago, to the detriment of their health. We're built to function best on ten hours of sleep a night, believe it or not, and before the invention of electric lights that's what most people got; people in cultures that don't yet have electricity or regimented jobs still sleep that much, reports sleep authority James B. Maas of Cornell University. But that doesn't prevent us from sleeping much less, with terrible effects on our health, safety, effectiveness, and happiness.

So it is with empathy. We're built for it, but we can still repudiate it, which is what seems to be happening. A massive study of empathy in U.S. college students from 1979 to 2009 found a sharp decline, especially since 2000. The research is valuable because it used a widely validated test in which people gauge themselves against various statements (for example, "I often have tender, concerned feelings for people less fortunate than me"). The test measures emotional components of empathy with statements like the example just cited plus more cognitive components (with statements like "I sometimes try to understand my friends better by imagining how things look from their perspective"). Measured comprehensively like this, empathy, at least among college students, is significantly down. This seems to be a generational change.

It's tempting to think that maybe people grow more empathetic as they age, but the evidence isn't there. To the contrary, a study of people aged twenty-two to ninety-two found that older people were less empathetic. Research that follows a large number of specific people over decades would be most helpful on the age question, and that hasn't been done. For now we have little reason to expect that today's less-empathetic students will grow out of it.

It gets worse. Reinforcing the evidence of a generational shift are findings that U.S. college students are becoming more narcissistic. As you would expect, higher narcissism is strongly correlated with lower empathy, and the elements of empathy that have declined the most since 1979 are the ones most strongly correlated in separate research with increases in the worst elements of narcissism—exploitativeness and entitlement.

What's going on? Probably a lot of things, starting with broadly shifting values. The researchers note a 2006 Pew survey in which 81 percent of eighteen to twenty-five-year-olds said that "getting rich was among their generation's most important goals; 64 percent named it as the most important goal of all. By contrast, only 30 percent chose helping others who need help." You have to wonder if the poor economy of the financial crisis and recession was a factor, but apparently not. The most pronounced decline in empathy began in boom years and continued in recession years.

The researchers speculate that rising use of personal technology could be a factor. The term "social network" has come to mean an online community, but it's exactly the opposite of the social networks we were built to rely on. Our extraordinary ability to sense the feelings and thoughts of others is based on seeing their faces, seeing their body language, and hearing their voices, none of which are available to us when texting or using social media. Obviously we do hear someone's voice on a phone call, but the activity for which young people use their mobile phones least is talking. Social media are the enemy of empathy, and, as we saw in chapter 4, they're winning.

An older technology, television, may also play a role. Over the past several decades, people in developed countries have been joining fewer organizations, eating dinner as a family less often, visiting friends less often, and generally becoming more disconnected from one another, as the extensive work of Harvard's Robert D. Putnam has shown. Other researchers have found that "people today have a significantly lower number of close others to whom they can express their private thoughts and feelings." Less interaction and fewer "close others" mean fewer opportunities for empathy. Many factors have contributed to those changes, but television seems to be the largest, and TV viewing, including online viewing, keeps increasing.

REBUILDING A WASTING MUSCLE

So here's our situation: We are designed to empathize. It's part of our essential nature. But in developed economies we live in an environment that has become hostile to empathy. We hunger for it.

We can't get it from computers because that's not what it is. It evolved in us as a human-to-human interaction. The opportunity for us to offer genuine empathy in an empathy-starved world is thus a chance to be truly valuable, to supply something that everyone wants and needs and isn't getting enough of. That's part of why employers are becoming so desperate to find it in employees. And we can do it in virtually any role that involves human interaction.

The challenge is that in today's world, especially in the developed world, many people just aren't very good at it. Back 100,000 years ago it was critical to our survival. Today, while we still yearn for it, we can earn a living with very little of it—texting, e-mailing, Facebooking, and going to meetings at which half the people are secretly texting, e-mailing, etc. Empathy has become a wasting muscle. To take advantage of the opportunity it offers, and to become excellent at the value-creating work of the coming economy, we have to build it back up.

Many people have recognized this new challenge and are developing ways to rebuild the muscle. Several of the efforts focus on children, who will face a broadly transformed economy as adults. A well-known program, Roots of Empathy, is aimed at kindergartners through eighth graders and uses the ingenious device of bringing a local baby into the classroom every three weeks during the school year. Lessons before, during, and after each visit prompt students to discern and label how the infant is feeling, what it wants and needs, and how it changes during the year. The model works because the baby is real and captivating, and students know it hasn't been told what to do. Considerable research has shown that the program is effective; it builds empathy, decreases aggression, and increases pro-social behaviors such as sharing and helping, and the benefits last for years.

Some programs focus on girls, targeting the "mean girl" phenomenon and the apparent rise in female bullying. Many researchers recommend that parents spend more time reading aloud to children. Stories, especially fiction in which authors richly describe characters' thoughts and feelings, help kids appreciate how others respond to events; reading aloud gives parents a chance to raise the subject explicitly by pausing to ask, "How do you suppose she felt?"

One of the simplest and most effective ways to build empathy in children is to let them play more on their own. Unsupervised kids are not reluctant to tell one another how they feel. In addition, children at play often take on other roles, pretending to be Principal Walsh or Josh's mom, happily forcing themselves to imagine how someone else thinks and feels. Unfortunately, free play is becoming rare. Boston College research professor Peter Gray has documented "a continuous and ultimately dramatic decline in children's opportunities to play and explore in their own chosen ways" over the past fifty years in the United States and other developed countries. The effects have been especially damaging, he argues, to empathy. Citing some of the same findings we examined earlier, he concludes that "a decline of empathy and a rise in narcissism are exactly what we would expect to see in children who have little opportunity to play socially."

HOW DOCTORS SAW THE LIGHT

Building empathy in adults is surprisingly similar to building it in children but harder, because adult brains are more difficult to alter. Much of the most vigorous and instructive work is being done in the same field that has been so heavily researched: health care.

That's partly because many doctors are embracing empathy with a convert's zeal. It's hard to believe—or maybe not, depending on your experiences—that as recently as the mid-1990s, many doctors felt they should work hard to avoid empathizing with patients. "Impersonality, neutrality and detachment are needed to achieve objective medical care that does not favor one patient over another" was the reigning view as summed up by Johanna Shapiro of the University of California at Irvine (who strongly disagrees with it). Another reason for doctors to avoid empathizing was that it would be debilitating in a constant swirl of profoundly life-changing issues for patients; "empathy and compassion automatically turn physicians into blobs of emotion," as a writer put it in the *New England Journal of Medicine*; they'd quickly become exhausted and burned out.

Doctors and hospitals have reversed their views in light of the clear evidence we've seen that empathy pays off in healthier patients, lower costs, and fewer lawsuits. In addition, doctors and hospitals have recently faced an even more direct financial inducement: Medicare reimbursements since 2012 have been based in part on patient satisfaction ratings, and empathy plays a major role in satisfying patients.

Now powerfully incentivized to empathize, doctors and med students are getting trained. Much like the kids in the Roots of Empathy program, students at Weill Cornell Medical College follow one or more patients through their four years of med school. Like those kids, who are asked to speak their thoughts about what the baby is feeling, students at Weill Cornell are asked to keep journals of their thoughts about the patients they see. As with kids, reading stories turns out to be an empathy builder for adults, and several hospitals and medical schools offer programs to encourage it.

The most effective way to build empathy, again reflecting the experience of children, involves role playing. That's no surprise, since the way great performers get better at anything is by practicing apart from the actual performance of their skill. At University of

Missouri Health Care, for example, over 1,000 doctors have gone through a program in which they practice with actors representing patients. Scenarios include "having a routine interaction in a clinic or hospital, delivering bad news, delivering a life-changing diagnosis, and checking a patient's understanding of a plan of care," the *Wall Street Journal* reported. Afterward, the doctor and actor meet with facilitators to review the doctor's performance and how to improve it.

That is exactly the template for improving performance of any skill in any realm, and it works. The emotionally hot crucible of medical care is particularly revealing about how it works specifically with the skill of empathy. The issues are the same as they are for any enterprise or individual wanting to build empathetic skills, and those issues come through more intensely in the world of medicine.

"We ask the staff to bring cases that have haunted them," says Dr. Adrienne Boissy, the multiple sclerosis specialist we met earlier. Her thoughts on empathy are well developed because she also runs Cleveland Clinic's innovative program for training doctors and everyone else at the clinic. Her examples include: "Cases where somebody died due to somebody else's mistake, and the physician went to talk to the family and was the source of incredible backlash and personal attacks. Clinicians being kicked out of rooms or having things thrown at them because a patient was upset or in denial. Children dying in the physician's arms. Some of the things these people talk about are unfathomable."

Then the staff members in the program work through those cases, with instructors following the classic approach to teaching any skill: Explain how it's done; show someone doing it well, in this case with videos; ask the trainees to do it; give them feedback. The basic skill in this case is building an empathetic relationship, a simple idea that required some getting used to. "The premise is that what we're doing in health care is creating relationships,"

Boissy explained. "To most health care providers, that's not what they think they're doing."

To make the process clear, the program breaks it into three parts: relationship establishment, development, and engagement. None of it is complicated, yet participants are often surprised that each step is important and that they can get better at each one. Convey value and respect with the welcome. Don't ask your usual series of closed-end questions; let patients tell their own stories, and talk first about what they want to talk about, not what you want to talk about. Ask about their ideas, their expectations and fears. Listen reflectively, responding with what you've heard them say, and making sure you include their emotions as well as the facts. Tell the diagnosis in normal language, and frame it in terms the patient cares about. Then engage the patient in the decisions about what to do next. "Most doctors have a spiel," says Boissy. "We need to resist it—this is dialogue, not monologue." At the end of the visit, say something like, "I'm so glad you came to see me. I'm walking on this journey with you." It's an awful lot better than "Do you have any other questions?"

"The concepts seem straightforward," says Boissy, "but they are not part of standard medical teaching."

YOU DON'T UNDERSTAND

Experience with thousands of people in the program has revealed important lessons that hold value for everyone. One is that in an interaction with a patient, many practitioners ignore the emotional cues at the beginning, planning to come back and talk about them later. That's a mistake. If those cues don't get responded to early, people escalate them or just stop bringing them, and the relationship can never be what it should be.

Another lesson: Don't say you understand. You don't understand. We all say "I understand" quite a lot, and it certainly sounds empathetic, but it isn't. "I wish we could strike those words from the health care vocabulary," says Boissy. "Unless you're the patient, you don't understand."

Peer-to-peer teaching is critically important. The teachers in the program aren't professional facilitators; they're Cleveland Clinic doctors who have been trained in how to lead the program. Further, "the doctors teaching surgeons should not be pediatricians; they should be surgeons," says Dr. James Merlino, the executive in charge of patient experience. Only then do trainees accept the instruction as credible and the feedback on their performance as valid.

Perhaps the most profound lesson is that merely participating in the training turned out to be at least as comforting—as healing—for the caregivers as the newly empathetic relationships are for patients. Many doctors were brought up in a culture that believes asking for help "is a sign of weakness," as a famous surgeon explained to me. It's difficult for them to be vulnerable. But when clinicians of all kinds bring their most haunting cases to the small groups that train together, they find that they're not alone. As they go through the training, they become empathetic with one another, and it's therapeutic for them. The skill is more broadly beneficial than anyone had expected. As Boissy says, "There's a hunger for it."

We're not all in the health care industry, but we all face many of the same challenges. Competition is getting more intense as performance is measured more rigorously, and we're being paid according to what we deliver. Technology is advancing and disrupting all around us, doing wonderful things but increasingly making our business, whatever it is, more commoditized, leaving us struggling to achieve and maintain some kind of competitive advantage. A friction-free economy—in which information costs, transaction costs, and switching costs are dropping rapidly to zero—is more efficient but also more merciless; in an always-on environment, stress and burnout are increasing. As technology takes over cognitive tasks, deep human connection becomes more economically valuable.

We're all discovering what the health care industry has already discovered—that empathizing responds to all those challenges.

TRUE EMPATHY IS A SKILL, NOT A TRAIT

Remember the scenarios at the beginning of the chapter? One involved a doctor who told a worried patient he'd be fine, even though the doctor had no idea, and evidence suggested the patient would not be at all fine. The other was about some doctors who tell patients they have multiple sclerosis, which the patients desperately want to believe, even though they don't have it. Were those doctors being empathetic? They certainly discerned the feelings of their patients, and they brought comfort with their responses. But they weren't really being empathetic. They lied to their patients and arguably violated their own professional ethics, and those patients were not truly better off.

Genuine empathy comprises two parts: discerning the thoughts and feelings of others, and responding appropriately. Those doctors blew the second part. Real empathy couldn't have been delivered in the simple responses they gave. It would have required much more listening, and responding carefully in ways that gave the patient comfort, support, and the truth. In the first case, the doctor who knew nothing about the patient's condition probably should have invited the patient to talk about his worries, then reassured him about the expertise of the physician who was actually looking after him and comforted him with a message that the doctor and a team were together with him in his treatment. In the second case, the doctor probably faced the problem of recommending psychological or psychiatric care to a patient who wouldn't want it. This is where building an empathetic relationship becomes crucial. Developing rapport and trust, asking about fears and emotions, emphasizing partnership with the patient: In the experience of doctors who have faced the situation, those steps prepare the way for the patient considering the possibility of psychological or psychiatric care.

That is true empathy. It's enormously valuable, and it is a human experience at the deepest level. Could a computer deliver it? Strictly speaking, it probably could in one sense; it's easy to imagine that a computer could say the right words and hear the responses and reply appropriately. But because we're hardwired to experience empathy as a human interaction, we're not able to receive it in its most powerful, person-to-person form from anything but a human. We see again that a critical factor in identifying high-value skills is not what computers are capable of, but what humans are incapable of.

A striking bit of data from the Cleveland Clinic's experience is that while 70 percent of program participants found the empathetic relationship training useful, only 10 percent expected it to be. Only 10 percent! Why did practically no one expect this exercise to do any good?

A likely explanation is that the whole notion seems kind of weird—learning how to do something that we innately do. Most people wouldn't even consider empathy a skill; they'd say it's a trait, something you just have. We will see that, in this, it's like many of the skills that turn out to be the high-value skills of the computer age—very deeply human, widely regarded as traits, not skills, and the kinds of things we don't even think of as trainable.

But we can get better at them—extraordinarily better—if we're willing to think about them in a new way. In fact, we know a great deal about how it's done. There exists a vast store of knowledge about how to make ordinary people much, much better at some essential abilities of human interaction, including the ones that will prove most valuable in the coming economy, and this knowledge resides in a most unexpected place.

CHAPTER SIX
EMPATHY LESSONS FROM COMBAT

How the U.S. Military Learned to Build Human Skills that
Trump Technology, and What It Means for All of Us.

The F-4 Phantom fighter jet was a technological marvel of the 1960s and early 1970s. Massive in size—sixty-three feet long—it was nonetheless blindingly fast, the fastest fighter jet in operation anywhere and for a time the fastest airplane of any kind in the world, having achieved 1,606 mph. So powerful were its engines that they could hurl the plane into the sky in a manner more like a rocket's; a modern commercial jet gets up to a high cruising altitude of 39,000 feet in about ten minutes, but an F-4 could do it in seventy-seven seconds. A navy pilot in an F-4 once roared up to 90,000 feet, flying at more than twice the speed of sound at a steep upward angle, then shut down the engines and glided upward another mile and a half above the earth, reaching the highest altitude ever attained by any plane at the time.

As equipped for combat in Vietnam, the F-4 was also fearsome. In addition to a six-barrel Gatling cannon that fired rounds over three-quarters of an inch in diameter, it carried the most advanced air-to-air missiles of the time. The Sparrow was a radar-guided missile; the Sidewinder was a heat-seeking missile that used infrared sensing. Either one of them could hit a target twenty miles away in about forty-three seconds, and the F-4 carried four of each. Overall, this airplane was a package of the world's most advanced military technology.

The North Vietnamese were flying Soviet jets, which were probably the world's second best, but they were not the equal of U.S. equipment. Their top-of-the-line plane, the MiG-21, had a short range and was hard to maneuver. The Soviets possessed a missile much like the Sidewinder—they had obtained an actual Sidewinder in 1958 and reverse engineered it—but they had nothing like the Sparrow, nor was their long-range radar as good as the F-4's.

In short, this was no contest. Except that in the skies over Vietnam it was a contest, and it wasn't going well for the United States. Success in air combat is often expressed as an exchange ratio or "kill ratio"—how many of the enemy's aircraft were destroyed for each one of ours that was lost. Some of the numbers are surely obscured in the fog of war, but it appears that U.S. exchange ratios in World War II and Korea were high, meaning the United States took out many enemy aircraft for each one it lost—5:1 or, in some accounts, 10:1 or even higher, depending on the types of aircraft and the period. In the first few years of the Vietnam War, America's ratio was an alarmingly low 2.3:1, and in early 1968 it was getting much worse; in the year's first three months, the navy shot down nine MiGs but lost ten planes. The great technology wasn't working. About 90 percent of the Sparrow missiles fired didn't hit a thing, and the Sidewinders weren't much better. During a particularly bad stretch in 1968, navy fighter pilots fired fifty of those wonder missiles in a row and missed every time.

The situation was so bad that at the end of 1968 the United States decided to halt bombing, eliminating the need for fighter jets to accompany the bombers, for a year. The navy and the air force then commenced an unprecedented natural experiment in training, the results of which were so dramatic that they sparked a genuine revolution. They have profoundly changed the entire U.S. military such that much training as it existed previously would be virtually unrecognizable to a young U.S. service member today. More important for our purposes, this revolution offers crucial guidance in how we can get better at the high-value skills of a changing economy—the skills that most of us don't think can be trained at all.

NOT OUR JET VS. THEIR JET—OUR PILOT VS. THEIR PILOT

The great experiment arose from two independent decisions: The navy decided to train its pilots in a new way during the one-year bombing halt, and the air force didn't. In the four years before the bombing halt, the exchange ratios of the navy and air force in Vietnam had been almost exactly the same. So here was about as good a controlled experiment as we're going to find in the real world. After a year, bombing and thus fighter missions would resume, and the military could see which training regimen had produced better results.

Until then, the training of fighter pilots had not included much fighting, and the little that was done was not realistic. That's because practicing a dogfight is, like a real dogfight, dangerous. "When you have a mishap in dogfight training, calamity rains upon you," Lieutenant Commander Ronald E. "Mugs" McKeown, who directed the navy's new training program, later told *Armed Forces Journal*. "The world will forgive an idiot, but fighter pilots are supposed to be pros and a [dogfight] accident is a big no-no." When a pilot did practice a dogfight, he faced an opponent in a plane just like his own, which of course was nothing like the experience he would actually have in Vietnam. McKeown summed up the training as it had long been done: "It was F-4 against F-4 and people were dedicated to not having accidents." Such training made pilots fluent in use of their equipment but not expert in what counted: winning dogfights against the enemy they would face. The air force continued this established type of training during the bombing halt.

The navy called its new program, conducted at a base near San Diego, the Navy Fighter Weapons School and established it on three entirely different principles, each of which will return time and again as we investigate how people get better at high-value skills:

- Everything that happened in practice would be recorded—every (simulated) shot or missile fired and its result, everything that was said, every movement of each plane. There would be no disputes afterward about what had happened. As a later chronicler of the program put it, "No longer would the first participant who got to the blackboard win."

- The enemy would be as real as possible, only better. Instead of flying F-4s like the trainees, the trainers would fly planes as similar as possible to North Vietnamese MiGs, even painted the same, and the pilots would follow North Vietnamese air combat doctrine. Within those constraints, they could do anything they liked to defeat the trainees. It was crucially important to the program that the trainers were the navy's very best pilots; the trainees were next best. That meant the trainers generally defeated the trainees, more so as time went on because the trainees spent two weeks at the school and then returned to their units, while the trainers faced a new group of green trainees every two weeks. Those trainers became extremely skilled at shooting down trainees.

- Each training exercise would be followed by a completely candid after-action review. Everyone involved would gather in a room and talk about what had happened, which usually meant the trainees tried to figure out why they'd been shot down. Why did you do that? What were you thinking? What if you had tried this? Brutal honesty and total openness were the only approach that made sense: The stakes for the trainees—survival in real combat—could not have been higher. Face-saving and self-delusion ("But I know I fired at you then!") were impossible because the exercise had been recorded. After the review, they'd go do the whole thing again, over and over for two weeks.

When the bombing halt ended after a year, air combat missions by navy and air force pilots resumed, and the final phase of the experiment began. By the war's end, the results were as follows: In the four years after the bombing halt ended, the air force's exchange ratio was almost exactly the same as it had been during the four years before the bombing halt began; it actually got a bit worse, declining from 2.3 to 2.0. The navy's ratio, however, improved so much that it seemed beyond belief. It rose from 2.4 to 12.5.

This was a result without precedent. In training of this kind, a 5 percent improvement is very welcome. This was a five-times improvement. It eventually dawned on leaders across the U.S. military that something extremely important had been discovered even beyond the astonishing effectiveness of the training principles used. It was something larger—that the technology was much less influential than the abilities of the humans using it. The clear superiority of the U.S. jet wasn't decisive because the battle wasn't just our jet versus their jet; it was mostly our pilot versus their pilot. As air force colonel John Boyd once put it, "Machines don't fight wars, people do, and they use their minds." Even a fighter jet dogfight, in which neither pilot would ever speak to or even see the other, was above all a human interaction. Few people would call it an exercise in empathy, but that's what it was—discerning what was in the mind of someone else and responding appropriately. Winning required getting really good at it.

As for the Navy Fighter Weapons School, it became far better known by its informal name, Top Gun, and continues to train the navy's best aviators, now at Fallon, Nevada.

GENERAL GORMAN SPREADS THE GOSPEL

The air force was first to embrace the lessons of Top Gun, quickly adapting its fighter pilot training to include all the same principles. But it was the army that realized most fully how profound Top Gun's lessons were and that applied them on the largest scale. Not that the army's leaders were sold on the idea right away—quite the opposite – and how they came to embrace the new concepts is a lesson for any organization.

The man who did the most to change their minds and eventually revolutionize U.S. military training, and a hero of this story, was General Paul F. Gorman. After service as a commander in Vietnam, Gen. Gorman was appointed to the army's Training and Doctrine Command as deputy chief of staff for training. He was convinced that Top Gun as well as the air force's experience after converting to the same principles carried huge implications, and, fortunately, another part of the army was testing how those ideas might be applied to army training. The experiment was simple: Small units were tested in simulated engagements against an expert opposing force. Then all units got a week or so of intensive training. Half the units received conventional training, which "tended to emphasize doctrine, principles, terminology, and procedures," as Gorman later explained, and they learned from the best instructors of that training. The other units followed Top Gun principles: simulations of real engagements followed by after-action reviews. Then the units were evaluated again just as they had been before the training and in a number of other ways, including exercises in which two units, one from each group, battled each other.

You can guess the results. In the posttraining tests against an opposing force, the conventionally trained army units performed just as terribly as they had before training, losing 70 percent of their members in the first fifteen minutes of simulated battle. The simulation-trained units lost only 30 percent and inflicted far more damage on the enemy. In the unit-versus-unit shoot-outs, the simulation-trained units were, as Gen. Gorman later marveled, "two to six times better." That much difference from just a week of training. As at Top Gun, those were results that you just didn't see.

In the late 1970s Gen. Gorman commanded the U.S. Eighth Infantry Division in Germany, where he further tested training based on simulated engagements, again with overwhelmingly positive results. This time he had better technology involving lasers attached to each weapon and target (yes, the army invented laser tag). He became ever more persuaded that the entire army must adopt these new training principles.

Gen. Gorman had a good reason to be passionate, and it bears thinking about from a business person's perspective. Businesses in general devote little time to training, and many devote none at all. You're not supposed to practice, you're supposed to get out there and perform, learning by doing; you'll make mistakes, of course, but that's how you learn. When it came to winning engagements with the enemy, the military took a remarkably similar attitude. That sounds impossible; since most military units spend only a tiny fraction of their time fighting real battles, training is their main activity. Yet as we've seen, conventional training came nowhere near the reality of fighting battles, and sobering evidence shows starkly that most military units learned to fight real wars by doing it. The big difference between them and businesses is that the military's inevitable mistakes were much more costly.

In World Wars I and II, as in the first years of Vietnam, fighter pilots experienced no realistic fighting until going up for their first actual engagement. That's where they were supposed to learn, but their chances of being able to apply whatever they learned were small, since few first-time pilots survived to go up a second time. Nonetheless, if through skill or luck they somehow returned from their first combat, their odds of surviving future engagements increased rapidly with each one. If they made it to a fifth engagement, their chance of prevailing was 95 percent, and once they were past that one, evidence from several air forces in several wars showed that those pilots who kept flying combat missions typically achieved 50 to 100 victories before being shot down.

But what did all those findings actually show? One view among analysts was that no significant learning took place; the data simply reflected survival of the fittest, which is also the view many business people take when evaluating someone in a new job. It's the common view that interpersonal ability is a trait, not a learned skill; the performers with a natural aptitude for the task make it, and the rest don't. But we know from the experience of Top Gun, the air force's training, and other programs that in fact a huge amount of learning was happening. The problem in air combat, and in many businesses, is that the learner may never get past one early mistake. The model is, as Gorman put it, "a kind of deadly tutorial."

The same phenomenon turned up everywhere. U.S. submarine commanders in World War II learned a lot in just a few engagements, if only they could survive to apply what they learned. A researcher found that "once a commander had scored a kill, his chances of further success as opposed to his chances of losing his submarine appear to improve by a factor of three." U.S. Army officers in France after D-Day experienced this also. In the first seven weeks of fighting, about 95 percent of officers lost in the Ninetieth Division infantry were lieutenants—the junior officers who lead platoons—and their odds of surviving were terrible. About 48 percent of those commanding rifle and weapons platoons died each week in those first seven weeks. "Thus the average longevity of the lieutenant was just over two weeks," observed General William E. DePuy, Gorman's boss at Training and Doctrine Command. The Ninetieth Division then spent five months fighting its way across France, eventually reaching the Ardennes and the pivotal Battle of the Bulge. This was by some measures the most ferocious battle of the war and certainly the costliest for the U.S.—108,000 casualties, including 19,000 dead and over 26,000 missing or captured. But it could have been worse. During the seven weeks in and around the battle, the average loss of lieutenants was only 10 percent a week. The reason for the sharply improved survival of lieutenants, DePuy explained, was that "during the five intervening months, the 90th Division had learned how to fight."

In the 1970s Gorman was studying all these findings, many of which had only recently been produced. He saw that on land, under the sea, and in the air, it wasn't just survival of the fittest. People learned quickly from real experience; the problem was that the experience often killed them. He saw also at Top Gun and at the air force's new fighter pilot training program at Nellis Air Force Base in Nevada that putting people through realistic but nonlethal experience produced stunning, unprecedented improvements in performance. Indeed, the whole objective, as Gorman said of the air force program, "was to enable each pilot to experience his first ten 'decisive combats,' and thereby make available to air commanders, on D-Day of any future war, the differential between 40 percent and 5 percent probability of pilot loss on sortie one, and the significant increase in pilots and aircraft that would be available for sorties two, or three or n."

FIGHTING THE INTERNAL ENEMY

The navy had Top Gun, the air force had Nellis, but the army had no way of applying these extremely powerful principles to benefit its land warriors. Gorman therefore advanced a proposal so audacious it makes the head swim: Let's take 1,000 square miles of the Mojave desert and turn it into a site for training whole brigades, 3,000 to 4,000 men, in realistic simulated battles—and not by splitting them into opposing forces, but by having a whole trainee brigade fight another whole brigade that is permanently stationed there to fight the units that would rotate through, just like Lt. Cdr. McKeown and the other pilots at Top Gun.

The evidence in favor of building the National Training Center, as it's known, was overwhelming, but no institution embraces fundamental change. The army's top leaders were deeply divided. "Half of the four-star generals thought the NTC and its engagement simulation process was vital to restoring the army after Vietnam," Ralph Chatham recounted, "and the other half felt the NTC would destroy the army because it would, among other things, expose to the soldiers how bad their lieutenants were."

In a particularly harrowing encounter, Gorman tried to sell the basic idea of engagement simulation to a group of retired four-star generals at the Pentagon. He stood onstage and presented his charts and graphs, demonstrating this training's remarkable effectiveness. Then he asked for questions. An imposing figure struggled to his feet. It was Hamilton Hawkins Howze, as formidable an embodiment of army tradition as ever lived. He'd been born at West Point, where his father, also a general, was commandant. His grandfather, another general, had charged up San Juan Hill with Teddy Roosevelt in the Spanish-American War. His great-grandfather, an army surgeon, had died in the Mexican War. Now four generations of high army distinction looked at Gorman and said, "If I understand correctly, you assessed casualties on both sides in these exercises."

"Yes, sir," Gorman replied.

"What did you do then with casualties?"

"Well, they were effectively out of play until the after-action review. Then they rejoined their unit."

"So anyone who became a casualty got no training for that day. Is that correct?"

"Well, not quite, sir. First of all they learned some valuable lessons about how to do it."

"That's what I suspected," Howze said, pointing a bony finger at Gorman. "I suspect you're teaching these soldiers how to die." He figured that if soldiers knew they could get the day off by being "killed," they would find a way to do it. Howze turned around and faced his fellow four-stars. "Gentlemen," he said, "this is despicable."

Gorman felt his crusade was finished. "We're dead," he told Gen. DePuy, who had asked him how the presentation had gone. "Ham Howze is on my case." They weren't dead, but the episode helped Gorman understand the challenge he faced. "What I described was different from the way they had been brought up. It was different enough to the point that they just couldn't stomach it." Which of course is exactly how those who are most invested in any organization respond to fundamental change.

The hardest change for the traditionalists to stomach happened to be the most important element of the whole system: the after-action review. This simple idea seems obviously valuable, so it's a bit surprising—and instructive—to find that bringing it into the mainstream of military training required a titanic struggle. It's surprising also to see how deeply and broadly it has changed military culture. "It has literally transformed the army," then-Colonel Tom Kolditz told me when he was in charge of teaching leadership at West Point (he later retired as a brigadier general and went on to teach at Yale's School of Management). Ralph Chatham agreed. "Everything [today's soldiers] do, large or small, they subject to the critical analysis process of the after-action review," he wrote. "Today's Army is the only large organization that has institutionalized introspection at all levels up and down echelons."

After every training exercise—and in real combat, after engagements—those involved get together to talk through what happened. That's the AAR as a procedure, but that's not what makes it effective. The secret is in how it's done:

- It happens immediately after the event or sometimes, if possible, during the event.
- Except in very large-scale events, everyone involved is there. If the event was a training exercise against an opposing force, and the exercise is over, even the opposing force's leaders can be present.
- The discussion stays focused on the issue of how well the exercise achieved its objective. What was supposed to happen, and did we do it?
- The discussion is continually assessing performance at three levels—soldiers, leaders, and the unit.
- The point of the review is not to assign an overall grade to the group's performance, which is nearly useless, but to identify specific strengths and weaknesses that will guide future training.
- More important than all the other elements combined: The discussion is brutally honest—"no-holds-barred" is the phrase that everyone uses. "The real key to this

process is candor," Kolditz says. "It's soldiers and officers together. Everyone takes their helmets off, which is
very symbolic. There is no rank in the room. Comments
are blunt. If the boss made a bad decision, often it's a
subordinate who points it out."

This last feature above all is what freaked out the traditionalists. They believed that a truly candid AAR "would destroy order
and discipline," Chatham told me. "The army was very afraid."
Gorman understood this. The forces of the established order wanted
to kill his idea from the moment they heard about it, and, as Gorman later observed, "It would be even worse when they would discover that, in the AARs, the private could criticize the lieutenant,
or the sergeant could criticize the company commander, and that
kind of no-holds-barred discussion frequently would come up."

It came up from the beginning. So concerned was the army about
this order-threatening innovation that it sent its second-highest officer, a four-star general, Deputy Chief of Staff Jack Vessey, to observe
one of the first army AARs. He later recounted to Chatham that as
he watched from the back of the room, a sergeant stood up and said,
"I got up over this hill and found that something was seriously [fouled]
up." His lieutenant then stood up and said, "I know. I was listening
to the wrong people and should have sent you to a different place. . . .
I am going to need some help." To which the sergeant replied, "That's
okay lieutenant, we'll fix it."

Such a seemingly innocuous exchange was in fact revolutionary,
in the U.S. Army or any other army. For a mere sergeant to state
that someone had made a serious mistake; for a lieutenant to admit
error and ask for help; for the sergeant to offer help and the lieutenant
to accept it (as he did); no orders, no chain of subordination, no regimented procedure—it was all unthinkable. Of course the old guard
hated it. Yet the AAR didn't destroy the army. It strengthened the

army enormously, and it's worth asking how. The answers apply far beyond the military world to all enterprises.

WHY EVERY ORGANIZATION NEEDS THE AAR

The AAR showed that truly human interaction is more powerful and effective than mechanical interaction between people. The human-versus-mechanical distinction isn't contrived. Much military interaction has always been mechanical, and much still is. For a West Point plebe responding to an officer, for example, only four phrases are permitted: yes, sir; no, sir; no excuse, sir; and sir, I do not understand. In less extreme form, many other interactions were strictly formalized. Before the AAR, training exercises or engagements concluded with officers telling subordinates what they had done wrong, and there was nothing more to say. In that routine, "soldier observations and comments may not be encouraged," notes the extremely restrained army training circular on AARs.

The AAR, in any organization, transforms interaction between people from machinelike to human, and the benefits are many:

- Everyone, including the leader, gets much more information. "No commander, no matter how skilled, will see as much as the individual soldiers and leaders who actually conduct the training," says the army's AAR guide. Bringing out more information is the foundation of reaching better judgments, and it also increases respect for the leader. So long as subordinates know that the decision maker lacks certain information, which they themselves know, they'll never fully embrace his or her decisions.
- We remember more and learn more when we participate in discovering what happened and why. Plenty of

research supports that assertion, but we don't need the research. As humans, we understand it immediately.

- When people discover for themselves how they performed and how they could get better, they're eager to do that. They're motivated to do more training. Again, research supports the point, but we already know in our bones that it's true.

To say that the AAR has made interaction in the army less mechanical and more human is not to say that the army has gone all loosey-goosey. It remains strictly hierarchical, orders are still orders, and prescribed procedures are beyond number. That's why its example is so important for other realms of activity. Within a continuing overall structure, a change where it mattered—liberating humans to unleash genuinely human abilities—has been truly revolutionary.

THE FIRST REAL-WORLD TEST

Gorman's audacious idea, the National Training Center, opened at Fort Irwin, California, in 1981, operating like a mammoth Top Gun and conducted on the same big idea—that combat is fundamentally person versus person and team versus team, not equipment versus equipment. A brigade would train there for three to four weeks, with battalions (600 to 800 soldiers) each fighting eight to ten simulated battles in which all movement, firing, and communication was recorded. The opposing force, which back then was modeled on a Soviet motorized rifle regiment, lived at Fort Irwin, so it knew the difficult terrain intimately and knew the mistakes that each fresh group of soldiers would almost certainly make; it defeated them about 85 percent of the time. Just like the resident fighter pilots at Top Gun, it was as much like the real enemy as possible, but better. The AARs would begin immediately after each mock battle.

These exercises showed, even more clearly than Top Gun did, that realistic simulation helped trainees understand the mind of the opponent, and it achieved something else. It also helped them understand one another, which often was still more important. To realize how other members of the unit think, to have confidence in each one's abilities in conditions approaching real combat—these would prove to be game-changing advantages.

The results of the early NTC training were at least as remarkable as anything seen in previous simulation training. Army researchers analyzed hundreds of mock battles and compared the performance of thoroughly trained units to units with little training. The odds of a rifle platoon winning its engagement increased by a factor of about 30 (not 30 percent, but 30 times); for company teams (scores of soldiers), by a factor of about 15; for battalion task forces (hundreds of soldiers), by a factor of about 5.

These were spectacular and unprecedented results, but everyone including Gorman knew that they were just guesses. All that counted was performance in real battle, especially in the first battle of a conflict, where America's record was terrible. In most U.S. wars since 1776, the first battle had been a disaster, and as historian John Shy concluded, the results of that initial loss were "at best bloody, at worst irremediable." The problem, Shy found, was "lack of realistic large-scale operational exercises before the first battle." He wasn't writing about the need for the National Training Center—it was still fairly new—but he might have been.

In 1990, Gorman wrote a paper for DARPA, the Defense Advanced Research Projects Agency, about military training. In it he reported that the army's chief of staff at the time, General Carl Vuono, had told him that as long as he was in office, the National Training Center would be funded because he regarded it as "the principal 'driver'—motivating influence—on U.S. Army training today, and insurance that, in the first battles of the next war, the U.S. Army will not repeat the military disasters which have been its openers in past conflicts."

Gorman's paper was published in December 1990, at which time no one knew when that fateful next first battle might occur. As it happened, it occurred about two months later.

This was Operation Desert Storm, the effort to reverse Iraq's invasion and annexation of Kuwait. It was the first real-world test of the National Training Center, the first time the army had fielded in combat a force that had almost entirely been trained there. The results are well known. Ground operations ended just one hundred hours after they began. Unlike all those disastrous first battles of the past, this war's first battle "was so successful that there was no need for a second battle," as Chatham notes. The conventional analysis of that victory is that it resulted mainly from America's far more advanced technology; American TV viewers for the first time saw video of laser-guided bombs destroying targets in the crosshairs of a bomber's sights. The Iraqis had Soviet technology, which was nothing to dismiss, but America's was undeniably better. Still, it appears that commanders on the ground disputed the conventional view that technology was their main advantage. They thought that the training of their troops was even more decisive. "Several generals of that era told me that, if they could have kept the NTC, they would have won even if they had traded equipment with the enemy," Chatham reports.

THE BATTLE OF 73 EASTING

One engagement proved especially significant as a demonstration of NTC-style training effectiveness in actual battle and also as a harbinger of another training revolution that continues today and is growing more important. On February 26, 1991, in the first hours of Desert Storm, three troops of the Second Armored Cavalry Regiment—tank units—received orders to advance east and identify the defensive positions of Iraq's elite fighters, the Republican Guard. A much larger U.S. force would then follow, using reconnaissance from the lead troops to plan its attacks.

The U.S. tanks moved forward in a V formation, with the middle tank carrying the commander of the middle troop, a twenty-eight-year-old captain named H. R. McMaster. The U.S. soldiers didn't realize it, but they were entering a key Iraqi training area, meaning that any forces they encountered would know every rise and fall of the terrain. Late that afternoon, an American staff sergeant unwittingly drove his Bradley fighting vehicle over an Iraqi observation bunker, and the fighting began.

At first the U.S. forces took fire only from a nearby village, but when they advanced over "an imperceptible rise" in the desert, as Captain McMaster later described it, they suddenly came upon eight Republican Guard tanks and soon far more tanks, other armored vehicles, and infantry, dug in and prepared to defend against the Americans. McMaster's unit was able to destroy those vehicles and disperse, capture, or kill the infantry, but soon he faced a key decision. He had completed his mission—he had located the Republican Guard's defensive position. He also had the enemy on the run, but his orders had authorized him to advance only to "the 70 Easting," a grid line on a map. Just as his unit had broken through the initial Iraqi defense, McMaster got a radio message from one of his lieutenants: "I know you don't want to know this right now, but you're at the limit of advance. You're at the 70 Easting." To which McMaster responded, "Tell them we can't stop. Tell them we're in contact and we have to continue the attack. Tell them I'm sorry."

Advancing further east, McMaster's unit crested another ridge

and this time, at the grid line 73 Easting, found itself far outnumbered by a large Iraqi force, dug in and ready to defend. McMaster's
unit nonetheless attacked as aggressively as it could. It managed to
destroy these Republican Guard units as well. In fact, it attacked
and destroyed everything it could see. As McMaster later explained
to a class of West Point cadets, "The troop stopped when we had
nothing left to shoot."

Results were as follows: McMaster's unit, with only nine tanks,
had destroyed fifty-seven Iraqi tanks, twenty-eight infantry fighting
vehicles, eleven light-armored tracked vehicles, forty-five trucks,
and three air defense artillery pieces. The United States suffered no
casualties. The whole thing had taken twenty-three minutes.

This engagement is known as the Battle of 73 Easting, and among
students of war it is a famous battle because it was such a lopsided
victory over a vastly superior force. Obvious question: Why?

It wasn't America's far larger military; in this battle Iraqi
troops and equipment heavily outnumbered the U.S. forces. Superior U.S. technology was definitely important. GPS navigation and
thermal sights enabled U.S. tanks to maneuver and fire much more
effectively in blowing sand than Iraq's Soviet tanks, and the U.S.
tanks' guns could be reloaded and fired three times as fast. Antitank
missiles fired from Bradley fighting vehicles were extremely accurate.

Yet McMaster believed technology was not the main factor in
the victory. Instead, it was the way the unit's members had learned
to work together, and the confidence they gained in one another. "I
believe that the most critical factors were the offensive spirit of our
soldiers and the aggressive actions of crews, platoons, and the unit as
a whole," he told West Point cadets. "All of our soldiers attacked
without hesitation a numerically superior enemy force that possessed
all the advantages of the defense." That vital "offensive spirit," he
said, "derives from genuine confidence based in tough realistic

training." McMaster continually emphasized the value of realism. "Conduct training under conditions that replicate combat as closely as possible," he told the cadets.

The recurrent lesson, as Chatham put it: "Training trumps technology." He wasn't talking about training in how to use the equipment. He meant the kind of training that helps service members learn to read the enemy and one another.

The 73 Easting victory was so stunning that McMaster was asked to explain it to the Senate Armed Services Committee. How had it happened? "You cannot understand that unless you understand what our training experience had been," he responded. The key elements of that experience, the authors of a report on the battle said, consisted of "dealing with simulated combat situations presented in numerous training exercises at places such as the National Training Center and, for leaders, in working through scenarios in a variety of simulations."

As the first real-world test of NTC-style training, 73 Easting turned out to be an even more persuasive natural experiment than it first appeared. When the U.S. forces captured the Iraqi commander, they got a surprise: He too had been trained by the U.S. Army. Years earlier, when Iraq was a U.S. ally, he had gone through the Infantry Officer Advanced Course at Fort Benning, Georgia. But neither he nor his soldiers had been to the NTC. This was thus a test of old training versus new; the other main factors in the battle, superior technology for the United States and superior numbers and knowledge of the battlefield for the Iraqis, more or less canceled out. Realistic training against a realistic enemy made the difference.

Back in the early days of Top Gun, it was reported that fighter pilots would often return to their aircraft carriers after an engagement and say of the enemy MiG pilots, "It was just like fighting Top Gun, only they weren't as good." Similarly, after 73 Easting, one of the U.S. tank gunners said that he never experienced fear because "we had trained so hard and so often that it just seemed like another field problem."

THE DIGITAL TRAINING REVOLUTION BEGINS

The Battle of 73 Easting was highly significant for another reason, which concerned the National Training Center's one big drawback: It's so big and elaborate that it can't be easily replicated, and it can handle only a limited number of trainees per year. Satellite centers were built in Louisiana and Germany, but that's about it, and they were much smaller than the NTC. The concept is spectacularly effective, but it doesn't scale well. Massive tracts of suitable land are limited, and running these centers is expensive. The Defense Department has never disclosed the costs, but the NTC program requires rotating thousands of troops into and out of the Mojave desert every few weeks along with all their equipment, including tanks and other weaponry. Most army units go to the NTC only once every three years, and many Army Reserve and National Guard units never get there at all.

The NTC model carries one more drawback that's a bit ironic in light of how insanely ambitious the project seemed when Gorman first proposed it: It isn't nearly big enough for simulating some of the fighting the military does or may do. A real battle may involve forces much larger than the one or two battalions that engage at the NTC, on a battlefield even bigger than the NTC, and involving carrier-based fighter jets or other distant elements. No physical training center could ever accommodate all that.

Limited capacity, expense, sprawl—even in 1991, the solution to these problems seemed clear. It was computers. You could re-create at least some of the training experiences on a screen, and you could network computers to involve as many land, sea, and air elements as you wanted, at a minor fraction of what any live simulation would cost. As a first step, the army did something fundamentally new. It re-created the Battle of 73 Easting as software.

Most of the needed information had been recorded, and the software writers interviewed the fighters to get more. Satellite imagery and GPS data enabled them to re-create the terrain. The result was a highly accurate representation of the battle that was a new kind of teaching tool. In some versions (several were created), you could view the battle from any perspective—high above the battle looking down, or that of a GI looking through the sight of a Bradley fighting vehicle, an Iraqi tank gunner, or any other participant, and you could switch from one view to another at any time. In other versions you could try out various what-ifs—what if the weather had been clear instead of blowing sand, what if the Iraqi tanks had been oriented differently when the U.S. forces came upon them? This software brought together two key characters in this story when Gorman and McMaster jointly demonstrated it to the Senate Armed Services Committee in May 1992. Senator Sam Nunn of Georgia, the committee chairman, called it "very, very impressive and fascinating."

By modern standards it was pretty primitive. But it was a giant step into a new world of improving human interaction that has become extremely sophisticated, in some ways working even better than live simulation, as we shall see.

A twenty-three-minute battle in the Iraqi desert is thus an important event in our understanding of how people in all domains become more effective in their interactions with other thinking, feeling humans. It was the first real-world test of the proposition that hyper-realistic training of groups and not just individuals, when done according to highly specific principles, would produce order-of-magnitude improvements in performance, and it validated that idea conclusively. It was also the bridge to the next generation of training, which applies the NTC principles in digital form.

Both kinds of training, live and virtual, remain effective and highly valuable in helping people become better performers in the way that counts most, in human interaction. But maybe you're thinking that combat doesn't have much to teach you, that it's too unlike the challenges you face. We'll see that the NTC principles apply far beyond combat and are exactly the ones that help people improve human interaction in every realm. But okay—you'd like to view this issue in a form other than massed forces on a battle-field. It turns out that the U.S. military, of all institutions, can do exactly what you're asking.

TRAINING CONVERSATION, NOT COMBAT

The military's mission changed radically when the United States invaded Afghanistan on October 7, 2001, and then Iraq on March 20, 2003. The enemy was now largely insurgents. They might be dressed as warriors or might appear to be civilians. Critical engagements occurred not on battlefields but typically in villages. Success hinged increasingly on human interactions of the kind we all engage in every day—conversations, negotiations, interrogations, idle chitchat—and on the almost indescribable human ability to sense trustworthiness, intentions, and values based on the tiniest details of another person's eyes, posture, or tone of voice, even though all those factors and more may hold different meanings in that other person's culture. The military had, as Gen. George Flynn noted in chapter 4, entered "the human domain."

In response to the new mission, the National Training Center transformed itself. Instead of preparing to stage thundering tank battles every three weeks, it built extremely realistic Iraqi villages across its 1,000 square miles, thirteen villages at the Iraq war's height. It hired hundreds of civilians, many of them Iraqi nationals, to portray villagers, disguised insurgents, Al Jazeera news crews, and others. It created scenarios and plot lines that the soldiers who rotated through would have to discover for themselves.

The ordinary routines of daily existence became matters of life and death. For a time the NTC cast member most adept at "killing" U.S. troops was a hot dog vendor (in reality a probation officer from Sparks, Nevada) who used the same ruse on each new group of trainees, as he explained to the *New York Times*. Soldiers would come to his stand, where he would chat with them and ask if he might be allowed to sell hot dogs inside the nearby American base "to make some extra money for his family." The soldiers would always agree, and soon he'd be driving his truck full of hot dogs and charcoal into the base every day. Soldiers would search the truck thoroughly on the first few days. Then, confident the vendor was trustworthy, they stopped bothering. A day or two later the vendor would replace the charcoal with explosives— actually Hollywood-style fakes—then drive his truck deep into the base and blow it up. The trick worked every time. He figured he had "killed" hundreds of Americans.

Similar issues would get played out in countless ways through interactions with village elders, local police, children, imams, and anyone else who might be encountered. Despite the strikingly different kind of training being done—for "nonkinetic" operations rather than maneuver warfare—the principles of success remained the same:

- The simulation is large-scale and highly realistic. Actors must never break character; if a character doesn't speak English, then he or she must never speak English and must always speak through an interpreter.

Trainers have found that the most important elements in making the environment realistic are sound, smell, and temperature, so they take great pains to match the sounds and smells of an Iraqi village; in the desert, the temperature takes care of itself.

- Everything that happens is recorded. All interactions are video recorded, just as simulated battles are tracked through lasers and other technologies.
- The trainers are much better than the trainees. The mock villagers know every nook, hiding place, and tunnel, and, like the hot dog vendor, they know from experience how to fool newly arrived U.S. soldiers.
- Intense, no-holds-barred after-action reviews are held after every simulation.

Just as the principles remained the same as for traditional warfare training, the results were similarly impressive. NTC cast members reported that soldiers who returned from their deployment sometimes sought out the actors to thank them. They said that if they hadn't been "killed" at the NTC, they would surely have been killed in Iraq.

NEW INSIGHTS INTO TEAM SUCCESS

On the military's long journey through its training revolution, one of its most important discoveries was the power of the new concepts in training not just individuals but also groups. Extremely realistic simulation-based training certainly turbocharged the proficiency of individuals, and it did something else: It made each person much more confident in the abilities of his or her teammates and in the abilities of the team; members would quickly develop signals, routines, understandings that multiplied their efficiency and effectiveness. The result was the overall confidence that McMaster cited as the most important factor in his team's success.

More than ever, work today gets done in teams, and every team is a social unit. The quality of its social interactions— intrateam and interteam—determines its success or failure. It may seem unlikely that there could be any new learning about what makes groups effective, but there is, and it bears looking at for insight into the high-value work of the coming economy.

CHAPTER SEVEN
WHAT REALLY MAKES TEAMS WORK

It Isn't What Team Members (Or Leaders) Usually Think. Instead, It's Deeply Human Processes That Most Teams Ignore.

Paul Azinger had two problems. His big, general problem was that he was captain of the U.S. Ryder Cup team, a position that offered him an excellent chance of being abused by the media and U.S. golf fans after being humiliated by the European team, which was the usual fate of the Americans. Every two years America's twelve best golfers face Europe's twelve best during a three-day tournament. Each time, the world's golf writers, broadcasters, and aficionados agree that the U.S. team is best, and then the Americans usually lose. They had lost five of the six previous tournaments. The captain, who is different each time, is not one of the players and thus doesn't hit a single shot, but the media nonetheless reliably lambaste him for America's failure.

Azinger's second, more particular problem was that the world's greatest golfer would not be on the team. It was 2008, the year Tiger Woods won the U.S. Open with a broken leg and a torn ACL in his left knee. Having achieved that historic victory—his doctors had ordered him not to play—Woods had knee surgery and literally sat out the rest of the season. He had been on the U.S. Ryder Cup team for the three previous tournaments, all of which the U.S. had lost. Now, captaining a team that had repeatedly failed despite having the world's dominant player, Azinger was trying to win without him. When the tournament began at the Valhalla Golf Club in Louisville, the European fans taunted the Americans by revising the lyrics of "What Shall We Do with a Drunken Sailor?" and singing "How Can You Win without Your Tiger?"

Azinger had been an excellent professional golfer in the 1980s and 1990s, winning twelve PGA Tour events including a major, the PGA Championship. Known universally as Zinger, he was popular with the other players and the fans, who enjoyed his quirky way of seeing the world. When he later worked as a golf analyst on TV, he might say, if a player left a putt six inches short, "Do you wonder what would have happened if he had teed it up six inches closer?"

Such jokes betokened an independent mind, which is what the U.S. Ryder Cup team badly needed. The very concept of team building is a troubled one in the world of professional golf, which is the ultimate individual sport. Somehow, twelve guys who have spent the previous two years trying to beat one another are supposed to come together for a week as one big mutually supportive family, knowing that the following week they'll go back to destroying each other. Yet the team is a meaningful concept during that one week, when the competitors play forms of golf that are otherwise unknown. For example, a pair of Americans and a pair of Europeans compete, with each pair hitting one ball, the members of the pair hitting it on alternate shots. Or the same two pairs compete, with each player hitting his own ball, and on each hole the pair is credited with the lower of its two members' scores—so if your partner gets into trouble, you're under pressure to save the team. And in any configuration, instead of trying to vanquish the American player next to you, you're trying to support and encourage him.

The U.S. team had never been very team-like. The indefinable but unmistakable chemistry wasn't there, and everyone noticed it. Azinger's unconventional solution had nothing to do with enforcing stricter discipline, as one former team captain advised him, or with pumping the golfers up by emphasizing the glory of representing your country, as another advised him. It focused instead on the most human interaction between them.

One week wasn't enough to meld twelve guys into a team, Azinger reasoned, so he would break them up into four-man groups, which he called pods. He would group them not according to each member's golfing strengths and weaknesses, but according to what kind of person each was—not what they knew but what they were like. These guys had to be supremely comfortable with and confident in one another; they had to understand one another's thinking and communicate effortlessly, and they had only a week to make it happen. Azinger's plan assumed that the tiny nuances of human interaction would be critical. "A well-placed comment spoken at the right time can make a difference and lead to positive outcomes," he later explained. "A pat on the back or just catching someone's eye and giving him a slight nod can reestablish confidence and change an outcome." Azinger had no way of knowing that researchers would later use clever technology to show how astoundingly true this is. "How you deliver a message is just as important as the message itself," he said. In fact, it's far more important.

Azinger put together a group of aggressive, confident players (Phil Mickelson, Anthony Kim, Justin Leonard, Hunter Mahan); a group of "people people" who were comfortable in social interaction and who inspired enthusiasm (Boo Weekley, Kenny Perry, J. B. Holmes, Jim Furyk); and a group of steady, unflappable types (Stewart Cink, Ben Curtis, Steve Stricker, Chad Campbell). Then, with all assembled in Louisville on the Monday evening of tournament week, he told each pod, "You will practice together, play together, and strategize together. You are a team this week. Barring injury or illness, I will never break you apart."

This approach was unprecedented, and so were the effects. Players virtually reversed their typical behavior. "I usually think about my own game in these team matches," said Jim Furyk, who had played on America's six previous Ryder Cup teams, "but in Louisville I was thinking about Kenny [Perry, a member of his pod], asking his caddie how Kenny was feeling, whether he wanted me to talk or keep quiet. That's usually not my style, but I tried to put myself in Kenny's shoes, playing before his people in his home state of Kentucky." The players communicated, supported— empathized. Their pods played like real teams.

And they won—by the largest margin of any of the rare U.S. victories over the previous twenty-five years. No one doubted the reason. "We all bought in to the pod strategy, then Paul set the tone by giving us ownership, and it worked," said Mickelson, who had played on America's six previous Ryder Cup teams, five of which had lost. Other U.S. captains had paired golfers for their matches based on complementary golfing strengths, which certainly seemed logical. It just didn't work. Social factors turned out to be far more powerful—even more powerful than having the world's greatest golfer on the team.

After 2008, America's Ryder Cup captains abandoned the social-factors model and went back to more traditional strategies in 2010, 2012, and 2014. The U.S. lost every time.

WHY TEAMS MATTER MORE THAN EVER

The Ryder Cup team doesn't compete against robots, at least not yet, but it can teach us a lot about the power of teams in today's world of brilliant technology, particularly how the success of teams depends crucially on the quality of the most deeply human behaviors of their members. Understanding how and why this is true is more valuable than ever because teams are becoming more important to the success of organizations and of individuals.

It's striking that as information technology has grown more powerful and influential, the importance of human groups—as distinct from individuals—in creating knowledge has increased enormously. That isn't necessarily what you'd expect. With more electronic computing power in a laptop than existed in the entire world in 1954, and access to a universe of knowledge just a few clicks away, why would a scientist, inventor, author, engineer, manager, or anyone else need more help from people? Information technology gives individuals what our forebears would have considered godlike power, which in theory should enable them to achieve world-changing breakthroughs in every field. Groups, by contrast, have a reputation for doing the scut work. "No grand idea was ever born in a conference," wrote F. Scott Fitzgerald. Or, as the great ad man David Ogilvy put it more memorably, "Search all the parks in all your cities / You'll find no statues of committees."

Yet in reality, the most important advances in virtually every field have always involved collaboration and are increasingly being achieved by clearly defined groups. The evidence is in a massive study of 20 million research papers in 252 fields within science and engineering, the social sciences, and the arts and humanities over 50 years, plus 2 million patents of all kinds over 30 years. The results are starkly clear. In nearly 100 percent of the fields, more research is being done by teams, and the teams are getting bigger. In addition, the most influential work, that which is cited most often in the scholarly literature, is also increasingly being done by growing teams.

Especially notable are the findings on the most influential work of all, those rare insights or breakthroughs that drive progress. These were the realm of individual thinkers fifty years ago in science and engineering, and in the social sciences; solo authors were more likely than teams to produce the most massively cited works. But now the tide has turned, overwhelmingly. In science and engineering, for example, work by a team is 530 percent more likely than an individual's work to be cited 1,000 times or more. The authors of this huge study conclude: "The process of knowledge creation has fundamentally changed."

A few factors have combined to produce this historic shift, and all of them are significant in business and organizations generally, not just in scientific and academic research. As knowledge increases, people must specialize in narrower slices of it to achieve mastery. The corporate position of chief financial officer didn't become commonplace until the 1970s, the chief marketing officer not until the 1980s, the chief information officer not until the late 1980s, and search engine optimizers and digital marketers weren't even imagined until the 1990s. For almost any given problem, more people's contributions are required to find the best response. The trend is so broad that it has apparently become self-reinforcing: As teams increasingly produce higher quality work than individuals, individuals become less likely to match it and thus more likely to become part of teams striving to produce even better work. The result is that humans working in groups are more crucial to the success of organizations (and whole economies), and the ability to work in groups is more crucial to the success of individuals.

THE DISCOVERY OF TEAM IQ

So we reach a large question as the economy transforms: What makes teams effective? People have been trying to answer that for centuries, but researchers from MIT, Carnegie Mellon, and Union College discovered something fundamentally new about the issue when they approached it in a new way. They had noticed that groups take on a character of their own. They become living things distinct from the individual natures of their members. So the researchers wondered if groups could be measured as integrated entities on one particular dimension: intelligence.

The idea is especially intriguing because individual general intelligence as measured by an IQ test is a concept that wouldn't necessarily even have to exist. An IQ test isn't just one test; it's ten subtests that require the test taker to perform widely different tasks. You have to demonstrate the extent of your vocabulary and do arithmetic and solve visual puzzles and even demonstrate hand-eye coordination, among other things. There wouldn't seem to be any reason all these abilities should be related. A large vocabulary and good hand-eye coordination don't appear to call on the same skills, for example. You could even suppose that performance on the subtests might vary in opposite directions; someone could do well on the tests of abstract verbal reasoning and vocabulary by reading all the time, thus having less time to work on arithmetic. Yet, rather amazingly, people's scores on the subtests are correlated. If you do well on one, you'll probably do well on all of them. The pioneers of modern psychology realized there was some common factor that influenced a person's performance on all the different subtests. They could have called that factor any number of things, but they called it general intelligence.

Might the same phenomenon occur in groups? Could there be some common factor that affects a group's performance on a wide range of disparate tasks? If so, it would be extremely valuable to know about because the measure of that common factor in individuals, IQ, turns out to be surprisingly powerful. IQ has long been controversial, and it certainly doesn't measure everything we want to know about a person, but its predictive power is solidly established. As the researchers observed, it "is a reliable predictor of a very wide range of important life outcomes over a long span of time, including grades in school, success in many occupations, and even life expectancy." What if something similar existed for groups—a

factor that measures the general effectiveness of a board of directors
or a sales team or a project group, and that also predicts performance beyond the tested domains?

That's what the researchers went looking for, and they found it.
They measured almost 200 groups performing many widely vary-
ing tasks that groups in real life may have to do, such as brainstorming, making collective moral judgments, and negotiating over
limited resources, for example. Just as with individuals, a group's
effectiveness on these separate tasks was positively correlated. The
common factor exists.

What's more, this factor, which researchers called c for "collective
intelligence," is a strong predictor of performance on tasks that weren't
used in measuring the factor to begin with. Some of the groups, after
being tested, were asked to do a simple group task, competing against
a computer at checkers. Others had to perform a much harder task, an
architectural design task modeled on a complex research and development problem. In both cases, c was a strong predictor of a group's performance. It does exactly what we would wish for.

Then the researchers asked a crucial question: Does c tell us anything we couldn't figure out just by measuring the IQs of a group's
individual members? So they measured all those IQs and found that
the average IQ of a group's members was worth little in predicting the
group's performance. The IQ of the smartest member was worthless.
That is, even the most effective group doesn't need the smartest person. The winning Ryder Cup team doesn't need the greatest golfer.

What the group has, the researchers said, "is a property of the
group itself, not just the individuals in it."

The researchers then asked the most important question: If
individual intelligence doesn't explain a group's effectiveness, what
does? They investigated some popular candidates: group cohesion,
motivation, and satisfaction. None of them meant a thing.

The stability of the team and its size mattered only a little.

How about such fine-sounding concepts as having a clear, challenging, meaningful vision, and specifying well-defined roles and responsibilities, and giving team members appropriate rewards, recognition, and resources? They were unimportant.

What meant a lot, however, was social sensitivity. Group members each took a widely used test called "Reading the Mind in the Eyes," which requires you to choose a word that best describes people's thoughts or feelings based only on photos of their eye region. If you wanted to predict a group's effectiveness, the best thing you could do was look at the members' average score on that test. Conversational turn taking also made a big difference; groups dominated by a few talkers were less effective than those in which members took more equal turns.

Another way to predict the most effective group was much simpler: Just count the number of women. That's because in this research and much other research, women perform a great deal better than men in measures of social sensitivity. That finding is just one of several reasons that women seem especially strongly positioned to excel in the emerging economy, as we'll see in chapter 10.

"Collective intelligence" seems too narrow a term for what the researchers detected; it's more than intelligence as we usually think of it. Because it's based in large part on tasks that groups really perform, it might better be called group effectiveness. And the keys to it—to a group's ability to come up with ideas or plan an activity or reach a moral judgment or solve a hard problem—are the subtlest elements of human interaction, sensing the proper meaning of a furrowed brow or noticing someone's silent wish to contribute to a conversation.

Group performance remains an increasingly valuable human activity even as computers learn to read facial nuance and otherwise detect feelings. The simple reason is that we, not computers, decide what our problems are and ultimately choose the best solutions, and groups can be far better at choosing solutions than can any individual.

"Can" is a key word. Groups aren't always better; our own life experience (and plenty of research) shows that some groups are utterly dysfunctional and achieve nothing. But when they work, they're superior. We've seen also that as the world grows more complex, more tasks are being handled by groups. As technology takes over more tasks, choosing our problems and how to solve them will be among the jobs reserved for people because—remember our first big assumption—people are in charge. Understanding how to do those jobs best, which means in groups, is therefore vital to our success.

WHAT REALLY HAPPENS INSIDE WINNING TEAMS

We've now seen that the number one factor in making a group effective is skill at deep human interaction. That's a remarkable finding in itself when we consider that groups are hardly ever evaluated on that basis. Everyone seems to think that other factors—leadership, mix of technical skills, vision, motivation—are more important. They matter, but not nearly as much as social skills. Still, we can't do much with that insight until we understand why it's so.

What's really going on inside those highly effective groups, and how do finely tuned social skills cause it to happen? The answers were a mystery until Alex Pentland's Human Dynamics Laboratory at MIT invented the sociometric badge, an unobtrusive device that people in a group wear on their clothing. It typically measures the tone of voice a person uses, whether people are facing one another while talking, how much they gesture, and how much they talk, listen, and interrupt one another. It does not record what people say; in explaining the mystery, the words themselves turn out to be practically irrelevant.

Pentland was one of the researchers in the study that detected c, and some of the groups in that research wore the badges. They revealed what was going on inside the groups. The members of the very best ones interacted in three distinctive ways. First, they generated a large number of ideas in short contributions to conversations; no one went on at great length. Second, they engaged in what Pentland calls "dense interactions," with group members constantly alternating between advancing their own ideas and responding to the contributions of others with "good," "right," "what?" and other super-short comments that signaled consensus on an idea's value, good or bad. Third, everyone contributed ideas and reactions, taking turns more or less equally, ensuring a wide diversity of ideas.

Social skills were the most important factor in group effectiveness because they encourage those patterns of "idea flow," to use Pentland's term. Slicing the data in another way, those three elements of interaction were more important than any other factor in explaining the excellent performance of the best groups; in fact, they were about as important as all the other factors—individual intelligence, technical skills, members' personalities, and anything else you could think of—put together.

Those patterns looked very familiar to Pentland, who has spent years studying highly successful, creative people and groups. They all do those same things. In this study of groups, performance "depended upon how good the group members were at harvesting ideas from all of the participants and eliciting reactions to each new one," he observed. It made sense that the groups with the best social skills would be most successful because what the "socially intelligent participants in our collective intelligence experiment may have been doing was enabling better idea flow by guiding the group toward briefer presentations of more ideas, encouraging responses, and ensuring that everyone contributed equally." The operational value of social skills was explained. The mystery of how those skills make groups more effective was solved.

The people who made teams most effective may or may not

have been the best knowledge workers. They were definitely the best relationship workers.

PUTTING THE DISCOVERIES TO WORK

Human interaction is so powerful that increasing it just a little improves group performance a lot. For example, Pentland and his lab investigated a huge Bank of America call center where the emphasis was on productivity; reducing the average call handle time at that one call center by just 5 percent would save the company $1 million a year. The bank grouped employees into teams of about twenty, but they didn't interact much, in part because their work was entirely solitary, sitting in a cubicle with a phone and a computer. They were unlikely to run into each other very often anyway because the bank staggered break times in order to keep staffing levels steady. Here was a team that barely justified the term.

Yet the members did interact a bit, and when Pentland asked them to wear the sociometric badges for six weeks, he found that the best predictor of team productivity was how much the members interacted in the little time they had, and what he calls engagement, the degree to which all team members were involved in the interaction. So Pentland proposed that managers try an experiment: Give a whole twenty-person team their coffee break at the same time. In a call center of over 3,000 employees, it was easy to shift others' breaks to maintain service. The result was that group members interacted more, though it still wasn't much; more of them were involved in the interaction; and productivity rocketed. The effects were so clear that the bank switched to team-based breaks at all its call centers, estimating the move would save $15 million a year.

The same thing seems to happen everywhere. Even when people work mostly on their own, the right patterns of interaction when they do get together—as distinct from individuals' personalities or anything else—are the main way groups get better. Pentland concludes that "being in the loop allows employees to learn tricks of the trade—the kind of tacit, detailed experience that separates novices from experts—and is what keeps the idea machine efficiently ticking along." When people actually do work together substantively, it's the same effect on steroids.

WHAT TEAMS LOSE WHEN THEY GO ONLINE

Which leads to a seemingly obvious conclusion: If lots of interaction and broad engagement are the most powerful drivers of a group's performance, then hasn't technology brought us to the doorway of nirvana? Aren't e-mail, texting, and social media the greatest gift to groups in history? The answer is no, or at least not necessarily. Social interaction is the very essence of being human, as we've seen—a phenomenon so highly evolved that we're still discovering all the ways in which it happens, sometimes affecting us deeply without our even realizing what happened. We didn't develop these wondrous abilities in the electronic age, and a lot of them just don't work online. For example, Pentland's lab experimented with groups connected only by technology and found that members continued to use body language, even though no one could see them, and of course we've all done the same thing. The trouble is that we're throwing away one of our strongest and most deeply-rooted tools for connecting with one another: mimicking. As we saw in chapter 3, we often mimic the postures and gestures of others, mostly unconsciously, and this process is extremely powerful in building empathy and trust between people, though neither party may realize it's happening. Even when we can't see each other, we can scarcely stop ourselves from trying to make it happen. But if we can't see each other in real time, it won't work.

Evidence is clear that face-to-face interaction is far richer and more effective than is the fragile, meager digital version in building trust, cooperation, and the patterns of behavior that make groups effective. Is anyone surprised? We humans were interacting face-to-face long before we developed language, and today even when we're talking, it isn't what we say that matters most. After badging hundreds of groups in face-to-face interaction and collecting billions of data points, Pentland and his colleagues realized that unspoken social signals—who's talking, how much, in what tone, interrupting or not, facing toward whom and away from whom, gesturing how—told them all they needed to know about the performance of a group. They didn't need to hear any words. Pentland's striking finding is that "usually we can completely ignore the content of discussions and use only the visible social signals to predict the outcome of a negotiation or a sales pitch, the quality of group decision making, and the roles people assume within the group." But most of those visible social signals aren't available in digital communication.

When digital interaction is effective, it's most likely between people who already have a face-to-face relationship. Some 61 million U.S. Facebook users got a "go vote" message on election day 2010, part of an experiment by political science professor James Fowler and Facebook researchers. A simple informational message about voting had no effect at all; people who got it were no likelier to vote than were those who got no message. But other users received the same message plus randomly selected profile photos of up to six of their Facebook friends who had clicked an "I voted" button on Facebook. Those users were more likely to vote; the message merely informing people that some friends had voted got an extra 60,000 users to the polls. But the real effect was in what happened next: When those users clicked the "I voted" button, triggering a message from them in their friends' newsfeeds, as distinct from the randomly generated message telling them some friends had voted, an extra 280,000 of their friends voted.

This would seem to be strong evidence of the power of online relationships. But actually it was just the opposite. When the researchers dug deeper, they found that these influential friends weren't just any friends. "Only close friends influenced users to vote in the real world," the researchers found. "Facebook users have an average of about 150 friends, but they are likely to have close relationships with only ten," they reported, and those few friendships, based on face-to-face interaction, made all the difference. "The closest ten friends on Facebook mattered; the other 140 didn't matter at all," Fowler said. "Online networks are powerful . . . but it is those real-world ties that we have always had that are making a difference."

That is, there are Facebook friends, and then there are actual friends. Other research underscores the difference, but your own experience with online-only relationships versus strong in-person relationships is all the evidence you need. Effective teams are built on person-to-person interaction, usually among small numbers of people. Digital media can help sustain strong relationships that were established face-to-face in the real world, but cannot create such strong relationships. It's the way we're wired.

It may seem ironic that few people have ever understood that fact better than one of the greatest digital geniuses, Steve Jobs. "Despite being a denizen of the digital world, or maybe because he knew all too well its isolating potential, Jobs was a strong believer in face-to-face meetings," reports Walter Isaacson in his Jobs biography. He quotes Jobs: "'There's a temptation in our networked age to think that ideas can be developed by e-mail and iChat. That's crazy. Creativity comes from spontaneous meetings, from random discussions. You run into someone, you ask what they're doing, you say 'Wow,' and soon you're cooking up all sorts of ideas.'"

It all has to happen in person. That's why Jobs famously designed the Pixar headquarters the way he did. Pixar is the animation studio that Jobs initially funded and eventually ran in the years before he returned to Apple and for several years thereafter. It's arguably the most successful film studio ever, since it has never produced a flop. The *Toy Story* films, *Finding Nemo*, the *Cars* films—of the fourteen features it had produced through 2013, every one was a major financial winner. Jobs wanted to keep it that way, so he insisted that Pixar's new headquarters be designed around a central atrium; he then placed the café, mailboxes, conference rooms, and other elements so as to force people to criss-cross it. "We designed the building to make people get out of their offices and mingle in the central atrium," he told Isaacson. He felt so strongly about this that he ordered just two giant bathrooms for the whole building, both off the atrium. That was going too far. An employee revolt killed the idea, but all of the bathrooms to be added were—guess where—near the atrium. Jobs knew what makes teams work, and it isn't e-mail.

MORE POWERFUL THAN ECONOMICS

Maybe you've been struck by how irrational all these findings seem to be. People are enormously more likely to vote if they know that a close friend has done so—but why should that make any difference? Teams are more effective if their members take equal turns in conversation and exhibit social sensitivity, and we've seen that they do this for reasons deeply rooted in our evolutionary past; but in a business setting, where dollars supposedly make the difference, does that make any sense? Yes, those behaviors make a team more successful, which is good for a business, but in the real world we know it's naïve to presume that all members of a successful team will share in the rewards; in any case, it's a stretch to imagine that people are taking equal conversational turns just because they think they'll earn more money. But then why are they doing it? In a business, where people are working to support themselves and their families, why on earth would they behave in a way that they don't feel confident will pay—and indeed may have no good reason to think will pay—sooner or later?

So let's just say it: Yes, such behavior is irrational. It does not fit the model of homo economicus—the rational, knowledgeable, wealth-maximizing person who forms the basis of neoclassical economics. That concept has been pretty well demolished by forty years of behavioral economics research that shows in a hundred ways how crazy our decisions often are. In explaining effective groups, though, we're looking at a slightly different type of irrational behavior. Behavioral economics focuses on our predictably faulty cognitive behavior. (Example: A pad and pencil together cost $1.10. The pad costs a dollar more than the pencil. What does the pencil cost? Almost everybody will immediately say ten cents, which of course is wrong.) That's why Daniel Kahneman called his monumental book on the subject *Thinking, Fast and Slow*—it's about thinking. Here, we're looking instead at social behavior. It's irrational in that it's a clear affront to economic man. But unlike the foibles revealed by behavioral economics, it doesn't lead us into error. On the contrary, our irrational social behavior leads us to great performance, to producing megahit movies and winning international golf tournaments and achieving undreamed-of efficiencies. How perfectly, essentially human: irrational behavior that somehow makes sense.

The contradiction appears most clearly in the pioneering work of Wharton's Adam Grant on givers and takers. In a company with a giver culture, Grant says, employees are "helping others, sharing knowledge, offering mentoring, and making connections without expecting anything in return." An economist would say they're nuts. In a taker culture, by contrast, "the norm is to get as much as possible from others while contributing less in return. Employees help only when they expect the personal benefits to exceed the costs." And is that not the very definition of economic rationality?

Yet which culture do you think produces better results?

We all know the answer. Extensive research shows that the answer is even more impressive than we suspect. A giant meta-analysis of studies involving 51,000 people in companies found that giver behaviors were associated with higher productivity, efficiency, and profit; lower costs, employee turnover, and absenteeism; and greater customer satisfaction.

The giver culture works even in environments where employees needn't interact much, as discovered in that petri dish of organizational research, the call center. Grant reports how a firm called Appletree Answers was plagued by a 97 percent employee turnover rate, a common problem in that industry. Desperate for a solution, the managers devised a program called Dream On that invited employees to request the thing they wanted most in their personal lives but believed they could never get. Then a secret committee started fulfilling those dreams—"from sending an employee's severely ill husband to meet his favorite players at a Philadelphia Eagles game to helping an employee throw a special birthday party for his daughter." With surprising speed, the culture was transformed. Employees started submitting Dream On requests on behalf of colleagues and more broadly started looking for ways to help each other. In six months the turnover rate plunged from 97 percent to 33 percent. Lower turnover means employees stay longer and can build closer bonds. The company immediately had its two most profitable quarters ever.

The power of economically irrational social bonding in improving team performance shows up even when researchers aren't looking for it. In the aftermath of the 9/11 attacks, the Intelligence Science Board asked Harvard psychologist J. Richard Hackman and Michael O'Connor of Mitre Corp. to figure out why some of the government's intelligence analysis teams were so much more effective than others. The researchers discovered that the most important difference was the fundamental basis on which a team was organized—cognitive or social. "The cognitive perspective puts the individual analyst at center stage," they reported. "The social perspective, by contrast, focuses more on the importance of collegial interactions. . . ." Their report therefore mostly compared these two kinds of teams—"a comparison that, we must note, was not the original purpose of the research."

They weren't looking to categorize teams in this way, but the distinction was unavoidable, and the differences in performance were stark. The socially based teams were 30 percent more effective than the cognitively based ones. The main reason, also unsought by the researchers, was likewise emphatically clear. It was the seemingly irrational culture of the socially based teams and the greater, deeper interaction that resulted. The members spent time teaching and helping each other without being exhorted to do so or having any system of rewards. Helping behaviors "unexpectedly turned out to be more powerfully associated with team effectiveness than any other factor assessed in the research." Just as other researchers found that social sensitivity was the most important element in team effectiveness, these researchers found also that social factors, in this case helping behaviors, were the key.

Seen in one way, this all makes sense. We can easily understand why a group that elicits everyone's ideas and everyone's reactions is more effective than a group dominated by a few blowhards, and why a group of people who help one another achieves far more than a group of people who don't. But in another way, this makes no sense at all. Why should any individual behave like the members of these highly effective teams? After all, these behaviors work only if everyone does them. Doing them alone may bring you nothing and could even hurt you; if you're the only giver in an office of takers, you may just get walked on. It would seem to be a miracle that effective teams ever occur.

WHY THE MIRACLE SOMETIMES HAPPENS

We are powerfully driven to do what we see a group of peers doing, so if the right behaviors get a foothold in a group, they may snowball. Of all the hardwiring in our brains, this conformity behavior is some of the hardest. For an early human on the savanna, belonging to a group was a matter of life and death because the group helped protect him or her from predators and could hunt prey and guard resources far more effectively than any individual could. Fitting in with the group meant survival; spurning it meant likely doom. Our group-joining imperative is even older than that. Primates that live in groups make distinctive sounds and movements to indicate what they think the troop should do next, in a process that leads to a consensus; once that consensus becomes clear, a troop member would be very foolish not to go along with it. That process lives on today through the similar signaling that happens in meeting rooms—the "uh-huh," "right," "what?" and body language that Pentland's team documented—through which a human group reaches consensus. Going along is rarely a matter of life and death, but group members act almost as if it is, tending to fall in line and behave like the rest of the group.

Improving the odds that helping behaviors might actually establish themselves in a group is the fact that participating in cooperative group behavior—working for the success of the group without regard to potential personal rewards—makes us high. Consider a crew of rowers. We know that the simple physical activity of exercise causes the body to produce endorphins, natural opioids; that's "runner's high." Rowers experience this when training individually on rowing machines. But put eight rowers into a boat and have them exert exactly the same amount of effort as they did individually on the machines, and their bodies produce more endorphins. The researchers who discovered this phenomenon observed that the increase was apparently "owing in some way to the effect of working together as a highly coordinated team." That result is especially meaningful because rowing is the ultimate team sport. Any attempt by a crew member to distinguish himself or herself individually merely unbalances the boat and degrades performance. That is, the extra endorphins seem to result from subsuming one's own efforts in the group's efforts. Members of the most effective intelligence analysis teams, and of the best teams in general, actually aren't behaving crazily. They get a highly rewarding buzz from rejecting the goal of personal gain in favor of the group's success.

Plenty of other evidence shows that working together in close coordination makes people happy and even euphoric. Activity as simple as singing together triggers the release of opioids. More broadly, and more significantly for understanding highly effective teams, such activities also promote exactly the social tendencies that contribute most to a team's performance—"cooperativeness and generosity" and "greater willingness to behave altruistically toward those with whom one performs such activities," say researchers from the University of Oxford. "Group-activity-generated endorphin release may thus play a . . . role in bonding human social groups."

The apparent mystery of effective teams is that the individual members behave in ways that don't seem to serve their individual interests—helping one another without expecting recompense, not dominating group activities—and why would they do this? It isn't rational. Yet the mystery has a solution. We're clearly ruled by more powerful forces, not always for the worse. In some settings nonrational behaviors can cause us considerable grief, but when a team is performing at high levels, it's in large part because ancient instincts and powerful brain chemistry are asserting their towering dominance over puny rationality.

WHY TEAMS NEED TIME

As we've observed before, we humans are not machines. We don't entirely make sense, and this sometimes baffling quirkiness is in fact understandable and key to our effectiveness and greatest value in the changing economy. In the context of teams, it means that individuals are not interchangeable parts. We do not all bring the same social skills, and group effectiveness depends on building up social capital between group members through earning trust and helping one another. It all takes time. An important implication of these findings is that since highly effective teams are rare and valuable, not easily or quickly replicated, keeping them together, once formed, is worth a lot.

Exhibit A was Apple's top team under Steve Jobs. The conventional view of Apple's success is that it derived from Jobs's genius and dictatorial management, but Jobs knew that wasn't nearly enough. He worked extraordinarily hard to assemble and keep a highly effective top team, which is an extremely difficult feat in a successful company. As the company prospers, other firms try to lure away its executives, usually with higher-level, higher-paying, more highly visible roles, and the temptation can be overwhelming. Nonetheless, by the time Jobs stepped down as CEO in August 2011, the six-executive inner circle he had assembled had been working as a team for thirteen years, meeting together for hours every week. This is virtually unheard of and appears to be unique among companies of Apple's size and success. The social capital this group had built was beyond imagining, and no one, least of all Jobs, doubted that this was a major reason the company became the most valuable in the world.

To see how wrong things can go when teams don't have a chance to build social capital, look at the statistics on airline mishaps, which are almost incredible. "The National Transportation Safety Board found that 73 percent of the incidents in its database occurred on a crew's first day of flying together, before people had the chance to learn through experience how best to operate as a team," reports Harvard's J. Richard Hackman, who also studied the intelligence analyst teams after 9/11 and is a preeminent researcher on groups. Scheduling crew members individually rather than as teams is more efficient for the airlines, but the results may give you pause next time you step onto a plane. "I once asked an operations researcher of an airline to estimate how long it would take, if he and I were assigned to work together on a trip, before we could expect to work together again," Hackman told the *Harvard Business Review*. "He calculated that it would take 5.6 years. Clearly this is not good from a passenger point of view."

As contrast, Hackman notes the practice of the Strategic Air Command, which oversaw the planes that would have delivered nuclear bombs during the Cold War. Those crews trained together and stayed together, and they performed much better than any other crews he studied. His conclusion: "When you're working together in real time and there can be no mistakes, then you keep your teams together for years and years rather than constantly change their composition."

The story is similar in another high-stakes field: surgery. Dr. John Noseworthy, CEO of the Mayo Clinic, told me about the considerable lengths to which he has gone in order to keep together a highly effective surgical team. The value of a team may seem surprising in surgery, since only one member is applying the scalpel to the patient, but it can actually make a significant difference to a patient's chance of surviving. Patients are far less likely to die when they're operated on by surgeons who perform a lot of operations—hardly surprising. But when a surgeon does the same operation at a hospital other than his home base, with a different team, the high-volume advantage evaporates. This somewhat disturbing discovery comes from Harvard Business School researchers who studied cardiac surgeons who practice at multiple hospitals. If they perform a lot of procedures at hospital A, their patients' mortality rates there are admirably low. But their unfortunate patients at hospital B don't get any of that benefit because over there, the surgeons perform no better than if they had never done all those operations at hospital A. A patient's chance of dying is just as great as if the surgeon hadn't accumulated all that practice. The explanation, say the researchers, is "a surgeon's familiarity with

critical assets of the hospital organization . . . which may be specific
employees, team structures, or operating routines."

Surgery and piloting are activities guided by strict and elaborate protocols, and the people who do them must go through years
of training and rigorous certifications. Airliner cockpits and operating rooms would thus seem to be the settings in which people are
as close to being interchangeable parts as they could possibly be.
Yet even there, social factors, which are entirely disregarded by all
those regulations and protocols, turn out to be critically important. The difference between teams whose members have learned
over time how to work well together—who have built up social
capital among themselves—and teams whose members have not
can be literally the difference between life and death, just as it was
on the savanna 100,000 years ago.

The world is doing ever more of its work in teams, and we
humans have been exquisitely fine-tuned over the millennia to work
together in this way. For that reason, we're not well suited to doing
this valuable type of group work with computers. It's not that computers couldn't bring at least as much knowledge to a team as people could. The issue, as we saw when we examined empathy, isn't
them; it's us. We form, exchange, improve, accept, and reject ideas,
and we improve our collective performance, through deeply human
processes that may happen even without our knowing it. These processes sometimes seem irrational, yet they're not mysterious. We
increasingly understand how and why they work.

A pattern is emerging: The activities that are becoming more
important in the economy are those that we are highly evolved to
do with other humans and that may seem irrational but that we
are understanding better. The pattern will keep turning up. As we
shall see next, it applies to how we reach people most effectively—
how we inform them, persuade them, motivate them, and influence their behavior.

CHAPTER EIGHT
THE EXTRAORDINARY POWER OF STORY

Why the Right Kind of Narrative, Told by a Person,
Is Mightier Than Logic.

Stephen Denning is a quiet, reserved lawyer who devoted most of his career to the World Bank, the lending organization that aims to reduce poverty in the world's poorest nations. Over decades he rose in the ranks to become director of the Africa Region, which accounts for about one-third of the bank's operations—an important job. Then one day Denning's orderly career began to fall apart. The bank's president died unexpectedly. Denning's own boss suddenly retired. New leaders pushed him out of his high-level post and into organizational Siberia, still employed but with no clear role in a sprawling enterprise famed as one of the most bureaucratic on earth. "Things were not looking too bright for me," he recalled later.

He pressed higher-ups for some kind of assignment and was finally told to "look into information," meaning the bank's huge troves of data and how they were handled—an area of operations, Denning noted, "that had about the same status in the organization as the garage or the cafeteria." So things were looking even bleaker for him. Denning did as he was told and found that the bank handled its data extremely inefficiently, spending huge sums for little benefit. But no one really cared.

As he pondered his depressing situation, Denning realized he was looking at an opportunity. The World Bank exists for a noble purpose, to help the world's poor, and over the previous fifty years it had amassed enormous knowledge about how to do it—by building schools, advancing agriculture, improving health, and much else. But hardly anyone could get at that valuable knowledge. Even within the bank, you had to know someone who happened to know what you were interested in, and if you were outside the bank you could forget about learning anything from it. This was crazy. Denning became fired up by a simple idea: Why don't we share our knowledge?

The more he thought about it, the more excited he got. This idea could reignite the plodding old World Bank, which was increasingly seen as a tired institution being surpassed by more innovative lenders, including commercial banks. "We could actually become a fairly exciting organization with a bright future," he realized. Denning tried selling his inspiring idea to his colleagues, and guess what? No one cared.

He figured he wasn't selling his idea the right way, so he tried doing it the way consultants do—"charts and slides with boxes and arrows." Everybody yawned.

And then, Denning recalled, "I stumbled on to something else." He started telling a little story. It wasn't much of a story—just a short account of how a health worker in a Zambian village logged on to the website of the Centers for Disease Control and Prevention in Atlanta to get information on treating malaria. This was in the mid-1990s, when getting online from a remote village in one of the world's poorest countries was new and amazing. In light of the effect the story would eventually have, it's worth paying attention to exactly the way Denning told it. It contained two key sentences. The first: "But the most important part of this picture for us in the World Bank is this: that the World Bank isn't in the picture." The bank held immense knowledge about malaria, but Denning pointed out that it wasn't organized or accessible, so the Zambian health worker couldn't get at it, just as millions of other people who were fighting poverty worldwide couldn't learn any of the bank's vast and useful knowledge. That is, the bank was failing at its mission. The second key sentence, which ended the story, followed a template that Denning later realized holds a special power: "Just imagine if we got organized to share our knowledge in that way; just think of what an organization we could become!"

Denning told that story a lot, and the people who heard it started retelling it. Bank leaders finally began to understand what Denning was talking about and to realize the power of it. The effect was remarkable. Within months, the bank's president told a meeting of finance ministers from around the globe that knowledge sharing was now a key part of the bank's strategy. The World Bank would become "the knowledge bank." With a story, an organizational outcast had moved an immovable bureaucracy and, as later evidence would show, had helped millions of poor people worldwide.

Complications ensued, of course, as they must in a big organization. Creating "the knowledge bank" was a multiyear effort, and all along the way Denning used stories to help people understand what they were doing and why. For the most part it worked, and outsiders began to cite the World Bank as a best-practice organization for knowledge sharing. The problem was that the bank's top leaders weren't hearing the stories, and in the cauldron of organizational politics, a movement was emerging to kill the whole program. It wasn't worth the cost, some said. They made their case with slides and bullet points. Denning got an e-mail on vacation that his program was in deep trouble. He returned to Washington and found that the movement against him was gaining momentum.

He had one opportunity to turn things around before the situation became hopeless, a lunchtime meeting of vice presidents and their deputies. He knew what to do. He told a story.

It was much better than the Zambia story. This one concerned a World Bank team leader in Madagascar helping the government reform its tax policy—not too exciting until you consider the hot-button conflict: whether to exempt medicine from a new value-added tax. The debate threatened to wreck the whole reform effort, so the team leader e-mailed a worldwide community of tax policy experts inside and outside the bank, assembled over time as part of the knowledge-sharing program, to get their experience with exactly this issue. The leader quickly heard back that international data clearly favored granting the exemption. He returned to the debate, armed not just with his opinion, but with a wealth of experience from around the world. The exemption was granted, and the reforms stayed on track.

Denning told that story about the power of knowledge sharing and then added the secret-ingredient closer: Just think what more we could do. What was learned by that team leader and a hundred others like him can now be placed in our knowledge base and made available to everyone, so "anyone can get answers to questions on which the World Bank has some explicit know-how and on myriad other subjects on which it has assembled some expertise." It was an inspiring vision, rooted in concrete experience, of how the bank could fulfill its mission.

As Denning later recalled, "the outcome of the meeting was not, as some had expected, my court-martial." Instead, the bank's statement of official strategy reaffirmed knowledge sharing "as a key strategic pillar for the future." Stories had succeeded where bullet points had failed; knowledge sharing survived, and the world's poor began getting help that had never been available to them before.

As for Denning, he eventually left the World Bank to become a consultant on knowledge management, in which he was widely regarded as an authority. But he found that many of his clients actually wanted to learn about storytelling. He wrote four books about it and ended up advising thousands of leaders around the world on how and why stories are so effective in changing organizations.

WE NEED TO HEAR STORIES FROM PEOPLE

The idea that stories are powerful is not exactly breaking news. Wise people have always known that stories are more memorable and more persuasive than facts. It's remarkable that even though we all know it, we mostly forget it when we become part of an organization. In our work we mostly understand what Stephen Denning believed through most of his career, that storytelling is "nebulous and ephemeral and subjective and unscientific," all qualities that are "very bad." In recent years it has become acceptable in many organizations to acknowledge the power of stories, and a small industry has grown up to explain it to corporate clients. That's an excellent development. As we shall see, research is showing that stories are even more powerful than we thought, affecting our deepest human tendencies. Every society on earth uses narrative; it's one of Donald Brown's human universals. We will see also why that is so—the chemical reactions that a story induces in our brains and that we cannot resist—and which narrative elements make some stories more powerful than others.

But even if we accept that stories are a central part of our essential humanity, can they really help us succeed in the era of ever more capable technology? We would seem to face a logical problem if we try to argue that stories will help humans create high and lasting value in that world, because after all, haven't we already seen that computers can write stories? They aren't especially gripping stories so far. Mostly they're just data—say, about a Little League baseball game or a company's financial results—put into narrative form. But all technology innovations are crummy when they're new. Software developers and researchers are working hard teaching computers to write better stories, to look into the data and find the conflicts that make a story move, to write in different styles. If we're being realistic, we have to admit that the day will come, sooner than we expect, when a computer will write genuinely compelling stories and do it faster than humans do. So isn't this just another field in which computers will perform better than us?

As an answer, consider that Denning's personal story at the World Bank includes a significant coda. Having witnessed the impact of stories, he and his staff wrote up twenty-five inspiring stories that had proven effective in meetings, and published them in a booklet and in newsletters distributed to the entire organization. "They had absolutely no impact," Denning found. "No excitement. No interest. No sign of any new activity."

Figuring that the written form somehow lacked punch, Denning's group produced videos telling those same stories. Result: "No discernible impact in the organization."

What was the problem? "If I am telling you a story, face-to-face, eyeball to eyeball, it's me and you interacting," he explained. "The listeners can see me and feel me and listen to me and can tell if I really mean what I'm saying. They may or may not end up believing me, but at least they can tell if it's authentic. And so we found that it was oral storytelling that in fact had the large impact." Denning had revealed something fundamental: "We discovered that it wasn't story that was having the impact but storytelling."

It turns out that good stories in written or visual form can actually have a major impact, as Denning later found, but he had identified a deeper issue that accounts for what he was seeing— and it doesn't bode well for computer-generated narratives. It's authenticity. Who is telling the story? We humans aren't moved by a story unless we can evaluate the teller, decide whether he or she is trustworthy, and gauge the true passion that he or she brings to it. A big problem with company-written stories—the problem Denning encountered—is that often they don't seem authentic. Sometimes we don't even know who wrote them, and when we do know, we still suspect the teller is just trying to please Wall Street or is pursuing some other undisclosed motive.

Imagine how we would evaluate a computer-written story. If it puts complicated data into interesting narrative form, we might appreciate it very much, and if it's also fun to read, we'd think it was just terrific. But if its objective is to use the power of story at its maximum—to move people to change—then it will fail no matter how good it is. We'll give it a score of zero for authenticity.

Thus the stories in any form that have the best chance of influencing us are those from tellers we already know and trust based on a preexisting in-person relationship. Lacking that, we'll be most influenced by storytellers whom we judge to be authentic based on whatever we can discern about them. That's why stories told in person are best: They let us bring our whole brains to the experience—our thinking, evidence-weighing brains and our ancient, judging-in-an-eyeblink brains. Research finds that we judge a person's trustworthiness and likeability in about a tenth of a second, and "our first impressions of others are generally accurate and reliable," says Harvard Business School researcher Francesca Gino.

Stories told in person are extra powerful in another way also. They create a two-way human relationship. "You get all sorts of cues in terms of expressions and body language from the audience as to how they are responding to the story, and you adjust the story to take that into account," says Denning. The resulting power cannot be matched. His bottom-line judgment: "If you're trying to do something difficult like take a change-resistant organization up by the scruff of the neck and hurl it into the future, then I've got a very simple, two-word piece of advice: Be there!"

Stories don't have to be human. Computers can write them. But we don't really care about stories. What we care about is effective storytelling, and that is entirely human—an innately, deeply human exchange. No matter what kind of work we do, as technology becomes more capable, we will become enormously more valuable if we can influence people in this uniquely powerful way.

WHY WE'RE TRANSFIXED BY STORIES

When U.S. forces captured Saddam Hussein on December 13, 2003, U.S. bond prices rose, meaning investors were seeking safety in ultrasafe U.S. Treasury securities. The headline on Bloomberg reflected investors' apparent aversion to risk: "U.S. Treasuries Rise; Hussein Capture May Not Curb Terrorism." Within an hour, however, prices had fallen back. So Bloomberg rewrote its headline: "U.S. Treasuries Fall; Hussein Capture Boosts Allure of Risky Assets."

This nonsensical behavior was noted by Nassim Nicholas Taleb in his book *The Black Swan,* and it gives a tiny glimpse of how deeply embedded in us is the power of story. In this case, the Bloomberg headline writer could not stop himself from seeing a story—a cause-and-effect sequence of events—in the news of that day, and he apparently didn't care that he told two directly contradictory stories, with a single cause leading to exactly opposite effects. If we want to make the most of storytelling's extraordinary power, we need to understand how it works. It operates within us deeply.

That headline writer needn't be ashamed. It appears that we are hardwired to see stories when we observe events, even if nothing in our experience tells us that those events would be related. Philosophers and scientists have not always believed that we operate in that way. On the contrary, for centuries the conventional view held that we are strictly rational in this regard, and only by observing repeatedly that, say, plants grow where seeds fall do we eventually figure out cause and effect. But more recent research shows that we see stories automatically and instantly, before we even realize it. The Belgian psychologist Albert Michotte showed this simply in the 1940s by creating a crude animation in which a square drawn on paper appears to move and bump into another square, which immediately shoots off in the same direction. Anyone seeing this knows what happened: The first square pushed the second one. Except that of course nothing really happened at all; the squares were just drawings—nothing real actually touched anything, and any adult knows how the animation was made. It doesn't matter. We all still insist on seeing causation, a little story, just as the headline writer insisted that Saddam's capture affected the bond market no matter which way it moved.

Daniel Kahneman, the Nobelist who popularized the notion of two separate and distinct modes of thinking in our minds called System 1 and System 2, summed up this tendency well. System 2 "allocates attention to the effortful mental activities that demand it," he explains, but "System 1 operates automatically and quickly, with little or no effort and no sense of voluntary control." That's why System 1 rules our brains and our behavior. System 1 just happens. We can overrule it only through the slow, arduous work of engaging System 2, and it's so much easier not to bother. As Kahneman puts it, "System 1 is adept at finding a coherent causal story that links the fragments of knowledge at its disposal." Seeing stories in random events is actually easier for us than not seeing stories.

Not only do we insist on seeing stories, but we insist on seeing stories about people, regardless of what appears before us. That's why we routinely attribute human motivations to dogs, cats, parakeets, goldfish, and other pets in creating stories to explain their behavior. Or consider again that crude animation created by Michotte. Imagine that instead of the first square hitting the second square, the second square had started moving just before the first square struck it. As psychologist Jason Goldman has written, could any of us fail to see a story in which the first square "wants" to catch the second one, and the second one "wants" to get away? We turn them into people, with desires and minds.

You can have some fun observing this phenomenon for yourself. Just Google "Heider and Simmel." Fritz Heider and Marianne Simmel, psychologists at Smith College, created a one-minute-thirteen-second film in 1944, and thousands of students and research subjects have watched it since. Like the Michotte sequence, this also is animation of the simplest, most homemade type. We see a big triangle, a small triangle, and a circle—no shading, depth, or color, just solid black shapes on a white background. There's also a black rectangle in outline, with part of one side able to swing out and back, opening access to the inside of the rectangle. What happens next is almost impossible to describe—for most of us—without using human terms. The triangles get into a fight, the large one being the aggressor, while the circle tries to hide and goes inside the rectangle, cowering in fear, pursued there by the big triangle. I may as well spoil the ending: The circle and the small triangle elude the big triangle and escape together, leaving the big triangle so furious that he destroys the rectangle in frustration.

But of course none of that actually "happens." A few geometric shapes appear, through animation, to move around. That's it. Yet almost instantly we turn them into people with personalities and motivations, and we create a story that explains their behavior in terms of a person's actions causing another person's actions. (The one exception is that viewers with autism tend not to see the shapes as people.) We may not all see the same story; Heider and Simmel asked their students to write descriptions of what they saw and got back many variations of the basic narrative outlined here. For example, some people described the small triangle as brave and heroic while others said "he"—most used that word—was clever or brainy. But nearly all created the same essential story from the movements of little shapes on a screen. As Kahneman says, "Your mind is ready and even eager to identify agents, assign them personality traits and specific intentions, and view their actions as expressing individual propensities."

The critically important point for our purposes is that we're born this way. For most of the twentieth century that claim was controversial; plenty of people would have argued that we see motivations and attribute causality only because we learn to do it, based perhaps on the culture in which we're raised. But it doesn't seem to be so. Kahneman's reading of the evidence is "that we are born prepared to make intentional attributions: infants under one year old identify bullies and victims. . . . " We seem to be inherently transfixed by stories about people and insist on seeing our world as a collection of such stories—even if we have to make them up.

STORIES CAUSE "NEURAL COUPLING"

It's a sign of narrative's remarkable power that we create stories from groups of random facts or from movements of random shapes—but then what happens? We've seen what we in effect do to stories, but then what do stories do to us? The answer shows how powerful they are and how they achieve their greatest power when they're part of the most directly human interaction.

When we hear or see a story, we begin to experience it—not just perceive what is happening but actually to experience being in the story as if we were really there. We see ourselves acting, which is why stories are so powerful in motivating action. We all know that, and it's one of the main reasons we love stories. A good story carries us outside ourselves and into outer space or fifteenth-century Japan or who-knows-where and refreshes us with an emotional experience, though we never leave our chairs. It's remarkable when you think about it—that we can be made to sweat, breathe faster, laugh, cry, or scream "Don't open that door!" while just sitting there. We can get that kind of experience from a movie, play, book, or in other forms.

When we hear a story in one particular form, direct from a human speaker, something even more amazing happens. The speaker's and the listener's brains align. We not only experience the story; we and the storyteller are having the same experience. Researchers at Princeton scanned the brains of a storyteller and of listeners and found "a surprisingly widespread neural coupling." The same parts of the brain were being energized in teller and hearer, and researchers can identify the functions of those brain regions quite specifically. The brains of the storyteller and hearer light up not just in areas controlling speech and language but also, more significantly, in "areas known to be involved in processing social information crucial for successful communication, including, among others, the capacity to discern the beliefs, desires, and goals of others." We're talking about empathy again. Storyteller and hearer are connecting in a deep way.

The phenomenon becomes much stronger when a storyteller is speaking to several listeners at once. The effect then, the researchers say, is "to induce similar brain activity across different individuals." That is, the storyteller and a group of listeners are all having the same emotional experience at the same time. Consider how much more powerful this is than when everyone merely possesses the same facts. We can newly appreciate the unequaled effectiveness, the motivating power of emotional, story-based oratory, whether it's William Wallace calling the ancient Scots to arms at Stirling Bridge or Lincoln at Gettysburg casting his speech as a narrative that began four score and seven years earlier with America's founding. We can also nod ruefully at the steady disappearance of such transformational experiences in our increasingly virtual lives.

HOW TO SQUEEZE THE PITUITARY

We have referred a few times to "good stories" and what they do, a shorthand way of acknowledging that not all stories are equally effective. Heider and Simmel's minidrama of triangles and a circle engages our emotions, but it doesn't haunt our dreams or inspire us to action. Yet some stories do. Why? Humans are the best storytellers, but to be most effective we must understand what makes the best stories.

In one sense the answer is simple. It's oxytocin. Stories that we deem effective cause our brains to release this chemical that has a broad range of intensely emotional effects. It makes us "more trustworthy, generous, charitable, and compassionate," says Paul J. Zak, of Claremont Graduate University, who has pioneered research into how stories affect us. It plays an important role in romance and sex—some have called it "the love hormone," others "the bonding hormone." Zak calls it "the moral molecule" because it makes us "more sensitive to social cues around us," often making us more inclined "to help others, particularly if the other person seems to need our help." It is therefore "the neurochemical responsible for empathy," he says. Oxytocin is the potent juice that a good story causes our pituitary gland to release.

This raises the obvious question: How do you make a story that does that? Zak's research yields an answer that proves and explains what dramatists have known for millennia. It's all about the story structure, and the classic structure became classic because it is unsurpassed at squeezing the pituitary. We all know the classic structure. John Doe is living an uneventful life until something shakes it up. John then finds himself in conflict—with himself or another person or an organization or society or something. Things get bad, and then things get worse. Eventually John faces the source of his conflict and must find some resource within himself that enables him to prevail in a climactic confrontation, which he does. Order returns to John's life, but he is forever changed.

That's the kind of story that moves people, by soaking their brains in oxytocin. Zak proved it in an intriguing way. He made a short film relating the true story of Ben, a two-year-old with terminal brain cancer, and his father. The father is our John Doe. His life is pretty ordinary until he learns that Ben has cancer. Ben doesn't know he has terminal cancer, and in fact we see him playing happily in the background as his father speaks to us. The father's conflict is with himself; knowing that Ben will die within months, he finds it difficult to be happy around the boy, yet he knows that his sadness merely deprives Ben of joy that he could and should otherwise have. Ben's father tells about his struggle and how he eventually finds within himself the courage to be joyful around Ben, genuinely grateful for the gift of the child's brief life. The conflict is resolved, and Ben's father is changed.

Zak showed this film to hundreds of people. Before and after the viewing, he measured oxytocin levels in their blood. The film made those levels rise. The research subjects were paid for their time and for being stuck twice with needles to draw blood, yet they were very willing to give some or all of the money to a childhood cancer charity, depending on how much oxytocin their brains had released.

Then Zak showed other people a different film, depicting Ben and his father visiting a zoo. Ben has no hair, and his father refers to him as "miracle boy"; it's clear that we're watching a father and son and that the son has cancer. But while there's narrative—first they do this, then they do that—there's no story. We're just watching a father and son enjoying a day at the zoo. The brain chemistry of the viewers barely blipped, and they did not become notably generous to the charity. The structureless, wandering narrative—so like the reports or other data presentations that most of us spend much of our time creating or consuming—lacked all power.

"TELLING IS REMEMBERING"

The classic story accomplishes other feats as well. Research shows that we remember information far better when it's included in a classically structured story—an ordinary day, something goes wrong, a climactic resolution, denouement—than when the very same information is presented simply as a collection of facts. The great biologist Edward O. Wilson has written that "[f]acts presented in stories, as opposed to lists, are much easier to remember." We all realize how true it is for ourselves, but we generally fail to appreciate just how powerful this tendency is generally. As psychology researchers Roger Schank and Robert Abelson observe, "Storytelling is not something we just happen to do. It is something we virtually have to do if we want to remember anything at all."

Note carefully what they said, because it reveals more about humans' remarkable reliance on stories. We've seen that just hearing a real story makes facts far more memorable. But Schank and Abelson didn't say that story hearing is key to memory; they said storytelling is. If we really want to remember something for a long time, we must tell the story after we experience it or hear it. That's what cements it in memory, and the more we tell it, the better we remember the details that compose it. As they put it, "Telling is remembering."

Further, they found, we inherently understand story structure so deeply that when we tell a story, we make it fit the classic story structure, even if the actual events were not so conveniently arranged (as they often aren't). That is, we turn facts into narratives, and then in telling those narratives we turn them into structured stories, omitting or even adding facts as needed. This is not what anyone would call rational, but we literally can't help it.

Our relationship to stories is irrational yet strong in another way. We absolutely love happy endings. While that sounds reasonable, it doesn't necessarily make sense. Consider the story of Jen, a woman who was never married and had no children, and who died instantly and painlessly in a car crash. She lived an extremely happy life—lots of time with friends, rewarding work, fun hobbies, great vacations. Based on that description, how would you rate Jen's life? Now suppose that Jen's life was exactly the same except that she lived an additional five years that were perfectly pleasant, just not as terrific as her life until those final five years. How would you rate Jen's life in that case?

As you've guessed by now, Jen is fictitious and was created for a research study. Participants were asked to evaluate Jen's life as described in each of the two scenarios. They overwhelmingly rated Jen's life lower—less desirable and less happy—in the second scenario. As Kahneman has observed, this seems utterly baffling. In the second scenario Jen lives five additional, pleasant years. How could this not be better than the first scenario? Yet in our human judgment, Jen's life is worse overall because her happiness declines at the end. You may suspect that older people wouldn't make that judgment, but they do; old and young participants in the study followed the same pattern. Plenty of other research has confirmed this tendency: Regardless of what happens along the way, our response to a story depends heavily on what happens at the very end. It's truly crazy. But it's the way we are.

WHY DARPA IS STUDYING STORIES

Effective storytelling has even become a significant factor in the security of the world. It stands to reason, as warfare is increasingly conducted in "the human domain." In the postsuperpower era, most of the world's war and violence involves terrorists and insurgents, what security analysts call nonstate violent actors—ISIS, al Qaeda, Boko Haram, and many other lesser known groups worldwide. They're largely volunteers, relatively few in number but supported by large populations, remarkably committed, resourceful, and effective. What accounts for their success in commanding the world's attention and forcing the United States and the other great powers to reset their security agendas? What motivates these fighters and the millions who support them? The answer, many believe, is stories—about injustices, outrages, ancestors, coreligionists, nonbelievers, stories from the past and present. The U.S. Defense Department is so convinced that stories are at the foundation of today's security environment that it has established a program called Narrative Networks in the Defense Advanced Research Projects Agency (DARPA), the agency that pioneered the Internet, GPS, and other world-changing developments. "Why are some narrative themes successful at building support for terrorism?" the program asks and intends to answer, says its official description. America's defense policy makers have decided that the national security of the United States requires understanding how stories work.

The ambition of the Narrative Networks program is considerable. It aims to understand the effects of stories in the most expansive way—how they "contribute to radicalization, violent social mobilization, insurgency, and terrorism among foreign populations"—and at the same time to understand how stories work in human brains at the molecular level. The program's goals include understanding "the neurobiological impact of narratives on hormones and neurotransmitters, reward processing, and emotion-cognition interaction." This appears to be the most intensive and advanced research on stories being conducted anywhere. Another goal is even to "develop sensors to determine [narratives'] impact on individuals and groups." Sensors? To gauge the effectiveness of stories? Just wait until Hollywood gets its hands on those.

The serious point is that, as former Narrative Networks program manager William Casebeer has said, "we need a more comprehensive understanding of how a failure to tell good stories can lead to an increased risk of insurgencies, violent social movements, and terrorist action." When a country achieves that understanding, it can develop what Casebeer called a "counter-narrative strategy" for "undermining the efficacy of [the enemies'] narratives" and can develop its own competing narratives. Casebeer's research has persuaded him that the most effective stories, for antiterrorism just as for any other purpose, follow the classic structure. Stories are becoming a battlefield, and waging war is increasingly a struggle to release oxytocin in people's brains.

Nations in conflict have always known that stories are powerful, but never before has a nation deemed them so important or deployed such resources to understand them at unprecedented depth. Effective storytelling has become a strategic imperative for any nation or company or person or other entity hoping to exert influence.

MORE POWERFUL THAN THEY KNOW

The power of human storytelling is apparent in one more setting, an unexpected one because the storytellers do not realize the considerable effect of their in-person, face-to-face stories, and they never will. Country Meadows is an assisted-living community in Hershey, Pennsylvania, that includes a memory-support unit for patients with Alzheimer's disease and related dementias. These patients are beyond any ability to function in the outside world and must live in a locked environment. Doctors find them challenging to work with. No effective medications are available, and getting reliable information from them about their history or even their current condition is virtually impossible. Medical students often feel hopeless and depressed around such patients, research shows; they may even come to regard elderly patients more negatively and then carry that attitude into future practice.

Faculty at Penn State College of Medicine decided to involve students in a novel intervention at Country Meadows. The students' job was to get the patients to tell stories. Not that the patients could tell a conventional story, since they lacked almost any sense of chronology. The procedure was to show them a photo; it might be surrealistic—an elephant sitting on a park bench, a man in a clothes dryer—or something simple like a boy and a dog. Then the students encouraged the patients to tell what was happening in the photo. One of the students recorded the comments—none were excluded—and assembled them into a story. At the end of the session the scribe read back the story and asked the patients what it should be called.

The resulting stories were generally a bit odd, often funny, and surprisingly engaging. A story about a man standing in the middle of a street holding a large American flag ended as follows: "When he gets home, he isn't going to do any math problems. He is just going to wait for something good to happen. All the people from the parade that he invited home will come to his house to see it, but all they will get is a piece of bread apiece and some water." The patients called their story "Flag Day in Washington, D.C." (Nothing in the photo suggested it was Flag Day or Washington.)

The researchers had measured students' attitudes toward dementia patients before the storytelling sessions began. After four sessions, they measured their attitudes again. The improvement was stunning. Most striking was a huge reversal in students' attitudes toward working with these patients—notably a new, strong belief that working with dementia patients is rewarding.

As anyone experienced with advanced dementia patients knows, most of those patients probably forgot within sixty seconds that a storytelling session had ever happened. Yet in creating their stories, they had deeply reached some of the most cognitively sharp people in the world. They had also quite possibly affected how at least a few elderly patients will be treated by their doctors years in the future, when medicine will be more technologically advanced and doctors will feel financially pressured to spend still less time with patients. Such is the human power of face-to-face stories, even when the storytellers don't know it.

Telling a story is a creative act. In doing it, we produce something that didn't exist before. Storytelling is thus an example of the larger phenomenon of creativity and innovation. Considering the huge value of innovation in today's economy, and the important role of our instinctive tendencies in creating and telling effective stories, we had better find out whether creativity and innovation more broadly are activities as deeply human, as immune to technology substitution, as storytelling is. So that's what we turn to next.

CHAPTER NINE
THE HUMAN ESSENCE OF INNOVATION AND CREATIVITY

Computers Can Create, but People Skillfully Interacting
Solve the Most Important Human Problems.

"People might say a computer can never be creative," said Matthias Kaiserswerth, director of IBM Research in Zurich, to a conference room full of corporate infotech executives. "I'm sorry to disappoint you, but we are teaching Watson to be creative—with cooking."

He's certainly right that many people believe computers can't be creative. It's conventional wisdom. Check any list of jobs that computers will never replace—you can always find plenty of such lists online, reflecting people's widespread anxiety about technology substituting for labor—and ranked high will be occupations like artist, poet, composer. The usual argument is that computers can do only what we tell them to do, and all they can deal with is strict logic; they merely flip trillions of ones and zeroes according to rules we give them. By definition, they have no capacity for the ineffable flight of fancy, the magical stroke of genius, the inexplicable leap of imagination that a human artist creates and that takes our breath away.

Kaiserwerth is correct also that Watson is learning to be a creative cook. I suspect we would all agree that a genius chef is someone who can, among other abilities, combine flavors and textures in ways that utterly surprise us and yet also appeal strongly to our existing notions of what tastes great. So IBM's computer scientists decided to start teaching creativity to Watson by teaching it to find those combinations better than any human could do. They began by making Watson read tens of thousands of existing recipes as guides to established, well-loved food combinations—tomatoes and oregano, for example, or chicken, mushrooms, and cream. They also told Watson the chemical composition and nutrient profiles of thousands of ingredients, and they told it how people have rated the flavors of thousands of food compounds in decades of testing. With all that knowledge, Watson was ready to create combinations that people were highly likely to love. Then the scientists realized they'd better tell Watson one more thing: Don't invent what we already know. Coffee and chocolate is indeed a great combination, but somebody thought of it a few centuries ago. Just give us combinations that, as far as you can tell, nobody ever thought of.

Which Watson proceeded to do. Some of the resulting dishes were served from a food truck at the 2014 South by Southwest festival in Austin, Texas. Attendees loved them. Their favorites included a version of chili that uses roasted pork belly, pickled green beans, skirt steak, lemongrass, and cubeb pepper, an obscure ingredient that conveys aroma but no heat. Another favorite included the Austrian chocolate burrito, featuring ground beef, dark chocolate, mashed edamame, apricot puree, grated Edam cheese, and more, wrapped in a flour tortilla. These were, for sure, combinations that human chefs were extremely unlikely to come up with, and people thought they were delicious. But were they creative?

At first Watson could offer only combinations of ingredients; it couldn't suggest how to prepare them, so IBM asked chefs from the Institute of Culinary Education in New York City to figure that out. Preparing the ingredients is at least half the battle in creating great food, so you could argue that humans were still doing much of the creativity. But IBM then started teaching Watson about preparation, starting with techniques learned from expert chefs, and before long it could offer several suggestions for how to prepare its combinations—for example, cook a chicken breast with yellow curry paste and a vanilla bean (among other things) *sous vide*, or a chicken thigh with red curry paste and coconut milk (among other things) on a grill; those are two possible beginnings of a more complex recipe called Thai-Jewish chicken. Watson is gradually taking over more elements of human creativity in this process. Of course the results are ultimately for humans to judge. This human thinks they're terrific. More important, plenty of other humans think so too, and if IBM decides to continue down this road, Watson can keep learning what we humans like, and the results will get continually better.

At this point, is Watson being creative? Clearly it is. If successful innovations are novel, nonobvious, and useful—commonsense criteria that also happen to be the requirements for patentability in many countries—then Watson is producing them. Those recipes are certified novel because Watson has screened them for originality against thousands of existing recipes. By the same argument, they're obviously nonobvious. And they're surely useful; they make people happy.

COMPUTERS CREATE AND ARE GETTING BETTER

More generally, the idea that computers can't be creative is observably false. Computers are already being creative in realms far beyond the kitchen. David Cope of the University of California at Santa Cruz has been programming computers to write music since the early 1980s, and the results—fake Bach, fake Mozart, fake Chopin, and more—can easily fool the great majority of listeners. The awestruck writer of an article in Britain's *New Scientist* magazine even deemed these machine compositions so good that they call into question the supposed magic of human creativity; he called them "a requiem for the soul." More recently, Sony's Computer Science Lab in Paris has focused on the same task, creating software that fairly convincingly improvises on the (computer-generated) sax like Coltrane and on the piano like Bill Evans.

Fully computer-generated pictures are everywhere. Computers write poems, and software is even producing novels. You could object rightly that none of this machine-created work is truly great, but that's hardly the question. To criticize software-written music because it isn't as magnificent as Bach is to hold it to a standard that no contemporary human composer is expected to meet. The relevant question is whether this work is creative, and there's no escaping the conclusion that it is. In fact, it seems a safe guess that most people would rate it at least as good as a great deal of today's human-generated creativity in the same field.

We can predict confidently that computer-produced creativity will get a lot better. It's easy to picture a near future in which computers know much more about what kinds of visual, auditory, and other experiences make people delighted, engaged, bored. Imagine millions of people wearing Alex Pentland's sociometers, recording what they're doing, watching, hearing; that's a plausible scenario as watches and other wearable computers take over the sociometer's functions. At the same time, millions of people already wear basic biosensors on their wrists as fitness monitors that collect some of the needed data about how you're responding to your activities; watches also are starting to do the same things, only better, continuously recording heart rate, temperature, galvanic skin response, and other metrics. All that combined data—including what you're watching, reading, hearing, and how you're responding to it—stripped of identifying information, will let computers produce music, stories, and other work that will be not only creative but also enormously popular and even targetable to various groups.

WHY HIGH-VALUE CREATIVITY WILL REMAIN HUMAN

It's sounding as if we humans had better get our novels written, paintings painted, and songs composed pretty soon, because before long our services will no longer be required in those fields. But it isn't so. As we've seen in other domains, computers are learning skills at a quickening pace and taking over jobs previously done by people, but that fact doesn't necessarily concern us. Our focus is the high-value skills, the ones that will bring us and our kids a rising standard of living. And in the many realms of creativity, as elsewhere, those high-value skills will remain human largely because of the humanity of those who consume the output of those skills. It may well be that computers will take over the composing of the music we hear in the supermarket. Maybe they've done so already—who would know and who would care? The highest-value creativity, by contrast, will remain ours to do, for two reasons.

First, there's more to high-value creativity than just creating. When Robert Galbraith wrote a detective novel called *The Cuckoo's Calling*, at least one publisher (Orion Books) rejected it, and when it was eventually published in 2013, it was well reviewed but sold poorly—readers bought all of 1,500 copies in its first three months. Then the *Sunday Times* of London revealed that Robert Galbraith was actually J. K. Rowling, author of the *Harry Potter* books. *The Cuckoo's Calling* instantly rocketed to number one on Amazon. Publications that hadn't bothered to review it now paid attention and suddenly saw creative virtues that no one had previously seen. "[Rowling's] literary gift is on display in this work," said the Associated Press reviewer, for example.

In a rational world, as distinct from the human world, this shouldn't have happened. The work is the work, to be judged on its merits. But we humans like to have people associated with creative works. If they're people we hear rumors about but never see—

J. D. Salinger, Banksy—so much the better; the mystery only feeds our interest. They don't even have to be alive, as great creators with compelling stories like Mozart and Van Gogh remind us. We're always more engaged when there's a real person involved. Have you eaten any Watson-invented food lately? Are you eager to? I can tell you that it's really good. Still, I'll bet that you're not yearning for it. Yet if Jean-Georges Vongerichten or Mario Batali and not a computer invented Czech Pork Belly Moussaka, you can be sure that foodies would be stampeding for it.

In many creative fields, the highest-value creativity is associated with a person, which is part of what makes it high value. That's one reason that high-value creativity will remain a human endeavor. But it's not the most important reason.

The second and more important reason is that the most valuable acts of creativity are unlike those we've considered so far in that they aim to solve real-world problems, and the nature of those problems is such that humans must innovate the solutions. Is there a more efficient way to stamp the door panels for the new model pickup truck? Is there a faster way to get medical supplies into Burkina Faso? In theory, computers could solve even those problems far better than people could, examining more data and weighing more options enormously faster than any human. But in practice, the problem inevitably changes as we're trying to solve it. We realize that our objective isn't what we thought it was, or our efforts reveal an opportunity we hadn't considered. Stamp the door panels the same old way but make them of aluminum instead, lightening the vehicle and improving fuel efficiency. Instead of getting those meds into Burkina Faso, it would be far more effective and efficient to get certain patients out for treatment elsewhere. Humans must solve these problems because in real life, we're seldom sure what the problem really is, and since humans are ultimately in charge of shaping an organization's goals, or their own, humans must continually redirect the most creative efforts to solve the problems.

Let's look more closely at this second type of creativity, what researchers have called "creativity in producing ideas and solutions relevant to business problems." Creativity like that is not just inherently the realm of humans. The more closely we look at it, the more intensely human it becomes.

"IF YOU WANT INNOVATION, YOU NEED INTERACTION."

Marissa Mayer faced a desperately hard challenge when she became Yahoo's CEO in 2012. One of the most glamorous start-ups of the Internet's early days, the company had fallen into steady decline, and history has shown that a failing Internet company is almost impossible to rescue. Mayer had left a stellar career at Google to take on the challenge anyway, and she immediately began a bold program of acquisitions, divestitures, and new strategies. The move that attracted the most attention wasn't any of those things, however; it was a message conveyed by a brief e-mail from Yahoo's HR chief to all employees. Headed "Proprietary and Confidential Information— Do Not Forward," it was of course immediately leaked to media worldwide. Its message: "We're asking all employees with work-from-home arrangements to work in Yahoo offices." Why? "Some of the best decisions and insights come from hallway and cafeteria discussions, meeting new people, and impromptu team meetings," it said. "Being a Yahoo isn't just about your day-to-day job, it is about the interactions and experiences that are only possible in our offices." And while the e-mail was "asking" work-at-home employees to work from the office instead, those employees were told separately that if they didn't want to do it, they should find another employer.

The move sparked a storm of criticism—many commenters

noted that today's employees want and even expect flexible work arrangements—but Mayer didn't back down. Regardless of Yahoo's or Mayer's fate (far from certain at this writing), academic research and real-world experience show that she was right. Yahoo was in a life-or-death struggle and needed the most creative new ideas it could find in response to the vague, shifting, vital problems that you can't ask a computer to solve. The best way to find such solutions is to bring humans into close physical proximity.

Mayer understood this well from her time at Google. The company is fanatical about forcing people to connect in person. Its famous policy of providing excellent food free is not a tool for attracting great employees; great people want to work at Google anyway. The real goal is to make sure employees go to the cafeteria and have to wait in line so they'll talk with one another. The company even measures the length of the lines; a three- to four-minute wait is optimal. When employees get their food, they have to sit at long tables set up high-school-cafeteria-style rather than at small individual tables, increasing the chances that they'll sit next to or across from someone they don't know. Google puts those tables a little too close together so that employees may well hit someone when they push their chairs back and thus meet someone new–the Google bump, employees call it. None of it happens by accident. John Sullivan of San Francisco State University, who has studied Google and innovation generally, calls it "serendipitous interaction." He has concluded that it's essential to innovation. People who work from home are often more productive than office workers, but they're less innovative, research finds. "If you want innovation, then you need interaction," Sullivan says.

That isn't necessarily obvious. Putting people together can sometimes destroy creative thinking by prompting groupthink, the phenomenon in which group members simply reinforce one another's belief in an idea that accords with what they all knew already. The result is overconfidence and often disaster. The term was coined by William H. Whyte in *Fortune* magazine in 1952; researchers later used the concept to explain various U.S. policy fiascos, such as the Bay of Pigs invasion and the conduct of the Vietnam War. Policy makers were interacting to solve problems, but this is not the kind of creativity anyone wants.

The key is following Google's example, throwing together people who wouldn't normally talk with each other. In fact, other companies have done exactly what Google does. Alex Pentland of MIT reports that a young company where he deployed his sociometric badges was trying to improve communication among employees. Holding beer busts and other events achieved nothing, the badges showed. But, he reports, "making the tables in the company's lunchroom longer, so that strangers sat together, had a huge impact."

More broadly, as we saw in chapter 7 on teams and groups, organizations in which people combine in ways that increase idea flow become far more productive. But do they also become more creative? The answer is a loud yes. Specifically, members of the most creative groups divide their social time between two kinds of activities: exploring, which means interacting with people outside the group, and engaging with group members. Pentland has observed this effect in multiple settings. He reports, for example, that a PhD student at MIT collected sociometric data from teams at two R&D labs in the United States and also used a highly regarded procedure for gauging their creativity. The results showed that creativity was all about these twin activities of exploring and engaging. It wasn't even complicated, he says: "A simple combination of the engagement and exploration measures was able to predict which days were the most creative with 87.5% accuracy."

These findings make sense. Exploring exposes group members to new ideas outside the group that they can bring back, avoiding groupthink; high engagement within the group trains many perspectives on the ideas and enables the group to accept, improve, or reject them.

CREATIVITY CAN'T HAPPEN WITHOUT TRUST

A closer look at engagement among group members underscores the importance of in-person interaction—as distinct from digital interaction—for highly creative groups, and shows how right Mayer was in ordering all hands back on the ship. A team of researchers from two U.S. universities and three European universities used sociometers to record the interactions within several different teams, and also gauged the creativity and quality of the teams' ideas; the teams were highly educated people working on projects involving computer science, economics, psychology, and other fields. The results show strikingly what a deeply human experience it is to be creative in a group. The more that group members faced each other, the more creative their output was. The more they looked into each other's eyes, the more creative they were. The more willing they were to confide in one another, the more creative they were.

Those behaviors might not have immediately signaled creativity to you, but they may well have suggested something else: trust. Facing each other, looking into the eyes, confiding—all those behaviors reflect and build trust. As it happened, the researchers measured trust within the groups and found that it was critical to the whole process; more trust led to more creative and higher quality ideas. Their conclusion: "There is no substitute for face-to-face interaction to build up this trust."

The finding that groups are more creative when their members trust one another helps explain a phenomenon frequently observed: that the most creative groups of all are often groups of two. The writer Joshua Wolf Shenk has pointed out the truly astounding number of pairs who have produced many of the world's greatest creative successes. Think of John Lennon and Paul McCartney, Steve Jobs and Steve Wozniak, James Watson and Francis Crick, Jean-Paul Sartre and Simone de Beauvoir—once you get started you can think of them all day without even mentioning less known two-member teams like C. S. Lewis and J. R. R. Tolkien. Shenk argues that they all developed mutual trust so deep that it became faith in one another. "What I saw . . . in creative pairs was trust developing in concert as pairs took risks together," he has observed, "like when Neal Brennan and Dave Chappelle pitched HBO an idea for a comedy show—and got shot down—or when Warren Buffett and Charlie Munger bought See's Candy and turned a solid profit." Two people can trust each other in a way that no larger group can do.

While two people are a very small group, they're still a group. Shenk found that in the dozens of creative pairs he investigated, all members agreed that they could never have achieved their creative success alone. And though it was just the two of them, they all followed the exploring-engaging pattern that Pentland observed. They didn't spend all their time together—sometimes far from it. Even Sartre and de Beauvoir, lifelong companions and lovers, "accumulated disparate experiences, wrote separate stories and lectures, nurtured individual interests," Shenk writes. They could sometimes be found at the same café, working at separate tables. And then they, like all the pairs Shenk studied and like all successful creative teams, would engage closely.

THE SQUARE-OF-THE-DISTANCE RULE

Exploring and engaging—in both essential parts of the creative group process the value of physical proximity is striking. That fact explicitly contradicts many learned predictions of how the Internet and mobile phones would change fundamentally the ways we operate. With today's technology, just think how much more widely we can explore for new ideas, and how much more easily we can engage with members of our group, than could the Neanderthals of the 1980s or before. An acclaimed book at the dawn of the Internet age, *The Death of Distance*, argued that "new communications technologies are rapidly obliterating distance as a relevant factor in how we conduct our business and personal lives." Heaven knows those technologies have indeed changed our lives, but when it comes to exploring, engaging, and creating, distance is at least as limiting as ever.

At the level of exploring, consider cities. It has long been obvious that cities produce far more innovation than other areas do, but why, exactly? It isn't just the simple explanation that more people produce more ideas; cities produce more innovation per capita, as measured by patents, than other areas do, in addition to being more productive generally. So again, why? Some researchers have said it's because with so many people in one place, it makes economic sense for them to be more specialized in their work—the Adam Smith argument that finer division of labor makes for more efficient production. Other researchers have argued that because cities are crowded, they're expensive places to live, and thus they attract smarter, more productive workers who will think up more new ideas. Those arguments make sense, but it turns out there's a simpler and more powerful way to explain why cities are so innovative. Just look at the number of social ties between people. If exploring—getting new ideas and information from a wide range of other people—is key to innovation, then areas where people develop lots of contacts with others should be more innovative. They are, and this fact alone predicts innovation with remarkable accuracy.

Researchers created a simple model in which the number of a person's ties is based on population density—that is, on physical proximity. The more closely people are packed together, the more ties each one will have. Following previous research on social networks, the researchers used a formula in which the likelihood of a tie between any two people decreases with the square of the distance between them; if they become twice as far apart, they become four times less likely to form a tie (remember that fact). This model accurately predicts all kinds of phenomena that you would expect to be associated with exploring for ideas: the number of acquaintances that individuals have on average, the amount of communicating they do. It predicts interactions that you might think have nothing to do with physical proximity, such as total phone call volume. And it predicts the innovative results of exploring for ideas—namely, patenting activity as well as the economic productivity that goes with it.

Note that all those things increase faster than population density—if you double the density, you get more than double the innovation, among other things—and this model based on social ties predicts this phenomenon (which mathematicians call "super-linear scaling"). Thus, the researchers conclude, "population density, rather than population size per se, is at the root of the extraordinary nature of urban centers."

Extraordinary is the right word. Even in the information age, physical proximity exerts a special power. You might expect that it would cause people to make fewer phone calls, since they can easily speak to more people in person, but actually it causes them to make more calls. Or you might suppose that near-universal global connectivity would make physical proximity irrelevant, but as these researchers observe, "metropolitan Tokyo has roughly the same population as Siberia," and while Siberians have the Internet and mobile phones, we don't see a lot of innovation originating there.

Research on industry clusters reinforces the point. Companies in the same industry—especially industries that rely most heavily on creativity and innovation—often locate in the same area. Besides Silicon Valley, famous examples include high-tech clusters in Research Triangle, North Carolina, and Austin, Texas. Everyone in those industries agrees that an important reason for locating in clusters is to make exchanging ideas easier. But patterns of communication between companies within these clusters hadn't been investigated until researchers looked at the biotech cluster in Cambridge,

Massachusetts. They found that the amount of communicating between people from different companies—in-person, by phone, and by e-mail—depended on the physical distance between them. Specifically, it varied by the square of the distance, so small differences in distance made big differences in the amount of interaction. As a result, people at companies in the center of the cluster did the most communicating of all. In the exploring phase of group creativity, the vital, constant hunt for diverse ideas, you might not suppose that the office address would make much of a difference. But it does.

In the engagement phase of group creativity, when team members interact with one another, the story is similar with a surprising detail. Physical distance still makes a big difference; the "global teams" that many companies organize are often necessary, but even with all the videoconferencing and collaboration software in the world, they still operate at a heavy disadvantage in creativity because the members aren't near one another. When all the members are in the same building, however, we might imagine that the problem is solved—but it isn't quite that simple. Even when group members are in the same building and on the same floor, physical proximity matters. Research has shown that communication between engineers about technical matters, the kind of engagement on which innovation is based, depends on how far apart their desks are. The amount of communication varies—wait for it—by the square of the distance.

So the distance between two people—ten miles or ten blocks or ten feet—is a critical determinant of how much communicating they do. That means communicating of any kind. And the effect is huge. We're in an era when distance is supposed to be dead, so we might be shocked if we were told, say, that today communication between people declines in proportion to the physical distance between them. But the real effect is far greater, that communication declines in proportion to the square of the distance. To put it in nonmathematical terms, we humans really, really like to be close to one another. The closer we are, the more we communicate, and the more we communicate, the more and the better we create. Advancing technology does not diminish those tendencies even a little.

THE HUMAN ELEMENT IN CREATIVITY GETS LARGER

We've seen that creativity and innovation remain high-value human activities because no matter how capable computers become, humans are still in charge of which problems need to get solved, and humans in real life are constantly revising their ideas of what their problems and their goals really are. In addition, two other real-world considerations place creativity and innovation even more in the arena of human endeavor, regardless of how technology advances.

One concerns the well-known finding that intrinsic motivation stimulates creativity far better than extrinsic motivation does. Researchers have confirmed this result many times—but not all the time. In some studies it just doesn't hold up. Adam Grant of the University of Pennsylvania and James Berry of the University of North Carolina surveyed the extensive literature and found an explanation: "[I]ntrinsic motivation has been more consistently linked to creativity in artwork and writing tasks than to creativity in producing ideas and solutions relevant to business problems." For producing innovations that organizations would actually value, intrinsic motivation isn't enough. Something more is required, and Grant and Berry identified it. In their lab experiments and studies of organizations, people who are other-focused as well as intrinsically motivated produce the most creative and useful ideas. Being other-focused means having a prosocial orientation, a fundamental wish to help others. It can also mean a habit of seeing the world through other people's eyes. It's not surprising that people with those traits come up with ideas that will be useful to others, and when combined with intrinsic motivation, it's a winning package. The important point is that we're encountering empathy again. Creativity alone is nice. Creativity plus empathy is valuable.

The other real-world factor that magnifies the human element in creativity is a variation on the same idea—that successful creativity is more than just creating. It also requires buzz, interest, excitement among a broad audience. MIT's Peter Gloor and many others have pointed out that no effective innovation springs fully formed from its creator's mind. It has to be developed, and the most successful innovators involve others in its development from the very beginning. The first collaborators are likely a small team, maybe just two people, as we've seen. With time the innovators invite other interested people to help, steadily expanding the ring of collaborators who find the innovation truly interesting. Eventually this group of cocreators develops something with a decent chance of succeeding, and these enthusiastic, emotionally invested collaborators build ever broadening interest in the innovation, helping to launch it strongly into the larger world. Human interaction, skillfully pursued, is a big difference between innovations and successful innovations.

A persuasive argument holds that creativity isn't inherently special, magical, or mysterious. Rather, it's a set of skills. Regardless of whether a person has them, he or she could develop them; that's the nature of skills. This argument leads to the conclusion that, as with any other skill, computers could be as creative as, and eventually more creative than, any human. So it's important to remember that the reason high-value creativity will stay a human task has nothing to do with its supposedly magical, inexplicable nature. Arguments that rely on magic are generally suspect. The explanation is that creativity is done ultimately for humans, and, for all the reasons we've seen, it's in our deep nature to require that it be done by and with other humans. It isn't because we couldn't do it any other way. It's because it wouldn't solve our most important human problems if it were done any other way. That's why an ability to innovate in collaboration with others will continue to command high value even as technology roars ahead.

When we observe that some people seem to possess that ability more than others, we often wonder why. It's unlikely they were born that way; rather, they developed the skills of creativity and collaboration. This prompts the larger question of whether the more general skills of human interaction can be learned. The answer is that they can be, as we've seen and will see further in chapter 11. But we've noted also that these skills are fundamentally different from the skills that have made people economically successful in the past. The new high-value skills are more about what we're like than what we know. And when it comes to those skills—in a different category from the skills that have historically been economically valuable—one group does seem to possess a natural, inborn advantage.

CHAPTER TEN
IS IT A WOMAN'S WORLD?

In the Most Valuable Skills of the Coming Economy,
Women Hold Strong Advantages over Men.

Did you notice a fact that was mentioned fleetingly back in chapter 7, about why some teams are smarter than others? You'll recall that teams have an intelligence all their own, c, much like the IQ of an individual, that accounts for the team's success at performing a wide variety of tasks. We saw that the big-picture explanation of team intelligence is not what most of us would have guessed; it isn't the IQ of the team's members nor even how motivated, cohesive, or satisfied the team is. The main factor is instead the members' social sensitivity—how well they can discern the thoughts and feelings of other people, and how well they share their roles in the conversation, with no one dominating. The fleetingly mentioned fact was that women in general score higher than men on measures of social sensitivity, so the best-performing teams in the research tended to be those with the most women. Now it's time to focus on that fact and all that it implies for the issue of high-value skills in the coming economy, which is a lot.

The stark conclusion that emerges from the work on group intelligence is that women make groups smarter. The researchers weren't looking to prove or disprove anything about gender, but they couldn't help noticing what was in the data. Note that this is not the conventional diversity argument. It has become a cliché to say that bringing women into a corporate team, for example, improves the group's thinking because it introduces a wider variety of thoughts and experiences. That assumes the team was mostly men, and greater diversity improves performance. But the finding of this research is exactly the opposite. It shows that the more women in a group, the smarter it is, plain and simple. The smartest groups in the research had zero gender diversity; they were all women. If the diversity argument held, then replacing a woman with a man would make the group smarter. But it didn't. On average, it made the group dumber.

That unsought result stunned the researchers, but it was later confirmed by a separate study. The investigators never suspected that women's greater social sensitivity would be as significant as it proved to be. This prompted them to ask another question. As you may recall, they measured the social sensitivity of everyone in the experiments by giving them a well-established test called Reading the Mind in the Eyes (the RME test). You look at thirty-six black-and-white photos of just the eye region of various people and try to choose from a group of responses ("sad," "angry," "frustrated," "afraid," for example) what they're feeling or thinking. Using that test made sense, because all the groups in the group intelligence research met face-to-face, meaning everyone could see everyone else's eyes. So the researchers wondered: What would happen if the group members couldn't see each other?

In the new experiments, group members were separated and communicated only online through typed messages. And guess what: The result was the same. Groups with the highest social sensitivity, measured solely through the visually-based RME test, had the highest collective intelligence even when they couldn't see one another. The effect was just as strong as in the original face-to-face groups. Since women score highest on the RME test, this meant that, once again, all-women groups were the smartest.

Elsewhere we've emphasized that face-to-face interaction is much more effective and therefore valuable than any other kind, so you may naturally wonder if this research result negates that claim. It doesn't. It shows that the RME test is an excellent predictor of a group's collective intelligence—in fact, the best predictor of any factor the researchers measured—and it predicted just as strongly with online groups as with face-to-face groups. But it didn't show that online groups are just as smart as face-to-face groups; in fact, their average collective intelligence score was slightly lower. So face-to-face is still a more effective way to interact, but if a group must interact online, then group members with high RME scores will produce the best results.

It's immediately clear that the RME test measures much more than eye reading. It captures a type of interpersonal sensitivity that operates not just face-to-face but also in the far sparser environment of typed text. These two sets of experiments, considered together, show that women's social sensitivity is much farther reaching than many people realized. Women may be rolling their eyes as they read this, thinking that of course every woman already knows this to be true. But maybe not; it seems plausible to think that many women, told about the design of these experiments, would have guessed that diverse groups would be the smartest. In light of all we've seen so far about the types of human skills that are becoming most valuable, it's obvious that the role of women in tomorrow's economy requires a much closer look.

INNATE DIFFERENCES ARE REAL—AND FAVOR WOMEN

As value moves to skills of social interaction, you don't need rigorously designed social science experiments to tell you that women will probably perform those skills best. Men and women both know it from life experience. The dispute for centuries has concerned which sex's strengths are more economically valuable. For a long time the rising power of technology seemed to favor male engineers and entrepreneurs, but now, ironically, the trend is reversing as technology increasingly takes over all but the most deeply and essentially human roles. What we'd like to know more about is where the skill differences between the sexes come from, whether they're likely to disappear, what they mean for organizations (more than we think), and whether men are doomed to irrelevance.

Step one is confronting the hot-button issue of whether differences between the sexes are innate or learned, hardwired or imposed by society. That one's easy—clearly both—which means that at least some of those differences are in us at birth. As noted in chapter 3, the view that humans are innately inclined toward anything at all was out of favor for much of the twentieth century, but the evidence now seems persuasive that there is indeed such a thing as human nature, and it differs by sex.

To take an example highly relevant to our topic, why do boys seem so interested in mechanical things while girls seem more interested in human relationships? When researchers studied one-year-olds, they found that boys would rather watch a video of cars going past than a video of a human face, but girls would rather watch the face. That finding didn't satisfy some people, who argued that even at the tender age of one, acculturation could explain the difference. But in fact researchers had previously studied one-day-old babies. Boys looked longer at a mechanical mobile than at a face, while girls looked longer at the face. It's hard to argue that acculturation did it. For that matter, it's possible to measure the testosterone in a baby's system before it's even born and predict how much eye contact it will make at age one; less prenatal testosterone means more eye contact. Such evidence and much more suggests strongly that the gender differences we care about are indeed partly hardwired.

EMPATHIZERS TRUMP SYSTEMIZERS

The deep distinction between men's and women's brains, argues Cambridge University research psychologist Simon Baron-Cohen, is that men's brains are "systemizing" and women's are "empathizing." Systemizing means figuring out the rules that govern any kind of system—a lawn mower engine, the weather, software, a golf swing. Empathizing means figuring out the mental state of another person and an appropriate "affective" or emotional response. Systemizing and empathizing are in many ways "almost the opposite of each other," Baron-Cohen says. Systemizing is the best way of "understanding and predicting the law-governed inanimate universe." Empathizing is the best way of understanding and predicting the social world.

It's obvious which kind of brain is better suited to a world that values interpersonal skills, and men will be distressed to learn that Baron-Cohen's evidence for his model is vast. A few highlights:

- Starting at age one, girls are more likely to respond empathically (through sad looks, sympathetic sounds, comforting) to the distress of others. By age three, they're better than boys at figuring out the thoughts and intentions of others, and they never lose their advantage.
- Women are better than men not just at reading eyes but also at nonverbal communication generally, such as reading tone of voice and facial expressions.
- Women value reciprocal relationships more highly than men do. Men value power and competition more highly than women do.

- Empathy disorders, such as psychopathic personality disorder, are far more common among men. Murder, which Baron-Caron rather drily calls "the ultimate example of lack of empathy," is of course overwhelmingly male instigated.
- The way girls talk is much more cooperative and collaborative than the way boys talk, and girls can keep a conversation going longer than boys can.
- Girls show more concern for fairness than boys do. Boys share less than girls.

There's more, but the men reading this are probably starting to sweat already. I hate to pile it on, but in addition to women's considerable advantages in an economy that increasingly values empathy, collaboration, and relationships, men have another reason to worry. Besides losing in competition with women, they are likely to lose disproportionately in competition with technology.

This seems odd, considering that men, on average, are attracted to technology and have been, on average, the sex most responsible for the technology revolution. Of course, a number of computer pioneers were unsung women—Ada Lovelace, Grace Hopper, Jean Jennings, to name a few—who are only beginning to get the recognition they deserve. But it's undeniable that the industry has been and remains dominated by men, a situation that many companies, schools, and governments worldwide are trying to remedy. Yet the surprising new trend is that for men in general, technology's advance is becoming a problem.

That's because in the systemizers-versus-empathizers model, systemizing is exactly what technology is taking over. Understand how an engine, the weather, or a golf swing works? Men may be hardwired to focus on such questions, but in a world increasingly filled with sensors and ever greater processing power, computers will analyze those systems and practically all other systems faster and better than people ever could. Yes, even your golf swing; sensors that attach to your clubs and send analytical data about your swing to your computer have been around for years and are improving all the time. As for some of the most important systems in our lives—computer systems—they're increasingly being created by computers themselves.

Obviously the world will need plenty of computer engineers as infotech proliferates, but, as we've seen before, the important issue isn't the number of jobs but rather the number of high-value jobs. Computer coding is becoming commoditized, with schools adding classes for students as young as five. The skill is becoming analogous to writing—everyone in a modern economy must be able to do it at some basic level, but the world needs very few people who do it for a living. Instead, coding, or at least a knowledge of how it works, becomes a skill that everyone brings to their work in other fields. The larger point is that, as technology transforms our world in new ways, men's innate tendency to systemize, which has served them well since humans' emergence as a species, becomes ever less of an advantage for them in the economy.

SCANNING TRUMPS FOCUSING

Since it never rains but it pours, here's another emerging problem for men. While multiple forces are challenging men's abilities to do high-value work in the changing economy, a number of female tendencies—or at least tendencies that women have evinced more strongly than men—are increasing in value for reasons even beyond the ones we've already examined.

An important one was articulated by Sally Helgesen in her prophetic 1990 book *The Female Advantage*: Based on her study of women CEOs, and on earlier studies of men CEOs, she says that women leaders' view of their work differs from men's in that it "encompasses a vision of society—they relate decisions to their larger effect upon the role of the family, the American educational system, the environment, even world peace." That was 1990, and what she describes is exactly what societies around the world have since come to expect from leading businesses. Many of the companies that now see their purpose as including benefit to the society or the planet are led by men, but it appears that women leaders may be a bit faster and more comfortable in taking their organizations down that road, and that's an advantage.

The phenomenon is one manifestation of a more general difference between men and women, which is that, on average, women take a broader view. It's true literally: Women's peripheral vision is wider than men's, while men focus more narrowly and at greater distances. This may be an evolutionary adaptation from the days when men were stalking game and women were scanning the landscape for edible plants while keeping track of offspring. In any case, the difference exists metaphorically too: Brain imaging shows that in general, women's attention is engaged by many different things simultaneously, while men tend to stay focused on a narrower set of items.

The perfect human being would have both abilities, but in today's fast-changing business environment it's especially easy to see the advantages of wide scanning—noticing things that the focused observer, locked onto what mattered the day before yesterday, might miss. It's certainly striking that two of the most iconoclastic voices of warning before the financial crisis came from women. Meredith Whitney, a financial analyst, predicted deep trouble for Lehman Brothers, Merrill Lynch, Citigroup, and Bank of America when conventional analysts, focused on conventional measures, remained upbeat. She gazed more broadly and saw signals that the others missed. Sheila Bair, who chaired the Federal Deposit Insurance Corporation, tried publicly to warn regulators about a potential subprime loan disaster while America's lending festival was still going strong, but was ignored. She too took a broader view and saw how trouble could erupt in new ways.

That way of seeing is what every company wants in an era when any business can be disrupted, and the disrupter is almost never one of its conventional competitors—the ones most managers are focused on when they get blindsided by a new start-up. Even when a disrupted company does change its business model and survives, the new model won't last nearly as long as the old one. That's why businesses increasingly need leaders who are comfortable with a permanently temporary mode of operating—a profoundly uncomfortable environment in most organizations. Yet women seem to handle it easily, as Helgesen observed in a different context. She notes that Margaret Thatcher claimed never to have set long-term goals for herself "but had rather seized opportunities as they came and made the best of them." Several of the women in Helgesen's study described the same pattern. She quotes one of them as saying, "I don't draft five-year plans—I just do the best job I can and trust that it will lead me to where I'm supposed to be next. I know that sounds kind of squishy, but it works." They're talking about their highly successful careers, but the point applies more widely. Scanning for opportunities and making the most of them, rather than setting and pursuing a multiyear plan, is a winning strategy when technology can transform industries in the blink of an eye.

TWO WAYS TO ERASE WOMEN'S STRENGTHS

Women's advantage in social sensitivity gives them, on average, a big head start in the competition for high-value work in the changing economy, and this advantage is extremely deeply rooted. It seems to be genuinely innate. Yet it can be erased entirely in at least a couple of ways, and the causes reveal more about how distinctly female the advantage is.

A quick and easy way to wipe out women's powers of social sensitivity, at least for some women, is simply to give them a tiny dose of testosterone. Doing so makes some women less able to recognize emotional facial expressions, and it reduces their mimicry of others in social interactions—the unconscious body-language signaling that builds rapport and strengthens relationships. In one experiment, a bit of testosterone virtually destroyed women's empathy as measured by the RME test—and the researchers discovered another significant finding in the process.

It has long been known that testosterone affects the brain in two ways: Before birth it affects how the brain is organized, depending on how much of the hormone the fetus receives; and after birth, especially starting in adolescence, the amount of it being produced within the body affects the brain's functioning from moment to moment. Both boys and girls receive testosterone as they develop before birth—boys much more than girls, obviously, though exact amounts vary within sexes—and we all produce it through our lives, males producing more than females. Much previous research had shown that testosterone affects social behavior in a big way. In children of both sexes, higher levels of fetal testosterone mean not only less eye contact at age one, but also poorer social understanding in general at age four and poorer social intelligence, as measured by the RME and other tests, at ages six to eight. That is, in the first way testosterone affects the brain, organizing it before birth, it seems to preprogram the brain for weaker social abilities.

The researchers who gave women small doses of testosterone—the effect of which is only temporary—were investigating the second way it affects the brain, activating various processes from moment to moment. In addition, they measured how much prebirth testosterone their test subjects had been exposed to. (They did this by measuring the index finger and ring finger of each person's right hand; the longer the ring finger is relative to the length of the index finger, the more prebirth testosterone a person was exposed to.) It turns out that while a dose of testosterone appears to erase women's ability to detect the motives, intentions, thoughts, and emotions of others, it does so only in those who had received a lot of testosterone before birth. The effect is so strong that it influences the data for the entire group. But in women whose prebirth levels had been low, being given a dose of testosterone produced no effect at all; it couldn't derail their abilities to empathize.

Thus a big deficit in empathy is apparently a two-step process. It requires a brain that has been primed by a lot of testosterone before birth plus extra shots of the hormone in daily life. In general, apart from laboratory experiments, only men have both. These findings underscore men's seemingly permanent disadvantage.

Yet women's superior social abilities can also be negated in a different way that's highly relevant to real-world conditions. You'll recall the striking research showing that the more women there are in a group, the higher its collective intelligence. After those results were published, some researchers thought of a clever variation to the experiment. They again tested many groups for collective intelligence, but they told some of the groups to elect a leader who would remain the same while the members worked through their many tasks; that is, the leader was set and unchangeable. They told other groups they should choose a leader and would later have another chance to vote; so in those groups, members might compete for status as they did their work.

The results were dramatic. In the first groups, with stable hierarchies, more women once again equaled smarter groups. But in the second groups, with competition for status, the effect was eliminated—completely. A group could be all-women, all-men, mixed; it didn't matter. They all had the same collective intelligence. And it was way,

way below the intelligence of an all-female group with stable hierarchy. Competing for status poisoned a group's effectiveness regardless of gender composition. It destroyed the performance advantages that women bring to a group.

The reason seems clear. The social sensitivity of women helps group members collaborate more effectively in two critical ways. First, it gets more ideas out onto the table. Because women are more likely than men to share the conversation equally, and are better at sensing when someone wants to speak, female groups get more contributions from everyone. Second, as group members discuss ideas, women are better able to sense how others feel about each idea. So female groups can more accurately gauge the group's collective judgment of all the options proposed.

More ideas and better judgments—those are what make groups effective. But when group members can compete for status, the female advantage, at least in creating collective intelligence, gets shut down. The conversational turn taking, the body language to build rapport, the subtle vocal cues to indicate approval or disagreement—they can all become disadvantages when someone is trying to establish dominance. In real-world settings, group incentives thus become crucially important. It's emphatically clear that women can make groups much more effective. But whether it actually happens depends on whether group members are given incentives to try to outdo one another. Not even ancient, inherent strengths can survive bad management.

HOW EXPERIENCES CAN LEVEL THE PLAYING FIELD

The nasty effects of status competition are a hint that innate tendencies, powerful as they may be, aren't the whole story. Social experiences can also alter social abilities and collaborative behavior in both men and women, for better or worse. For example, early experiences can cause people of either sex to be more collaborative or less so.

People who grow up in larger families tend to be more "prosocial" as adults; prosocials try to maximize outcomes for themselves and for others, seeking greater equality in their interactions. They cooperate more. These are the effective collaborators of the world, the people whose value is increasing in the changing economy, and it's significant that, regardless of genes, our likelihood of being such a person is affected by something as basic as family size.

Experiences and inherent tendencies interact. The same researchers who discovered that family size affects prosocial behavior also found that the number of sisters in particular is significant: The more sisters a man or a woman has, the more likely that person is to be prosocial. Why? No one has nailed down an explanation, but there would seem to be something in the very nature of sisters. Similarly, these same researchers found that prosocial behavior increases with age, for reasons that may combine experiences with genes. Much previous work had shown that people become more cooperative through childhood and early adulthood, and these researchers found that the pattern continues all the way to people in their eighties. Maybe it's because people learn with time that prosocial behavior usually works out better for them. Or maybe it's because testosterone levels in men and women decline with age. Or maybe it's both those factors and perhaps others.

The fact that our social abilities can be affected by experience is hardly surprising, but the big-picture effects may be. In chapter 4 we saw that empathy in general appears to be declining, at least in the United States. The findings on prosocial tendency, obviously a related quality, add evidence on a broader scale. We see that bigger families produce offspring who are more prosocial, on average—and family size is declining worldwide. Similarly, much research has shown that children raised in settings with "high levels of collectivism, personal closeness, and interdependence," as one paper puts it, tend to be more cooperative and collaborative. Those settings are mostly rural and in small towns; as people globally live increasingly in cities, fewer are growing up in such environments. At just the moment when organizations are seeking more and better work from teams, large-scale forces may be shrinking the number of highly adept potential team members. Surging demand plus dwindling supply—that's the formula for high value.

We should not assume that women, with their marked natural strengths, have a lock on capturing this value. Variations caused by life experiences can level the playing field, possibly diminishing some women's abilities and enhancing some men's. In addition, even the innate tendencies of the two sexes are not divided by a clear line. Baron-Cohen, who proposed the distinction between the systemizing male brain and the empathizing female brain, emphasizes that all normal brains do plenty of both. The difference is that more males than females tilt toward systemizing, and more females than males tilt toward empathizing. Which means, as he says, that "some women have the male brain type, and some men have the female brain type, or aspects of it."

So as technology advances, raising the value of personal interaction and its many related skills, it's almost but not quite right to say that it's a woman's world. The more precise conclusion is that it's becoming a more female world. The traits, tendencies, and abilities for which women have long shown greater strength than men will prove highly valuable for people of either sex who possess them. That is, on the whole, a great thing for women and maybe not so great for men. At the same time, the changing economy presents large opportunities for both. It represents a balancing of an economic world that had long favored male abilities. Now members of both sexes have much to gain by acquiring the abilities they don't have. Empathizing men, systemizing women—those people are winners in a world that increasingly favors a combination of high technological literacy and deep social sensitivity.

But hold on. While there may indeed be much to gain by acquiring the skills of human interaction that one doesn't already have, how easy is it to acquire such skills? We've heard so much about hardwiring, about how deeply rooted these tendencies are in our evolutionary past, that you can't help wondering whether we have much control over them at all. As technology takes over more of the work that people now do, and does so faster than ever in history, can we actually make ourselves into the kinds of people who will excel at the high-value work of the future? That's the one big question left, to which we now turn.

CHAPTER ELEVEN
WINNING IN THE HUMAN DOMAIN

Some Will Love a World That Values Deep Human Interaction.
Others Won't. But Everyone Will Need to Get Better—And Can.

Southwest Airlines once hired a high-level employee for its information technology operations and quickly began to suspect it had made a mistake. After he'd been on the job for only a week or so, the company's HR chief asked him how things were going.

"People here are strange," he replied. "They want to talk to me in the hallway! They ask how my day has been, and they really want to know! And I just want to go back to my cube and work."

An IT guy who wants to be left alone in his cube is not exactly a surprise. It's practically a stereotype. But it was a big problem at Southwest.

This company succeeds in one of the world's most miserable industries. All three of its largest U.S. competitors—American, Delta, and United—have gone bankrupt at one time or another, in some cases more than once. Yet Southwest has earned a profit in each of its forty-plus years of existence. It prospers because, as its managers have always understood, it knows the value of human interaction externally and internally. The ability of employees to engage customers with humor, energy, and generosity is crucial to creating value in an experience that is not, on its face, all that appealing. This is an airline that won't give you an assigned seat, serve you a meal, or transfer your luggage to or from other airlines. But when you're dealing with nice people in a good mood, somehow it's okay. For employees who work strictly with one another behind the scenes, the business is as grindingly competitive as it is for any other airline, and doing the job is not a walk in the park. Coworkers who ask about each other and like to tell a joke are key to keeping everyone going.

So an employee who's uninterested in human interaction is trouble. His immediate depressive effect on those around him, bad enough by itself, could start to spread. Even if it doesn't, it's a problem. The company's culture is a big reason, maybe the main reason, that so many people want to work there. It's why, when the company has 3,000 jobs to fill, it gets 100,000 applications. If a newly hired young person comes to work on his first day and meets this guy, he'll conclude that the Southwest culture isn't at all what he thought. He'll be unhappy, possibly resentful, and he'll spread the word.

So Southwest's managers decided that their new IT guy, despite his excellent credentials, had to go. He was fired in short order.

That story, told to me by the HR chief involved, shows us a couple of important realities about the world we're entering. First, it shows that in a company whose success is built on skills of human interaction, those skills are at least as valuable as patents, economies of scale, or other assets that are the basis of other strategies. Even companies that say they value interpersonal abilities don't usually value them as highly as more traditional assets; they think they're nice to have but not essential. But, they are essential. When they're central to the strategy, as is becoming the case in companies of every kind, then even one person who threatens that strategy is one too many and cannot be tolerated.

Second, the story shows us something important about human nature in a world where the skills of human interaction are becoming the key to creating value. It's this: Just because everybody is human doesn't mean everybody will be good at those skills.

DON'T WASTE YOUR TIME TOGETHER

For most people, whether they're any good at those skills is largely a matter of chance. For starters, there's what you're born with; a man's Y chromosome and, in either sex, levels of prebirth testosterone affect social abilities, as we've seen. Then, in the realm of what we can control, it has also been largely chance. The size of your family, the number of sisters, and how you were raised can influence how successfully you engage with other people in later life, but those aspects of one's upbringing are partly or entirely random, not deliberate. Children whose "parents are very attentive to their elementary needs are likely to develop trust and security, which may promote prosocial orientation," note psychology researchers, but those parents probably weren't consciously trying to create cooperative, collaborative adults; they were just being good, attentive parents. After childhood, we typically encounter nobody who tries deliberately to improve our social abilities, and we generally don't try to do it ourselves. As a result, the question of who does and doesn't possess these supremely important skills is answered almost totally by a roll of the dice.

That situation has begun to change, as it must. As individuals and institutions see how the world is transforming, they're finding ways to develop people's social abilities deliberately and effectively. The institution that has done the most work by far is the U.S. military, and we've seen much of that work already. In addition, companies that realize where their fortunes lie are using innovative methods to build the social abilities of employees. The corporate efforts are mostly in early stages, and the military allows only some of its work to become public. Yet it's already clear that opportunities to improve people's social abilities are everywhere.

It's revealing that preeminent business schools are on top of the trend and are radically reforming their curricula in response. They're strongly motivated to produce the kinds of graduates who will succeed in the coming environment, and increasingly they're moving away from classroom teaching of subjects like finance, economics, and accounting—knowledge that's being commoditized— and instead are putting students through experiences of personal interaction. "We're changing how students interact," Stanford business school dean Garth Saloner told me, "and it starts in their first quarter." That's when they're required to work as small teams in exercises and realistic simulations of high-pressure business situations, then analyze their own behavior through army-style after-action reviews. That first quarter culminates in a day-long event when the teams must engage in high-stakes interactions with groups of experienced alumni who take the role of boards of directors; the teams are told their assignments in advance, "but there's always a curve ball thrown in," said Saloner. Then the students get detailed assessments of their behavior—listening, speaking, attention to body language—from the alumni and faculty.

The Harvard Business School similarly puts all first-year students through a series of team-based simulations and exercises. Then they're forced into the real world. Each team works with a real company in an emerging market—Lenovo in China, say, or Viet Capital Bank in Vietnam—on a real project proposed by the company, such as developing a new financial service to attract people who have never had a bank account, for example, or creating a new line of household fans. After developing an idea on campus, the teams travel to their markets in January and spend eight days doing market research and then presenting their proposal to the company's top leaders.

When they return to school, the work gets more intense and personal. Each team is told to start its own business, a real one, in ten weeks using $3,000 of seed money provided by the school. Each year that's 150 teams, 150 LLCs that get set up, 150 business ideas that have included premium underwear for men, a service to connect language tutors with students worldwide, a sari rental service, and widely varied others. All students buy and sell "stock" in all the businesses through a simulated market, giving everyone a view of how outsiders rate each idea. Most important, as dean Nitin Nohria noted, students must respond to human realities: "team members of varying skill and motivation, vendors who may be more or less reliable, and customers with their own views of what they want as opposed to what one wants them to buy." It's all a long way from learning the capital asset pricing model in a classroom.

Not many people will go to Harvard or Stanford business schools, but everyone can learn lessons from the way those schools are reallocating students' time. The truth is the capital asset pricing model is still important for business students to learn, but it no longer makes sense for them to learn it in classrooms, gathered together in physical proximity but scarcely interacting at all.

Learning basic concepts online is enormously faster and more effective than doing it in a classroom. For example, DARPA developed software for the U.S. Navy to use in teaching students to repair infotech systems on ships, a classic knowledge task without human components. The classroom course took sixteen weeks, but students who used the software instead mastered the material in two weeks and then kept going. They outperformed the classroom students by huge margins and achieved skill levels comparable to those of classroom-trained students with twelve years' experience.

Or consider what happened after Stanford professor Sebastian Thrun launched the era of massive open online courses (MOOCs) in 2011, when he put his graduate-level course on artificial intelligence online and opened it to anyone. This too was largely technical material without human elements, and tests could be scored by computer. To Thrun's amazement, 160,000 students from 190 countries signed up. Even more surprising, when the final exam was scored, the top 400 performers were all online students; those top 400 all did better than even the best of the elite Stanford students who took the course in the classroom.

So why spend valuable classroom time—why should any of us spend our time with other humans—doing tasks that not only don't require in-person gathering but that can actually be done faster and better without it? Those are wasted opportunities, which is why schools are moving the teaching of basic knowledge online. Students can learn the material more efficiently and can still get help from professors if needed. Their freed-up time can then be spent with others developing the in-person skills that are supplanting basic knowledge as the foundation of success.

The lesson from the business schools for all of us could be thought of as, Don't spend time with others if it's better spent alone. But there's a more useful way to say it: If you're going to spend time with others, make the most of it. Getting together in a classroom to learn basic corporate finance is no longer making the most of everyone's time. In companies, gathering for meetings in which people don't listen or encourage others to speak, don't try to sense the unexpressed thoughts and feelings of others, and don't speak their minds or communicate in ways that reach others deeply is nowhere near making the most of the opportunity. When family and friends get together it's the same, or often worse, because we let ourselves be distracted by digital devices. We're not fully there and thus not fully together. As Sherry Turkle has written, "It is easy for people to end up unsure if they are closer together or further apart." By not making the most of our time together, we are, in the business context, wasting time and becoming uncompetitive. In the personal context, we are losing our bonds with the people who are most important to us. In both contexts, our interpersonal abilities are weakening at exactly the time when we need to strengthen them. And, in profoundly unscientific terms, we are starving our souls.

INFOTECH TO THE RESCUE, BELIEVE IT OR NOT

You probably noticed an irony in the discussion of how we must rethink the way we allocate our time. Advancing technology is at the root of why we must improve our social abilities, but it's also enabling us to spend more time doing exactly that, if we choose. If we can now learn basic knowledge skills in weeks rather than months or years, using infotech, then we can focus increasingly on developing interpersonal abilities, just as those business students are doing. It's a hint that as technology creates a new world in which millions of people's jobs are threatened, it can also help us succeed in that world. In fact, it can do so in a much more direct way than we've seen so far.

It turns out—please sound the irony alert—that information technology can sometimes help us acquire interpersonal skills more effectively and efficiently than actual in-person experience can. Most of the evidence comes from the military. An early indication of what is possible turned up at a training facility in San Diego.

An important task on which certain teams of soldiers and Marines are trained is "clearing a room"—entering a room and making it safe, shooting any bad guys but not good guys—and doing it as fast as possible. Speed is the goal, but mistakes are obviously very costly. Rarely is well-coordinated teamwork more important. The established method of training is to send four-man teams repeatedly into a highly realistic setting, called a "shoot house," shooting real weapons with simulated ammunition—soap bullets that don't kill but do hurt. That's how soldiers and Marines were training in San Diego when, in the early 2000s, the trainers tried something new.

They digitally re-created the training area so it could be explored on a computer. Before ever seeing the real room, trainees could wander around it and the surrounding area on a PC screen; there was no action in the software, just observation. Then they were formed into teams and sent into the room, and their room-clearing times were compared with those of teams that hadn't seen the virtual room and its surroundings. Faster times—the goal—mean team members are working better together.

Teams that hadn't seen the virtual room got faster on every run through the shoot house, as you would hope and expect. But teams that had seen the virtual room in advance for just ten minutes were faster on their very first run—that is, team members were interacting better—than the other teams were after four runs. Those who had seen the virtual room on a big, projected video display rather than on a PC screen were faster still. Spending ten minutes with simple software improved team interaction better than spending hours in real-life practice. As an added benefit, when trainees who had first used the software then entered the real room for the first time, their heart rates were as low as the other trainees' heart rates were on their fourth run.

Those results surprised everyone. Other early efforts were showing similarly impressive results. Software created for the army as a demonstration project called Think Like a Commander took officers through a series of seven complex, ambiguous battlefield vignettes, requiring them to, say, relieve an encircled unit, and then asked them to identify the most critical information in light of what a thinking enemy commander might do, among other factors. They were developing empathy—discerning what was in the enemy commander's mind. Again, the results were striking. Captains who used the software but had never been deployed to Iraq were almost twice as good at identifying critical information, including that related to the enemy's thinking, as those who had actually been deployed to Iraq but had not used the software.

The next step was software that let team members train together in a realistic virtual setting. That came along in a program called Darwars Ambush (a somewhat droll name reflecting the program's creation by DARPA) to help squads on their way to Iraq deal with the growing number of deadly ambushes that U.S. forces were facing there. This was a multiplayer environment that required trainees to imagine what the enemy might have done and then work together to avoid harm and complete their mission. The software was adopted widely by the army and Marines.

None of this software brought trainees face to face with the native people they would meet in Iraq or Afghanistan, where interacting with them successfully could be literally a life or death matter. Soldiers could get an excellent and highly effective in-person simulation at the National Training Center, but it was impossible for every soldier being deployed to go there. One response was software called the Tactical Iraqi Language and Culture Trainer, and another version for Afghanistan. Trainees learned elementary spoken Arabic (or Pashto) and met, in realistic settings, avatars of village elders, soldiers, children, parents, and people whose roles were unclear.

Some computer games are called first-person shooters, but this was a first-person talker; U.S. soldiers couldn't shoot. The software put them in sticky situations, such as quelling an unruly crowd, where talking—saying the right thing to the right person at the right time—was the only way out. Trainees gauged how well they were doing by a "trust meter" at the bottom of the screen. How effective was the software? A beta tester, back from Iraqi deployment, told the developer, "I learned more in one day with this than I learned in my whole tour in Iraq."

That kind of software continued to improve as designers gained experience and technology advanced. Soon the software could understand soldiers speaking in their beginner's Arabic or Pashto, for example. Scenarios became more realistic. Darwars Ambush even let soldiers in the field create their own scenarios based on new situations they encountered.

How much difference such software made to soldiers on the ground is impossible to test rigorously because "we don't want to go to war again, this time without the training," said Ralph Chatham, whom we met in chapter 5, a DARPA program manager who developed Darwars Ambush and the tactical language and culture trainers. His conclusion: "I feel sure that Darwars Ambush and the tactical language tutors saved lives, but I don't know whose lives they saved."

Then, in 2011, DARPA aimed to go far beyond all that. Its ambition was much greater than simply teaching specific languages and cultures. Rather, it aimed to uncover the master keys to interpersonal relations at any time or place, in any culture or language, by studying "the science of social interactions and human dynamics," in the words of DARPA's official description. The program was called Strategic Social Interaction Modules, which quickly became known informally as Good Stranger. It would train service members "to approach and engage strangers in unfamiliar social environments," wherever they might be, to "recover from social errors, de-escalate conflict, integrate tact and tactics," and otherwise manage those engagements so as to advance the mission. DARPA saw only one way to achieve those goals, which was to go to the very heart of interpersonal relations and achieve a complete understanding of them. The grand objective was nothing less than to "identify and codify the constitutive elements of successful social interaction skills."

That's obviously a tall order, maybe too tall. DARPA declined my repeated attempts to learn more about the program, which was continuing as of 2015. But give the agency credit for once again identifying a centrally important issue. Good Stranger's objective is the right objective not just for the U.S. military but for everyone in the modern economy. What DARPA wanted to know is what we all need to know.

HOW COMPANIES ARE BUILDING THE HIGH-VALUE SKILLS

Do companies need to be as diligent as the military in making sure employees are skilled in social interaction? We're long past the days when millions of assembly-line workers were little more than low-maintenance machines, doing the same repetitive motions, yet some might still argue that for certain successful companies, personal interaction just isn't all that important. Consider Google—one of the world's most valuable companies. We've seen that it takes great pains to get employees talking with one another, but whether they're socially skilled is a separate question. The company is famous for prizing sheer brainpower above all. At one time it hired only graduates of elite schools with near-perfect—or absolutely perfect—SAT scores. In job interviews, applicants have been asked how much they should charge to wash all the windows in Seattle, or how many golf balls would fit in a school bus. There are no correct answers; the interviewer just wants to see how an applicant thinks.

But in fact, skills of human interaction are key even at Google. The company no longer hires only from top schools or only people with stunning test scores. It does, however, ask every applicant for any job how he or she "has flexed different muscles in various situations to mobilize a team," executive chairman Eric Schmidt has reported. The company is also interested in every applicant's "collaborative nature." You'd still better be really smart, but you won't have a chance of working there if you aren't also off-the-charts good at interacting with others.

And then, if somehow you're in that fraction of 1 percent of applicants who get hired, Google makes sure you and your colleagues interact, through such tactics as the carefully calibrated lunch line and the cafeteria-style tables described in chapter 9. The company also may well try to make you still better at interpersonal skills, using tools much like the military's. Google developed a cloud-based mobile game for helping team members work together better, starting with exercises to understand themselves and their teammates ("You have strong interpersonal skills and a compassionate nature. People gravitate toward you as a teacher. . . ."). The curricula embedded in the game could last from a month to a year. The game was created at the University of Central Florida's Institute for Simulation and Training, which has developed a great deal of military simulation technology, such as an app called Combat Hunter used in Marine Corps training. As you might suspect, even it includes training in skills of human interaction. One Marine reported that the training "helped me understand how to think and plan like the enemy would." Discerning another person's thoughts and responding appropriately—it's empathy again.

Growing numbers of companies have discovered what the military learned long ago, that the supposedly ineffable, intractable, untrainable skills of deep human interaction are in fact trainable. Managers' mind-sets are the highest hurdle to realizing the benefits. Businesses can't even begin to get better until leaders acknowledge that these skills are the key to competitive advantage, that methods of developing them may be unfamiliar, and that measuring the results will never be as easy as gauging operating efficiencies. If companies can get past those obstacles, which in most organizations are more than enough to stop managerial innovations dead in their tracks, then they have a chance. Here are some examples of what vanguard companies have done so far:

- Several companies, such as Avon and Lowe's, have used basic computer simulations to train customer-facing employees. The simulations' value is high repetition and feedback; trainees experience many different scenarios quickly, so they make their mistakes with fifty virtual customers before encountering a real one.

- More sophisticated and advanced, and less widely used, have been live simulations and exercises. For example, managers at Japan's Uniqlo, Grupo Salinas in Mexico, and Charoen Pokphand Group in Thailand—all multibillion-dollar enterprises—have used a technique that forces them to understand relationships within specific teams. The team members go through a series of deliberately artificial activities, such as guiding blindfolded members through an obstacle course under highly restrictive rules, and then must confront how well they communicated, handled conflict, showed sensitivity to others, and elicited ideas, and they must figure out how to fix the behaviors that need fixing. The technique, developed by the University of Michigan's Noel Tichy, is effective at building interpersonal skills when teams follow the multistep protocol, which is much more detailed and pedagogically sound than the old close-your-eyes-and-fall-backward exercises that some corporate veterans remember unfondly.

- A few firms have even run realistic live simulations. For example, a biotech company faced a severe problem of back orders and delayed shipments. Those were potentially company-killing failures because this firm made proteins and other materials that had to be grown in a lab and then shipped to researchers on time for experiments. Late orders risked being canceled, and the company was losing customers. So, in an empty building the company created a miniature version of itself, with mock production stations, packing areas, and a shipping department,

plus four teams of workers from those functions. The
teams were given goals—orders filled, costs, revenue,
on-time status, and others—but absolutely no instructions on how to reach them. The teams simulated a
twelve-week quarter in five hours. A real-time dashboard
projected on a wall showed each team how its decisions
were affecting the company's financial performance.

In the first run-through, every team failed to meet the targets. In
fact, they achieved almost exactly the same terrible results the company was actually recording. The researchers who studied this and
similar simulations say the first round is always like that. Even though
the teams were told explicitly to achieve hugely better results, they
mostly did what they had always done, just working faster and harder.

In the second and final round, held a week later, all the teams
behaved differently. They didn't try to work faster or harder, and
people in the various functions stopped focusing on their own specific goals. Instead, they pursued top-level financial goals like
company revenue and profit, and they figured out how their own
actions had to mesh with others' in order to meet those goals. All
the teams redesigned the shop floor to shorten how material and
information moved. And this time every single team beat the goals
they'd been given. The company adopted the most successful
team's solution, though in truth it was only a little better than the
others, and the back-order problem dwindled almost to nothing.
In simulation the workers had figured out how to interact, and in
real life they may well have saved the company.

- Several organizations have devised clever ways to
  encourage "giver" behavior as described by Wharton's
  Adam Grant. Givers are people who do things that
  benefit others with no expectation and sometimes no

possibility of recompense. For example, the person in the car ahead of you pays for your food at the drive-through; they're gone before you even realize what they've done. Or in a work setting, a colleague stays in the office late helping you create a presentation that has nothing to do with his own assignments. Such behavior is wonderful, but how could it help build social interaction more broadly?

Consider a simple bit of software called the Love Machine, developed at Linden Lab, the digital entertainment company that created the enormously popular Second Life. As Grant notes, tech companies face a virulent strain of a common problem: "Many employees aim to protect their time for themselves and guard information closely, instead of sharing their time and knowledge with colleagues." With the Love Machine software, when a colleague breaks that pattern and does you a kindness, you can send him or her a thank-you message that's viewable by everyone. The public acknowledgment creates new incentives. An employee told Grant that the software is a way to get "tech geeks to compete to see who could be the most helpful."

More generally, anything that encourages people to become givers is probably useful to an organization because givers are more empathetic; they "are more attentive to others' behaviors and more attuned to their thoughts and feelings," Grant writes. In addition, the software encouraged people not only to interact, but to interact in a spirit of openness and sharing—exactly the kind of interaction that people value most highly and that produces the best results from teams.

* Dozens of medical schools around the world encourage or even require the reading of fiction, because it helps build skills of social interaction. It "helps to develop and

nurture skills of observation, analysis, empathy, and self-reflection—skills that are essential for human medical care," says a statement from New York University Medical School's medical humanities program. Of course, it isn't just med students who can benefit. Research has shown that reading literary fiction improves the empathy of people generally. Reading nonfiction or so-called genre fiction—the kind churned out very profitably by the Danielle Steeles and James Pattersons of the world—doesn't do it. But reading fiction in which the characters are more complex and the action is often driven by their inner lives seems to make us more sensitive to what's going on in the minds of others. It's a rare way in which we can improve our interpersonal abilities by doing something all by ourselves.

Those findings and more offer new hope to humanities majors, who could certainly use it. While the best-paying college majors are almost entirely in engineering, as we've seen, the worst-paying are mainly in humanities and social sciences. Yet in the emerging world of work, the abilities that the humanities nurture are precisely those that the economy will increasingly value. It isn't just because an appreciation of the humanities will help technologists create better, friendlier, more appealing technology, though that is emphatically true. It was one of Steve Jobs's favorite themes—that his education at Reed College, a rigorous liberal arts school in Portland, Oregon, led directly to the superior look, feel, and experience of Apple products. He named his son Reed.

But now we see also how the humanities bestow another advantage. Far more than engineering or computer science, the humanities strengthen the deep human abilities that will be critical to the success of most people, regardless of whether they work directly in technology. Consultants Christian Madsbjerg and Mikkel B. Rasmussen, arguing that "we need more humanities majors," observe that "when you study the writings of, say, David Foster Wallace, you learn how to step into and feel empathy for a different world than your own. His world of intricate, neurotic detail and societal critique says more about living as a young man in the 1990s than most market research graphs." The benefits in real-world pursuits are direct, they argue: "The same skills involved in being a subtle reader of a text are involved in deeply understanding Chinese or Argentinian consumers of cars, soap or computers. They are hard skills of understanding other people, their practices and context." Skills that employers badly want—critical thinking, clear communicating, complex problem solving—"are skills taught at the highest levels in the humanities."

As we've seen, the most valuable people of all will be those who combine technical knowledge with the skills and sensibilities built by study of the humanities, as Jobs did. This is a marked contrast to the apotheosis of STEM subjects that became conventional in the late twentieth and early twenty-first centuries. STEM education will remain important for a long time. But humanities majors, take heart. The world is turning not away from you, as you've been led to believe, but toward you.

IDENTIFYING WINNERS AND LOSERS

Everyone can get better at the skills that will be most valuable in the changing economy, and it seems logical to see all this as the latest step in a long progression. For centuries people have improved their living standards by mastering new skills that a new economy rewards. But the skills that are becoming most valuable now, the skills of deeply human interaction, are not like those other skills. Learning to be more socially sensitive is not like learning algebra or how to operate a lathe or how to make a well functioning blog in Wordpress. Those skills, and virtually all the skills that ever-changing economies have rewarded in the past, are about what we know. The skills that become increasingly valuable as technology advances are about what we're like.

That means that some people will have a much easier time adapting than others will. We've seen that, on average, women are better at some of these skills than men are, and within genders are enormous differences in the interpersonal abilities that people bring to adulthood, even before any training they may receive, which for most people is little or none. Everyone can get better, but it will be hard for some people, and some just won't want to do it. Think of the IT guy at Southwest Airlines. It isn't about what they know. It's just the way they are.

Life will be increasingly tough for those people. Organizations used to have a place for them, in solid middle-class jobs in factories or back offices. But those are the jobs that technology is rapidly taking over. As the shift in valuable skills continues, organizations are finding not only that they have no jobs for the disengaged and socially inept, but that such people are toxic to the enterprise and must be removed. That was Southwest's conclusion. At the Cleveland Clinic, whose efforts to make the whole organization more empathetic we examined in chapter 5, they learned the same thing: "Off-board people who don't belong," concluded Dr. James Merlino, who led the transformation effort. "One disengaged employee who does not support the organization or the mission can have negative consequences for an entire department. The hardworking and engaged employees will resent these people being around." Adam Grant's advice to organizations is similar: "Keep takers out."

Joe Liemandt has been ahead of the overall trend for a long time. He dropped out of Stanford as a senior in 1989 to start a software company in Austin, Texas, that he called Trilogy. His father, a high-level General Electric executive, thought he was "a moron" for doing so. Joe hired graduates of Stanford, MIT, and other top technology schools to write the software; it helped giant corpora-tions keep track of the millions of different items they made and enabled salespeople to configure those items properly for customers and quote an accurate price instantly—tasks that previously took days or weeks. Trilogy signed up Ford, IBM, AT&T, and other high-profile customers, and it prospered. In the dot-com boom of the late 1990s, Joe's net worth was estimated at over $1 billion. But he was wise enough not to take Trilogy public, so when the bust followed, the company was wounded but survived.

Then, in the early 2000s, Joe started telling me that things were changing. It no longer made sense to hire coders from top American schools. "At Princeton there are 30 computer science graduates," he told me. "At a good school in China there are 700, and the top 30 will be better than the 30 from Princeton." And they'll be a lot cheaper. "The quantity and percentage of our software development that we do in China increases every year," he said.

The implications seemed clear: "Basic engineering skills are going to be less valuable because you're going to have ten times more engineers in the world," he said. Back then he didn't realize that advancing technology, as well as a flood of Chinese engineers, would devalue basic engineering skills, but now he does. "If the U.S. wants to stay ahead of commoditization, then the person who used to be an engineer will now have to be a team leader."

Which requires an entirely different set of abilities. To be a team leader, "you have to learn different skills, and they're definitely trainable," Joe told me in 2014. "Those are the high-value skills." Years earlier he had started explaining this to his American coders, telling them they'd have to upgrade their skills or probably lose their jobs. Some adapted and became successful team leaders; others chose not to and eventually had to leave. It's just the way they were.

When Joe and his wife were talking about the education of their two young daughters, their views were classically different.

Joe thought the girls had to learn coding, not because it would give them a competitive advantage but because it's the basic literacy of the modern economy. In contrast, "My wife said networking, teamwork, and leadership," he recalled. The skills of social interaction. "I think there's a good chance my daughters won't need to learn to drive. But my wife believes fundamentally that those skills she mentions are learned skills, and she's teaching them. One of our daughters is not outgoing, and since she was four my wife has been encouraging her to connect."

Joe's company and his daughters seem likely to do well as the economy changes.

TO CREATE A NEW AND BETTER LIFE

The current transformation of how people create value is historically quite sudden. Most people's essential skills remained largely the same from the emergence of agriculture 12,000 years ago to the dawn of the Industrial Revolution in the mid-eighteenth century. The transition to an industrial economy in the Western nations, and the accompanying shift in skill values, took well over a hundred years. The subsequent turn to a knowledge-based economy took most of the twentieth century. Now, as technology drives forward more powerfully every year, the transition to the newly valuable skills of empathizing, collaborating, creating, leading, and building relationships is happening faster than corporations, governments, education systems, or most human psyches can keep up with. That's disorienting, and it gets more so as the fundamental nature of value shifts from what you know to what you're like.

As economies have evolved over the millennia, we've always looked outward to get the new skills we require—to elders, schools, trainers, and employers that knew and could teach us what we needed to know. Now, for the first time, we must also look inward.

That's where we find the elements of the skills we need next. Developing those abilities will not be easy or comfortable for some, and it will likely get harder for everyone, because as the abilities become more valuable, standards will rise. Even those who are good at them will have to get better.

If the prospect sounds worrying, it shouldn't. On the contrary, it's wonderful news. Just think of what we're being asked to do—to become more essentially human, to be the creatures we once were and were always meant to be. Odd as it may sound, that's a significant change from what we're used to. For the past ten generations in the developed world, and shorter but still substantial periods in many emerging economies, most people have succeeded by learning to do machine work better than machines could do it. Now that era is ending. Machines are increasingly doing such work better than we ever could. We face at least the opportunity to create new and better lives.

Staking our futures to our profoundest human traits may feel strange and risky. Fear not. When you change perspectives and look inward rather than outward, you'll find that what you need next has been there all along. It has been there forever.

In the deepest possible sense, you've already got what it takes. Make of it what you will.

ACKNOWLEDGMENTS

As always, I want to thank the many people who were more indulgent, patient, generous, and kind than they needed to be as I worked through the process of creating a book.

At Portfolio/Penguin, Adrian Zackheim encouraged me always while applying his formidable intellect to the concepts I was developing. Will Weisser's perspective as a marketer was invaluable. Every suggestion from my editor, Emily Angell, improved the book.

Fortune editors supported me in writing about this book's themes in the printed and online magazine. Thank you Alan Murray, Andy Serwer, Stephanie Mehta, Cliff Leaf, Brian O'Keefe, and other colleagues who contributed ideas and data.

Countless people helped me with ideas, information, access to sources, personal stories, and reactions to the text. I particularly want to thank Marc Andreessen, Tom Baptiste, Dominic Barton, Adrienne Boissy, Jim Bush, Ashton Carter, John Chambers, Ram Charan, Ralph Chatham, Tony D'Amelio, Sally Donnelly, Christopher Dowling, Bran Ferren, George Flynn, Michael Gazzaniga,

Anne Greenhalgh, Peter Hancock, Rob High, Chester Kennedy, John Kelly, Rik Kirkland, Tom Kolditz, the Library of Congress staff, Joe Liemandt, Thomas Malone, Bill McDermott, James Merlino, David Metcalf, Steve Nakagawa, Nicholas Negroponte, Nitin Noria, Charles Phillips, Garth Saloner, Marc Scibelli, Danny Stern, and Noel Tichy.

Robert Barnett represented me superbly, as he has always done.

And again I must thank most of all my tolerant family for putting up with the demands of an author's job, which they generally budget for much more accurately than I do.

NOTES

CHAPTER ONE

2   **Realize that Watson . . .** General information about Watson is available at www.ibm.com. See specifically http://www.ibm.com/smarter planet/us/en/ibmwatson/what-is-watson.html; accessed 15 January 2015. Information about the built-in delay was told to me by Watson developers on-site at the NRF convention.

3   **The company has a whole fleet . . .** http://www.nytimes.com/2010/10/10/science/10google.html?_r=2& .

3   **Computers are better than humans at screening documents . . .** John O. McGinnis, "Machines v. Lawyers," in *City Journal*, Spring 2014, published by the Manhattan Institute for Policy Research (New York).

3   **Computers are better at detecting some kinds of human emotion . . .** Marian Stewart Bartlett, Gwen C. Littlewort, Mark G. Frank, Kang Lee, "Automatic Decoding of Facial Movements Reveals Deceptive Pain Expressions," *Current Biology*, vol. 24, no. 7, 31 March 2014.

3   **As I write, it has shrunk to the size . . .** http://www-03.ibm.com/press/us/en/presskit/27297.wss.

3   **In fact, as we shall see, substantial evidence suggests . . .** See detailed citations on all these assertions in chapter 2.

5   **The relentless advance of computer capability . . .** It's enlightening to read Gordon Moore's famous (and surprisingly short) paper, available at http://www.monolithic3d.com/uploads/6/0/5/5/6055488/gordon_moore_1965_article.pdf.

5   **Sony's first transistor radio . . .** The story is related at Sony's own website: http://www.sony.net/SonyInfo/CorporateInfo/History/SonyHistory/1-07.html.

5   Intel's latest top-of-the-line chip . . . https://software.intel.com/sites/
     default/files/forum/278102/327364001en.pdf.

CHAPTER TWO

7   In the movie *Desk Set* . . . Twentieth Century Fox Film Corp., *Desk
     Set*, released 2 August 1957.

9   "We're not intending to replace humans . . ." http://www.cnn.com/
     2014/05/29/tech/innovation/big-idea-swarm-robots/.

9   IBM has always said that . . . Rob High, *The Era of Cognitive Systems: An
     Inside Look at Watson and How it Works* (IBM Corp., 2012), pp. 1-10.

10   When he demonstrated it . . . D. Acemoglu and J. Robinson, *Why
     Nations Fail: The Origins of Power, Prosperity, and Poverty* (Random
     House Digital, Inc., 2012), p. 182f.

10   After the royal slapdown . . . Events of Lee's story are from http://
     www.britannica.com/EBchecked/topic/334614/William-Lee.

10   Yet weavers campaigned . . . http://www.cottontimes.co.uk/John
     Kayo.htm.

11   For decades, the U.S. economy . . . Data on length of job recovery after
     postwar U.S. recessions are at http://blogs.wsj.com/economics/2014/
     06/06/its-taking-longer-after-each-recession-to-get-back-to-normal/.

12   And why did wages begin stagnating . . . Data on wage stagnation in
     the United States and the developed world are at http://www.econo
     mist.com/news/finance-and-economics/21615589-throughout-rich
     -world-wages-are-stuck-big-freeze.

12   In a significant lecture . . . Lawrence H. Summers, "The 2013 Martin
     Feldstein Lecture: Economic Possibilities for Our Children," printed
     in *NBER Reporter*, no. 4, 2013.

12   The Pew Research Internet Project . . . Pew Research Center, "AI,
     Robotics, and the Future of Jobs," August 2014. Available at: http://
     www.pewinternet.org/2014/08/06/future-of-jobs/.

13   The company produced a version . . . http://www.nytimes.com/2014/05/
     28/technology/googles-next-phase-in-driverless-cars-no-brakes
     -or-steering-wheel.html?_r=0.

13   In a world like that . . . Loukas Karabarbounis and Brent
     Neiman, "The Global Decline of the Labor Share," National Bureau
     of Economic Research, October 2013. The authors find that "the
     decrease in the relative price of investment goods, often attributed to
     advances in information technology and the computer age, induced
     firms to shift away from labor and toward capital."

14   Economists aren't the only experts . . . Quotations in this paragraph are
     from Pew Research Center, op. cit.

14 **Microsoft founder Bill Gates . . .** He made these remarks during a session at the American Enterprise Institute in Washington, D.C., 13 March 2014. Video available at http://www.aei.org/events/from -poverty-to-prosperity-a-conversation-with-bill-gates/.

15 **Thus Summers's conclusion . . .** Summers, op. cit.

15 **But in Eli Whitney's Connecticut gun factory . . .** "Arms Production at the Whitney Armory," published by the Eli Whitney Museum and Workshop in Hamden, Connecticut. At https://www.eliwhitney.org/ 7/museum/eli-whitney/arms-production.

15 **The second turning point arrived . . .** Claudia Goldin and Lawrence F. Katz, *The Race Between Education and Technology* (Belknap Press of Harvard University Press, 2008), pp. 109–111.

16 **The high school graduation rate . . .** Ibid., pp. 164–165.

16 **But then the third major turning point arrived . . .** This development is explained most thoroughly in David H. Autor and David Dorn, "The Growth of Low-Skill Service Jobs and the Polarization of the U.S. Labor Market," *American Economic Review* 2013, 103(5): 1553–1597.

17 **That may seem outlandish . . .** http://www.nytimes.com/2011/03/05/ science/05legal.html?pagewanted=all.

17 **It can detect patterns . . .** Ibid.

17 **Computers then started moving up the ladder . . .** McGinnis, op. cit. (chap. 1, n. 3).

17 **Humans still have to identify . . .** Ibid.

18 **Advancing even higher into the realm of lawyerly skill . . .** Theodore W. Ruger, Pauline T. Kim, Andrew D. Martin, and Kevin M. Quinn, "The Supreme Court Forecasting Project: Legal and Political Science Approaches to Predicting Supreme Court Decision Making," *Columbia Law Review*, vol. 104:1150, pp. 1150–1209.

18 **Companies such as Lex Machina and Huron Legal . . .** See http://bits .blogs.nytimes.com/2014/08/01/in-legal-field-using-technology -to-stay-on-top-of-a-shifting-market/?_php=true&_type=blogs&_r =0 as well as company Web sites: www.lexmachina.com and http:// www.huronconsultinggroup.com/Company/Organization/Huron _Legal.

18 **"The rise of machine intelligence . . ."** McGinnis, op. cit. (chap. 1, n. 3).

18 **The breakthrough of this technology . . .** This general explanation and the examples are from Rob High, *The Era of Cognitive Systems: An Inside Look at Watson and How it Works* (IBM Corp., 2012), pp. 1–10.

19 **That's why the Internet entrepreneur Terry Jones . . .** Personal interview with Terry Jones, 8 October 2014.

19 **For *Jeopardy!*, Watson downloaded . . .** http://www.pbs.org/wgbh/nova/ tech/smartest-machine-on-earth.html.

19   **Memorial Sloan Kettering Cancer Center in New York City uses Wat-
      son** . . . http://www.mskcc.org/blog/msk-trains-ibm-watson-help
      -doctors-make-better-treatment-choices.

19   **Corporate Insight, a research firm** . . . http://public.corporateinsight
      .com/blog/will-ibms-watson-make-your-financial-advisor-obsolete.

20   **A company called Narrative Science** . . . Much of the description of the
      company comes from Steven Levy, "Can an Algorithm Write a Bet-
      ter News Story Than a Human Reporter?" *Wired*, 24 April 2012.
      Updated at www.narrativescience.com.

20   **In mid-2014, the Associated Press assigned** . . . "The A.P. Plans to
      Automate Quarterly Earnings Articles," *New York Times*, 1 July
      2014, p. B5.

20   **Schools from the elementary level** . . . "Essay-Grading Software Offers
      Professors a Break," *New York Times*, 4 April 2013, p. A1.

21   **Jeff Pence, a middle-school teacher in Canton, Georgia** . . . "Essay-
      Grading Software Seen as Time-Saving Tool," *Education Week*, 13
      March 2014.

21   **EdX, the enterprise started by Harvard and MIT** . . . The software is
      called Discern; for a description see http://code.edx.org/discern/.

21   **The Hewlett Foundation offered two $100,000 prizes** . . . http://getting
      smart.com/2012/10/the-hewlett-foundation-announces-asap-com
      petition-winners-automated-essay-scoring/.

21   **So researchers had a group of human teachers** . . . Mark D. Shermis
      and Ben Hammer, "Contrasting State-of-the-Art Automated Scor-
      ing of Essays: An Analysis," http://www.scoreright.org/NCME
      _2012_Paper3_29_12.pdf.

22   **In 1997 a computer** . . . This is known as Moravec's paradox; see,
      among many discussions of this topic, Hans Moravec, *Mind Children*
      (Harvard University Press, 1988), and Pamela McCorduck,
      Machines Who Think (A. K. Peters Ltd., 2004).

22   **Google's autonomous cars** . . . Jennifer Cheeseman Day and Jeffrey
      Rosenthal, "Detailed Occupations and Median Earnings: 2008."
      U.S. Census Bureau, http://www.census.gov/people/io/files/acs08
      _detailedoccupations.pdf.

22   **You can train a Baxter robot** . . . http://www.rethinkrobotics.com/baxter/.

23   **Robots went into the wreckage** . . . "Meet the Robots of Fukushima
      Daiichi," *IEEE Spectrum*, 28 February 2014, http://spectrum.ieee
      .org/slideshow/robotics/industrial-robots/meet-the-robots-of
      -fukushima-daiichi.

23   **By 2008 about 12,000 combat robots** . . . "Pushing the Boundaries of
      Traditional HRI," *Science and Technology Innovations*, Fall 2013, p. 7.
      Published by the University of Central Florida Institute for Simula-
      tion and Training.

23   **Some, barely larger than a shoebox** ... See, for example, the iRobot "FirstLook" robot, http://www.irobot.com/For-Defense-and -Security/Robots/110-FirstLook.aspx#Military.

23   **Larger ones dispose of bombs** ... See, for example, the iRobot "Kobra" robot, http://www.irobot.com/For-Defense-and-Security/ Robots/710-Kobra.aspx#Military.

23   **A few robots armed with guns** ... "The Inside Story of the SWORDS Armed Robot 'Pullout' in Iraq: Update," *Popular Mechanics*, 1 October 2009, http://www.popularmechanics.com/technology/gadgets/4258963.

23   **Nonetheless, General Robert Cone** ... "U.S. Army Studying Replacing Thousands of Grunts with Robots," *Defense News*, 20 January 2014. http://archive.defensenews.com/article/20140120/DEFREG02/ 301200035/US-Army-Studying-Replacing-Thousands-Grunts-Robots.

23   **But the army realized this model was inefficient** ... The description of RoboLeader is based on an article by Jessie Chen of the U.S. Army Research Laboratory, "Multi-Robot Management," in *Science & Technology Innovations*, Fall 2013, p. 12. Published by the University of Central Florida Institute for Simulation and Training.

24   **Consider a robotic hand** ... The description and quotes are from "A Better Robotic Hand," *Harvard Magazine*, March/April 2014 (unpaginated).

25   **In fact, a researcher named Paul Ekman** ... For a review of his work, see "Paul Ekman," *American Psychologist* 47 (4), April 1992, pp. 470–471.

25   **But Ekman, one of the most cited** ... S. J. Haggbloom, et al. (2002). The 100 Most Eminent Psychologists of the 20th Century. *Review of General Psychology*, vol. 6, no. 2 (2002), pp. 139–45.

26   **Ekman built a successful business** ... Paul Ekman Group has continued for many years—see www.paulekman.com.

26   **The possibilities of such technology** ... For the founders and advisers of Emotient, see www.emotient.com.

26   **Point a video camera at any person's face** ... "This Google Glass App Will Detect Your Emotions, Then Relay Them Back to Retailers," *Fast Company*, 6 March 2014, http://www.fastcompany.com/ 3027342/fast-feed/this-google-glass-app-will-detect-your-emotions -then-relay-them-back-to-retailers.

27   **Affectiva, a spin-off from MIT's Media Lab** ... See www.affectiva.com.

27   **A separate project within the Media Lab** ... For a description, see http://affect.media.mit.edu/pdfs/14.Hernandez_et_al-DIS.pdf.

27   **Researchers led by Dr. Marian Bartlett** ... Bartlett, et al., op. cit. (chap. 1, n. 4).

28   **For example, computers analyzed the faces of college students** ... Jacob Whitehill, Zewelanji Serpell, Yi-Ching Lin, Aysha Foster, Javier

R. Movellan, "The Faces of Engagement: Automatic Recognition of Student Engagement from Facial Expressions," *IEEE Transactions on Affective Computing*, vol. 5, no. 1(2014), pp. 86–98.

29   MIT's stress-monitoring car . . . http://affect.media.mit.edu/pdfs/ 14.Hernandez_et_al-DIS.pdf.

31   For Cowen's observations on competition in chess, see his blog entry at http://marginalrevolution.com/marginalrevolution/2013/11/what -are-humans-still-good-for-the-turning-point-in-freestyle-chess-may -be-approaching.html.

CHAPTER THREE

33   **The case in Arizona Superior Court . . .** The research is described in D. A. Krauss, J. G. McCabe, and J. D. Lieberman, "Dangerously Misunderstood: Representative Jurors' Reactions to Expert Testimony on Future Dangerousness in a Sexually Violent Predator Trial," *Psychology, Public Policy, and Law*, 25 July 2011. Advance online publication, doi: 10.1037/a0024550.

36   **Jeremy Rose, a trial consultant . . .** "How Jurors Perceive Expert Witnesses," *Trial*, June 2000, pp. 51–57.

37   **"Natural selection mandated us . . ."** Michael Gazzaniga, *Human: The Science Behind What Makes Us Unique* (HarperCollins, 2008), pp. 82–83.

37   **"We are social to the core . . ."** Ibid., p. 83.

38   **"The intellectual faculties required . . ."** N. K. Humphrey, "The Social Function of Intellect," first published in *Growing Points in Ethology*, eds. P. P. G. Bateson and R. A. Hinde (Cambridge University Press, 1976), pp. 303–317.

38   **For many years the reigning view . . .** An excellent survey of the tabula rasa view, and a powerful refutation of it, are in Steven Pinker, *The Blank Slate: The Modern Denial of Human Nature* (Viking Penguin, 2002). This is also the source of the Ortega y Gasset quotation and the mentions of Mead's and Thomas's research and its subsequent refutation.

39   **The full scope of the argument . . .** The quotation and the list of human universals are from Donald E. Brown, *Human Universals* (McGraw-Hill Humanities, 1991).

40   **Early researchers in computer translation of languages . . .** A broad description of the disappointing progress of artificial intelligence in translating languages, playing chess, and performing other tasks as of 1972 can be found in Hubert L. Dreyfus, *What Computers Can't Do: A Critique of Artificial Reason* (Harper & Row, 1972).

40   **Now Google translates written language for free . . .** See https://trans late.google.com/. Regarding Skype, see "Skype Update Translates

English and Spanish in Real Time," *Christian Science Monitor*, 15 December 2014.

40 **Economists Frank Levy and Richard J. Murnane** . . . Levy and Murnane, *The New Division of Labor: How Computers Are Creating the Next Job Market* (Princeton University Press, 2004).

40 **Steven Pinker observed in 2007** . . . Steven Pinker, *The Stuff of Thought: Language As a Window Into Human Nature* (Penguin Books, 2007).

41 **Yet iRobot soon thereafter** . . . For product descriptions, see www.iro bot.com.

42 **And yet, in 2014, when I asked Dominic Barton** . . . Personal interview, 24 September 2014.

43 **Judges make parole decisions** . . . The research is described in Dan Ariely, *Predictably Irrational: The Hidden Forces That Shape Our Decisions* (HarperCollins, 2008).

44 **We want to hear our diagnosis from a doctor** . . . For more on the powerful effects of being heard, see Emile G. Bruneau and Rebecca Saxe, "The Power of Being Heard: The Benefits of 'Perspective-Giving' in the Context of Intergroup Conflict," *Journal of Experimental Social Psychology* (2012), doi: 10.1016/j.jesp.2012.02.017.

44 **Ask employers which skills they'll need most** . . . Oxford Economics, *Global Talent 2021: How the New Geography of Talent Will Transform Human Resource Strategies*, 2012, p. 6.

44 **The biggest increases by far** . . . http://www.npr.org/blogs/money/2012/03/20/149015363/what-america-does-for-work.

45 **The McKinsey Global Institute found** . . . McKinsey Global Institute, *Help Wanted: The Future of Work in Advanced Economies*, 2012, p. 2.

45 **Harvard professor William H. Bossert, a legendary figure** . . . I was a student in Bossert's class, Natural Sciences 110, and describe it from still-vivid memory.

46 **The phenomenon has been explained most persuasively** . . . Goldin and Katz, op. cit.(chap. 2, n. 17), p. 2.

46 **"College is no longer the automatic ticket to success . . ."** Ibid., pp. 352–353.

47 **Researchers at the University of British Columbia** . . . Paul Beaudry, David A. Green, Benjamin M. Sand, "The Great Reversal in the Demand for Skill and Cognitive Tasks," National Bureau of Economic Research Working Paper 18901, March 2013, http://www.nber.org/papers/w18901.

48 **Average lawyers "face a bleak future"** . . . McGinnis, op. cit. (chap. 1, n. 3).

49 **It has been excellent advice for quite a while** . . . http://www.payscale.com/college-salary-report/majors-that-pay-you-back/bachelors.

50   **"At the beginning of Iraq and Afghanistan . . ."** All quotations from
     Flynn are from a personal interview with Gen. George Flynn
     (USMC, Ret.), 18 February 2014.

50   **A jarring alert came in 2004** . . . Gen. George W. Casey Jr. (U.S. Army,
     Ret.), "Leading in a 'VUCA' World," *Fortune*, 7 April 2014, p. 76.

51   **Lieutenant Colonel Chris Hughes was leading a small unit** . . . Dan
     Baum, "Battle Lessons," *New Yorker*, 17 January 2005.

51   **"Well, I did this . . ."** Leonard Wong, "Developing Adaptive Leaders:
     The Crucible Experience of Operation Iraqi Freedom," Strategic
     Studies Institute, U.S. Army War College, 2004, p. 9.

51   **"Planning for success in the Army . . ."** "'Human Domain' Enters
     Future Army War Plans," www.military.com, 20 February 2013.

52   **"I hope we never have to fight our enemies . . ."** Personal interview with
     Ashton Carter, 26 February 2014.

52   **This is what military leaders mean** . . . Ralph Chatham, "Toward a
     Second Training Revolution: Promise and Pitfalls of Digital Experien-
     tial Learning," in K. Anders Ericsson, ed., *Development of Professional
     Expertise: Toward Measurement of Expert Performance and Design of
     Optimal Learning Environments* (Cambridge University Press, 2009).

53   **It was designed to be that way** . . . Ford's quotation has been rendered
     with a great many slight variations, but always with the same theme.
     See http://thinkexist.com/quotation/why-is-it-every-time-i-ask
     -for-a-pair-of-hands/1206105.html.

CHAPTER FOUR

55   **For five springtime days** . . . Yalda T. Uhls, Minas Michikyan, Jordan
     Morris, Debra Garcia, Gary W. Small, Eleni Zgourou, Patricia
     M. Greenfield, "Five Days at Outdoor Recreation Camp without
     Screens Improves Preteen Skills with Nonverbal Emotion Cues,"
     Computers in Human Behavior 39 (2014), pp. 387–392.

58   **Nor can we assume that the kids will build those abilities** . . . These
     points are substantiated later in the chapter.

59   **These are primarily the "symbolic analyst" jobs** . . . Robert Reich, *The
     Work of Nations: Preparing Ourselves for 21st Century Capitalism*
     (Alfred A. Knopf, 1991).

59   **For a marked contrast, consider touch** . . . Joshua M. Ackerman,
     Christopher C. Nocera, John A. Bargh, "Incidental Haptic Sensa-
     tions Influence Social Judgments and Decisions," *Science*, 25 June
     2010, pp. 1712–1715.

60   **Job applicants who shake hands** . . . Greg L. Stewart, Susan L. Dustin,
     Murray R. Barrick, Todd C. Darnold, "Exploring the Handshake in

Employment Interviews," *Journal of Applied Psychology*, vol. 93(5), September 2008, pp. 1139–1146, http://dx.doi.org/10.1037/0021 -9010.93.5.1139.

60 **We judge people who shake hands . . .** Francesca Gino, "To Negotiate Effectively, First Shake Hands," HBR Blog Network, 4 June 2014.

60 **It is literally an electric experience . . .** Sanda Dolcos, Keen Sung, Jennifer J. Argo, Sophie Flor-Henry, Florin Dolcos, "The Power of a Handshake: Neural Correlates of Evaluative Judgments in Observed Social Interactions," *Journal of Cognitive Neuroscience* 24:12, pp. 2292–2305.

61 **Keeping in mind that digital media use . . .** Data for all countries mentioned in the paragraph are from *AdReaction: Marketing in a Multiscreen World*, 2014, results of a survey conducted by MillwardBrown.

61 **Across a broad, representative sample of U.S. teens . . .** All data in this paragraph are from "Teens, Smartphones & Texting," Pew Internet & American Life Project, 19 March 2012.

62 **Among American preteens and teenagers . . .** All data in this paragraph are from "Generation M Squared: Media in the Lives of 8- to 18-Year-Olds," the Henry J. Kaiser Family Foundation, January 2010.

62 **Researchers at the University of Michigan studied young adults who used Facebook . . .** Ethan Kross, Philippe Verduyn, Emre Demiralp, Jiyoung Park, David Seungjae Lee, Natalie Lin, Holly Shablack, John Jonides, Oscar Ybarra, "Facebook Use Predicts Declines in Subjective Well-Being in Young Adults," *PLoS ONE* 8(8): e69841, doi: 10.1371/journal.pone.0069841.

63 **When preexisting pairs of friends talk in person . . .** Lauren E. Sherman, Minas Michikyan, Patricia M. Greenfield, "The Effects of Text, Audio, Video, and In-Person Communication on Bonding between Friends," *Cyberpsychology: Journal of Psychosocial Research on Cyberspace*, 7(2), article 3, doi: 10.5817/CP2013-2-3.

64 **People who use social networks, for example . . .** Sabatini, Fabio, and Francesco Sarracino. "Online networks and subjective well-being." *arXiv preprint arXiv:1408.3550* (2014).

64 **When two people talk to one another face-to-face . . .** Jing Jiang, Bohan Dai, Danling Peng, Chaozhe Zhu, Li Liu, Chunming Lu, "Neural Synchronization During Face-to-Face Communication," *Journal of Neuroscience*, 7 November 2012, 32(45); pp. 16064–16069.

65 **Besides our basic cognitive skills . . .** Oscar Ybarra, Piotr Winkielman, Irene Yeh, Eugene Burnstein, Liam Kavanagh, "Friends (and Sometimes Enemies) with Cognitive Benefits: What Types of Social Interactions Boost Executive Functioning?" *Social Psychology and Personality Science*, 2010, doi: 10.1177/1948550610386808.

67   MIT's Sherry Turkle, who has been studying relations . . . Quotations
     are from her book *Alone Together: Why We Expect More from Technol-
     ogy and Less from Each Other* (Basic Books, 2011), p. 11.

CHAPTER FIVE

69   Dr. Timothy Gilligan and another doctor . . . Timothy Gilligan, "If I
     Paint a Rosy Picture, Will You Promise Not to Cry?" *Journal of
     Clinical Oncology*, vol. 30, no. 27, 20 September 2012.

70   Dr. Adrienne Boissy is an eminent multiple sclerosis specialist . . . Personal
     interview with Adrienne Boissy, 27 March 2014. See also Adrienne R.
     Boissy and Paul J. Ford, "A Touch of MS: Therapeutic Mislabeling,"
     Neurology 11 May 2012, doi: 10.1212/WNL.0b013e318259e0ec.

72   When journalist George Anders scanned an online employment
     board . . . George Anders, "The 'Soft Skill' That Pays $100,000+,"
     Forbes Online, 26 June 2013.

72   Those results reinforce the findings . . . Sir Roy Anderson, "Careers
     2020: Making Education Work," *Pearson Education*, January 2014.

72   The chief technology officer of one of the United Kingdom's largest retail-
     ers . . . Spoken not-for-attribution at a private conference, 27 May 2014.

72   Charles Phillips, CEO of the enterprise software company Infor . . . Per-
     sonal interview with Charles Phillips, 21 July 2014.

72   Maybe, but when Bill McDermott . . . Personal interview with Bill
     McDermott, 29 September 2014.

73   And Meg Bear, a high executive at yet another enterprise software com-
     pany . . . Meg Bear, "Why Empathy Is the Critical 21st Century
     Skill," posted at LinkedIn, 24 April 2014, https://www.linkedin.com/
     pulse/20140424221331-1407199-why-empathy-is-the-critical-21st
     -century-skill.

73   When Jim Bush was in charge of American Express's call centers . . .
     Personal interview with Jim Bush, 29 March 2012. See also Jim
     Bush, "How American Express Transformed Its Call Centers," *HBR*
     Blogs, 19 April 2011.

73   Belinda Parmar, a U.K. technology commentator . . . Belinda Parmar,
     "Can Empathy Really Work in a Business World Dominated by Tes-
     tosterone?" *The Guardian*, 18 June 2014.

74   Columbia University business professor Rita McGrath . . . Rita
     McGrath, "Management's Three Eras: A Brief History," *HBR* Blog
     Network, 30 July 2014.

74   Research shows that when caregivers . . . Mohammadreza Hojat, Daniel Z.
     Louis, Fred W. Markham, Richard Wender, Carol Rabinowitz, Joseph
     S. Gonnella, "Physicians' Empathy and Clinical Outcomes for Diabetic
     Patients," *Academic Medicine*, vol. 8, no. 3, March 2011, pp. 359–364.

74 By contrast, internal medicine residents who rate low in empathy . . . Colin P. West, Mashele M. Huschka, Paul J. Novotny, Jeff A. Sloan, Joseph C. Kolars, Thomas M. Habermann, Tait D. Shanafelt, "Association of Perceived Medical Errors with Resident Distress and Empathy," *JAMA*, vol. 296, no. 9, 6 September 2006.

75 In two studies involving over 21,000 diabetes patients . . . See Hojat et al., op. cit, and Stefano Del Canale, Daniel Z. Louis, Vittorio Maio, Xiaohong Wang, Giuseppina Rossi, Mohammadreza Hojat, Joseph S. Gonnella, "The Relationship Between Physician Empathy and Disease Complications: An Empirical Study of Primary Care Physicians and Their Diabetic Patients in Parma, Italy," *Academic Medicine*, vol. 87, no. 9, September 2012, pp. 1243–1249.

75 It makes patients less likely to sue . . . Francis Fullam, Andrew N. Garman, Tricia J. Johnson, Eric C. Hedberg, "The Use of Patient Satisfaction Surveys and Alternative Coding Procedures to Predict Malpractice Risk," *Medical Care*, vol. 47, no. 5, May 2009, pp. 553–559.

75 One study shows that even a surgeon's tone of voice . . . Nalini Ambaddy, Debi LaPlante, Thai Nguyen, Robert Rosenthal, Nigel Chaumeton, Wendy Levinson, "Surgeons' Tone of Voice: A Clue to Malpractice History," *Surgery*, vol. 132, no. 1, July 2002, pp. 5–9.

76 When we're newborns, just hours old . . . The material on emotional contagion is from Gazzaniga, op. cit., pp. 165–171.

77 The size of the pupils in someone's eyes . . . Michael Trimble, *Why Humans Like to Cry: Tragedy, Evolution and the Brain* (Oxford University Press, 2012), pp. 143–144.

78 As Gazzaniga observes . . . Gazzaniga, op. cit. (chap. 3, n. 3), p. 162.

78 "Mutual aid between and among members . . ." James Harris, "The Evolutionary Neurobiology, Emergence and Facilitation of Empathy," chapter 10 in *Empathy in Mental Illness* (Cambridge University Press, 2007).

78 Some scientists even speculate . . . Trimble, op. cit., p. 113.

79 Ability to discern the feelings of others . . . Gazzaniga, op. cit., p. 169.

79 Michael Trimble concludes, in scientific language . . . Trimble, op. cit., p. 95.

80 We're built to function best on ten hours of sleep a night . . . James B. Maas, *Power Sleep: How to Prepare Your Mind for Peak Performance* (Villard, 1998), p. 6.

81 A massive study of empathy in U.S. college students . . . Sara H. Konrath, Edward H. O'Brien, Courtney Hsing, "Changes in Dispositional Empathy in American College Students Over Time: A Meta-Analysis," *Personal and Social Psychology Review* 15(2), pp. 180–198, doi: 10.1177/1088868310377395.

81 As you would expect, higher narcissism . . . Konrath et al., op. cit., p. 183.

82   Over the past several decades people in developed countries . . . Robert
      D. Putnam, *Bowling Alone: The Collapse and Revival of American
      Community* (Simon and Schuster, 2000).

83   A well-known program, Roots of Empathy . . . For an overview, see
      www.rootsofempathy.org.

84   Some programs focus on girls . . . "Little Children and Already Acting
      Mean," *Wall Street Journal*, 26 May 2014.

84   Unfortunately, free play is becoming rare . . . Peter Gray, "The Play
      Deficit," http://aeon.co/magazine/culture/children-today-are
      -suffering-a-severe-deficit-of-play/.

85   "Impersonality, neutrality and detachment are needed to achieve . . ."
      Johanna Shapiro, "Using Literature and the Arts to Develop Empa-
      thy in Medical Students," chapter 25 in Tom F. D. Farrow and Peter
      W. R. Woodruff, eds., *Empathy in Mental Illness* (Cambridge Univer-
      sity Press, 2007).

85   Another reason for doctors to avoid empathizing . . . Howard Brody,
      reviewing *Empathy and the Practice of Medicine: Beyond Pills and the
      Scalpel* in the *New England Journal of Medicine*, vol. 330, no. 4, 27
      January 1994, pp. 296–297.

85   Much like the kids in the Roots of Empathy program . . . Antonio M.
      Gotto, "Teaching Empathy in Medical School," Huffington Post, 4
      September 2013.

85   At University of Missouri Health Care . . . Laura Landro, "The Talking
      Cure for Health Care," *Wall Street Journal*, 8 April 2013.

86   "We ask the staff to bring cases that have haunted them . . ." Quotations
      and the description of the program are from the cited personal inter-
      view with Boissy.

88   Further, "the doctors teaching surgeons . . ." Personal interview with
      James Merlino, 19 March 2014.

90   A striking bit of data from the Cleveland Clinic's experience . . . James
      Merlino, *Service Fanatics: How to Build Superior Patient Experience
      the Cleveland Clinic Way* (McGraw Hill Education, 2015).

CHAPTER SIX

91   The F-4 Phantom fighter jet . . . See http://web.archive.org/web/
      20110604105623/http://www.boeing.com/defense-space/military/f4/
      firsts.htm. Also http://en.wikipedia.org/wiki/McDonnell_Douglas
      _F-4_Phantom_II, which directs to various statistical sources.

92   Their top-of-the-line plane, the MiG-21 . . . See http://en.wikipedia.org/
      wiki/Mikoyan-Gurevich_MiG-21.

92   In the first few years of the Vietnam War . . . Description of the history
      and operations of the Navy Fighter Weapons School, and later

quotations from "Mugs" McKeown, are from "'You Fight Like You Train' and TOP GUN Crews Train Hard," *Armed Forces Journal International*, May 1974, pp. 25–26, 34.

94 **The navy called its new program** . . . The principles of the Navy Fighter Weapons School are described in the *Armed Forces Journal* article cited, and are described more fully in Ralph Chatham, "The 20th Century Revolution in Military Training," in K. Anders Ericsson, ed., *Development of Professional Expertise: Toward Measurement of Expert Performance and Design of Optimal Learning Environments* (Cambridge University Press, 2009).

94 **As a later chronicler of the program put it** . . . Chatham, ibid.

95 **It rose from 2:4 to 12:5** . . . "'You Fight Like You Train,'" op. cit.

95 **As air force colonel John Boyd once put it** . . . Greg Wilcox, "People, Ideas, and Things in that Order: Some Observations," Boyd Symposium, 12 October 2012, http://fasttransients.files.wordpress.com/2010/03/wilcox_people_ideas_things.pdf.

96 **The man who did the most to change their minds** . . . Paul F. Gorman, "Cardinal Point: An Oral History—Training Soldiers and Becoming a Strategist in Peace and War," Combat Studies Institute, 2011.

96 **The description of the test and its results are in** Paul F. Gorman, "The Military Value of Training," Institute for Defense Analysis, December 1990.

98 **That's where they were supposed to learn** . . . Data regarding losses in air combat and, later, submarine combat are from Gorman, ibid.

98 **A researcher found that "once a commander had scored a kill . . ."** The researcher was Herbert K. Weiss, quoted in Gorman, ibid.

98 **U.S. Army officers in France after D-Day** . . . The description, statistics, and quotation of DePuy are from W. E. DePuy, "Battle Participation and Leadership," remarks to the TRADOC Commanders' Conference, USAC&GSC, Fort Leavenworth, Kansas, March 1989, quoted in Gorman, "The Military Value of Training."

99 **This paragraph is based on** Gorman, ibid.

100 **Gorman therefore advanced a proposal** . . . Ibid.

100 **"Half of the four-star generals . . ."** Chatham, "The 20th Century Revolution in Military Training."

100 **In a particularly harrowing encounter** . . . Gorman, "Cardinal Point."

102 **"It has literally transformed the army . . ."** Personal interview with Thomas Kolditz, 17 December 2007.

102 **"Everything [today's soldiers] do, large or small . . ."** Chatham, "The 20th Century Revolution in Military Training."

102 **The secret is in how it's done** . . . *A Leader's Guide to After-Action Reviews*, Army Training Circular 25-20, 30 September 1993.

102   "The real key to this process is candor . . ." Personal interview with
       Kolditz, op. cit.

103   They believed that a truly candid AAR . . ." Personal interview with
       Ralph Chatham, 5 March 2012.

103   The forces of the established order wanted to kill his idea . . . Gorman,
       "Cardinal Point."

103   The story is recounted in Chatham, "The 20th Century Revolution
       in Military Training."

104   In that routine, "soldier observations and comments may not be encour-
       aged . . ." The quotation and the one following are from A Leader's
       Guide to After-Action Reviews, op. cit.

106   The odds of a rifle platoon winning . . . Analysis by Robert H. Sulzen
       cited by Gorman in testimony to the U.S. Senate Committee on
       Armed Services, 21 May 1992, p. 712.

106   All that counted was performance in real battle . . . The summary of
       America's military performance in first battles is based on John Shy,
       "First Battles in Retrospect," from Charles E. Heller and William
       A. Stofft, eds., America's First Battles, 1776–1965 (University Press of
       Kansas, 1986).

106   In 1990, Gorman wrote a paper for DARPA . . . Gorman, "The Military
       Value of Training."

107   Unlike all those disastrous first battles of the past . . . Chatham, "The
       20th Century Revolution in Military Training."

107   "Several generals of that era told me . . ." Ibid.

108   On February 26, 1991, in the first hours of Desert Storm . . . The basic
       facts of the Battle of 73 Easting are summarized in Gorman's testi-
       mony to the U.S. Senate Committee on Armed Services, 21 May
       1992, pp. 689–695. Then-Captain H. R. McMaster also testifies.

108   Late that afternoon, an American staff sergeant . . . This fact and the
       description of the battle are based on Gorman's and McMaster's testi-
       mony to the Senate Armed Services Committee and on a talk that then-
       Colonel McMaster gave at West Point, reprinted in Leaders In War:
       West Point Remembers the 1991 Gulf War (Frank Cass Publishers, 2005).

110   Back in the early days of Top Gun . . . "'You Fight Like You
       Train . . . ,'" op. cit.

110   Similarly, after 73 Easting . . . The quotation is taken from McMas-
       ter's talk in Leaders in War, op. cit.

112   It re-created the Battle of 73 Easting as software . . . The project was
       described and demonstrated during Gorman's and McMaster's testi-
       mony to the Senate Armed Services Committee (ibid.). Details are
       from W. M. Christenson and Robert A. Zirkle, "73 Easting Battle
       Replication—a Janus Combat Simulation," Institute for Defense
       Analyses, September 1992.

113   In response to the new mission, the National Training Center transformed itself . . . The transformation is described in Chatham,
"Toward a Second Training Revolution," in *Development of Professional Expertise*. Its operation during the conflicts in Afghanistan
and Iraq is described in "Deep in a U.S. Desert, Practicing to Face
the Iraq Insurgency," *New York Times*, 1 May 2006. An overview of
NTC operations is at http://www.irwin.army.mil.

CHAPTER SEVEN

117   Paul Azinger had two problems . . . Azinger tells the story of captaining the 2008 U.S. Ryder Cup team in *Cracking the Code* (Looking
Glass Books, 2010), which he cowrote with Ron Braund, a clinical
therapist who helped him devise his strategy.

117   They had lost five of the six previous tournaments . . . Data on Ryder
Cup history and players are from www.rydercup.com and http://
en.wikipedia.org/wiki/Ryder_Cup.

117   His doctors had ordered him not to play . . . Reported in Hank Haney, *The
Big Miss: My Years Coaching Tiger Woods* (Three Rivers Press, 2012).

121   "No grand idea was ever born in a conference . . ." http://classiclit
.about.com/od/fitzgeraldfsco/a/F-Scott-Fitzgerald-Quotes_2.htm.

121   Or as the great ad man David Ogilvy put it . . . Reported in Kenneth
Roman, *The King of Madison Avenue: David Ogilvy and the Making of
Modern Advertising* (Palgrave Macmillan, 2009).

121   The evidence is in a massive study . . . Stefan Wuchty, Benjamin F. Jones,
Brian Uzzi, "The Increasing Dominance of Teams in Production of
Knowledge," *Science*, vol. 316, 18 May 2007, pp. 1036–1039, doi:
10.1126/science.1136099.

122   People have been trying to answer that for centuries . . . The landmark
research is Anita Williams Woolley, Christopher F. Chabris, Alex Pentland, Nada Hashmi, Thomas W. Malone, "Evidence for a Collective
Intelligence Factor in the Performance of Human Groups," *Science*, vol.
330, 29 October 2010, pp. 686–688, doi: 10.1126/science.1193147.

126   The answers were a mystery until Alex Pentland's Human Dynamics
Laboratory . . . Pentland describes sociometric badges in *Honest Sig-
nals: How They Shape Our World* (MIT Press, 2008), and in *Social
Physics: How Good Ideas Spread—the Lessons from a New Science*
(Penguin Press, 2014). He describes his lab's role in the collective
intelligence research in *Social Physics*.

128   For example, Pentland and his lab investigated a huge Bank of America
call center . . . Pentland reports this story in *Social Physics*, and with
additional detail in "The New Science of Building Great Teams,"
Harvard Business Review, April 2012.

129   Pentland concludes that "being in the loop . . ." Pentland, *Social Physics*.

129   For example, Pentland's lab experimented with groups connected only by technology . . . Ibid., p. 111.

130   Pentland's striking finding is that "usually we can completely ignore the content of discussions . . ." Ibid., p. 132.

130   Some 61 million U.S. Facebook users got a "go vote" message on election day 2010 . . . "Facebook Experiment Boosts U.S. Voter Turnout," *Nature*, 12 September 2012, doi:10.1038/nature.2012.11401.

131   "Only close friends influenced users to vote in the real world. . ." Ibid.

131   "Despite being a denizen of the digital world . . ." Walter Isaacson, *Steve Jobs* (Simon and Schuster, 2011), p. 430.

131   That's why Jobs famously designed the Pixar headquarters the way he did . . . The story is told in ibid., p. 431.

133   The contradiction appears most clearly in the pioneering work of Wharton's Adam Grant . . . See Adam Grant, *Give and Take: Why Helping Others Drives Our Success* (Penguin Books, 2013).

133   In a company with a giver culture, Grant says . . . These quotations are from Grant, "Givers Take All: The Hidden Dimension of Corporate Culture," *McKinsey Quarterly*, April 2013.

133   A giant meta-analysis of studies involving 51,000 people . . . Nathan P. Podsakoff, Steven W. Whiting, Philip M. Podsakoff, Brian D. Blume, "Individual- and Organizational-Level Consequences of Organizational Citizenship Behaviors: A Meta-Analysis," *Journal of Applied Psychology* 2009, vol. 94, no. 1, pp. 122–141, doi: 10.1037/a0013079.

134   Grant reports how a firm called Appletree Answers . . . Grant, "Givers Take All."

134   In the aftermath of the 9/11 attacks . . . J. Richard Hackman, Michael O'Connor, "What makes for a great analytic team? Individual vs. Team approaches to intelligence analysis," Washington, DC: Intelligence Science Board, Office of the Director of Central Intelligence (2004).

136   Consider a crew of rowers . . . Emma E. A. Cohen, Robin Ejsmond-Frey, Nicola Knight, R. I. M. Dunbar, "Rowers' High: Behavioural Synchrony Is Correlated with Elevated Pain Thresholds," *Biology Letters* 15, September 2009, doi:10.1098/rsbl.2009.0670.

138   Nonetheless, by the time Jobs stepped down as CEO in August 2011 . . . See biographies at www.apple.com for the tenures as of August 2011 of Eddy Cue (twenty-two years), Phil Schiller (fourteen years), Jonathan Ive (nineteen years), Scott Forstall (nineteen years), and Tim Cook (thirteen years).

138   To see how wrong things can go . . . "Why Teams Don't Work: An interview with J. Richard Hackman by Diane Coutu," *Harvard Business Review*, May 2009.

139   Dr. John Noseworthy, CEO of the Mayo Clinic, told me about the considerable lengths to which he has gone . . . Personal interview with John Noseworthy, 4 December 2012.

139   But when a surgeon does the same operation at a hospital other than his home base . . . Robert S. Huckman, Gary P. Pisano, "The Firm Specificity of Individual Performance: Evidence from Cardiac Surgery," *Management Science*, vol. 52, no. 4, April 2006, pp. 473–488, doi: 10.1287/mnsc.1050.0464.

CHAPTER EIGHT

141   Stephen Denning is a quiet, reserved lawyer . . . Denning told his story at a symposium on organizational storytelling, held under the auspices of the Smithsonian Associates in April 2001. It was reprinted in *Storytelling in Organizations: Why Storytelling is Transforming 21st Century Organizations and Management* (Elsevier Butterworth-Heinemann, 2005), pp. 97–133.

147   Research finds that we judge a person's trustworthiness and likeability in about a tenth of a second . . . Gino, op. cit. (chap. 4, n. 6).

148   This nonsensical behavior . . . Nassim Nicholas Taleb, *The Black Swan: The Impact of the Highly Improbable* (Random House, 2007).

148   On the contrary, for centuries the conventional view . . . This is explained in Daniel Kahneman, *Thinking, Fast and Slow* (Farrar, Straus and Giroux, 2011), p. 76.

149   The Belgian psychologist Albert Michotte . . . Ibid.

149   Daniel Kahneman, the Nobelist who popularized the notions of two separate and distinct modes of thinking . . . Ibid., pp. 20–21.

149   As Kahneman puts it, "System 1 is adept at finding a coherent causal story . . ." Ibid., p. 75.

149   As psychologist Jason Goldman has written . . . Jason G. Goldman, "Animating Anthropomorphism: Giving Minds to Geometric Shapes," *Scientific American*, 8 March 2013, http://blogs.scientifi camerican.com/thoughtful-animal/2013/03/08/animating -anthropomorphism-giving-minds-to-geometric- shapes-video/.

150   Heider and Simmel asked their students to write descriptions of what they saw . . . Ibid.

151   As Kahneman says, "Your mind is ready and even eager to identify agents . . ." Kahneman, op. cit., p. 76.

151   Kahneman's reading of the evidence is "that we are born prepared to make intentional attributions . . ." Ibid.

152   The speaker's and the listener's brains align . . . Greg J. Stephens, Lauren J. Silbert, Uri Hasson, "Speaker-Listener Neural Coupling

Underlies Successful Communication," *PNAS*, vol. 107, no. 32, 10 August 2010, pp. 14425–14430, doi: /10.1073/pnas.1008662107.

153 It makes us "more trustworthy, generous, charitable, and compassionate . . ." Paul J. Zak, "How Stories Change the Brain," *Greater Good*, 17 December 2013, http://greatergood.berkeley.edu/article/item/how _stories_change_brain.

154 Zak proved it in an intriguing way . . . Ibid.

155 The great biologist Edward O. Wilson has written . . . Edward O. Wilson, "The Power of Story," *American Educator*, Spring 2002, pp. 8–11.

155 As psychology researchers Roger Schank and Robert Abelson observe . . . Roger C. Schank, Robert P. Abelson, "Knowledge and Memory: The Real Story," in Robert S. Wyer Jr. (ed.), *Knowledge and Memory: The Real Story* (Lawrence Erlbaum Associates, 1995), pp. 1–85.

156 Consider the story of Jen . . . The research is described in Kahneman, op. cit., p. 387.

157 "Why are some narrative themes successful at building support for terrorism?" . . . http://www.darpa.mil/Our_Work/BTO/Programs/Nar rative_Networks.aspx.

157 The serious point is that, as former Narrative Networks program manager William Casebeer has said . . . William D. Casebeer, "Identity, Culture and Stories: Empathy and the War on Terrorism," *Minnesota Journal of Law, Science & Technology* 9(2), 2008, pp. 653–688.

158 The power of human storytelling is apparent in one more setting . . . Daniel R. George, Heather L. Stuckey, Megan M. Whitehead, "An Arts-Based Intervention at a Nursing Home to Improve Medical Students' Attitudes Toward Persons With Dementia," *Academic Medicine*, vol. 88, no. 6, June 2013, doi: 10.1097/ ACM.0b013e31828fa773.

159 The resulting stories were generally a bit odd . . . The storytelling program described in the research is known as Timeslips and is now used widely. For a large collection of pictures that have been used and stories that dementia patients have created, see http://www .timeslips.org/stories.

CHAPTER NINE

161 "People might say a computer can never be creative . . ." Personal notes from Kaiserwerth's talk at a private industry conference, 27 May 2014.

162 So IBM's computer scientists decided to start teaching creativity to Watson . . . The process is described in *Cognitive Cooking With Chef Watson: Recipes for Innovation* from IBM and the Institute of Culinary Education (ICE, 2014).

163   David Cope of the University of California at Santa Cruz . . . For Cope's
      story and samples of his computer-written music, see http://artsites
      .ucsc.edu/faculty/cope/experiments.htm.

163   The awestruck writer of an article in Britain's *New Scientist* maga-
      zine . . . Cited in Eliot Handelman, "David Cope: Virtual Bach," in
      Computer Music Review, vol. 29, no. 1, http://www.computermusic-
      journal.org/reviews/29-1/handelman-cope.html.

164   More recently, Sony's Computer Science Lab in Paris . . . Described in
      William Hochberg, "When Robots Write Songs," *The Atlantic*, 7
      August 2014, http://www.theatlantic.com/entertainment/archive/
      2014/08/computers-that-compose/374916/.

164   Computers write poems, and software is even producing novels . . . For a
      summary, see "Computers Are Writing Novels: Read a Few Samples
      Here," *Business Insider*, 27 November 2014, http://www.businessin
      sider.com/novels-written-by-computers-2014-11.

165   When Robert Galbraith wrote a detective novel called *The Cuckoo's Call-
      ing* . . . "J. K. Rowling revealed as author of *The Cuckoo's Calling*,"
      BBC News, 14 July 2013, http://www.bbc.com/news/entertainment
      -arts-23304181.

165   "[Rowling's] literary gift is on display . . ." Deepti Hajela, "Review:
      J. K. Rowling's 'The Cuckoo's Calling,'" Associated Press, 25 July
      2013, http://bigstory.ap.org/article/review-jk-rowlings-cuckoos
      -calling.

167   Let's look more closely at this second type of creativity . . . The quota-
      tion is from Adam M. Grant, James W. Berry, "The Necessity of
      Others Is the Mother of Invention: Intrinsic and Prosocial Motiva-
      tions, Perspective Taking, and Creativity," *Academy of Management
      Journal*, vol. 54, no. 1, 2011, pp. 73–96.

167   The move that attracted the most attention . . . The e-mail is widely
      available, for example, at http://allthingsd.com/20130222/physically
      -together-heres-the-internal-yahoo-no-work-from-home-memo
      -which-extends-beyond-remote-workers/.

168   The company is fanatical about forcing people to connect in person . . .
      For a description and the quotation from John Sullivan, see "'Seren-
      dipitous Interaction' Key to Tech Firms' Workplace Design,"
      National Public Radio, 13 March 2013, http://www.npr.org/blogs/all
      techconsidered/2013/03/13/174195695/serendipitous-interaction-key
      -to-tech-firms-workplace-design.

168   The term was coined by William H. Whyte in *Fortune* . . . http://fortune
      .com/2012/07/22/groupthink-fortune-1952/.

169   Alex Pentland of MIT reports that a young company . . . Pentland, "The
      New Science of Building Great Teams."

169   Specifically, members of the most creative groups divide their social
       time . . . Pentland explains the importance of exploration combined
       with engagement in *Social Physics*, pp. 96–103.

169   It wasn't even complicated . . . Ibid., p. 102.

170   A team of researchers from two U.S. universities and three European
       universities . . . Peter A. Gloor, Francesca Grippa, Johannes Putzke,
       Casper Lassenius, Hauke Fuehres, Kai Fischbach, Detlef Schoder,
       "Measuring Social Capital in Creative Teams through Sociometric
       Sensors," *International Journal of Organisational Design and Engi-
       neering*, vol. 2, no. 4, 2012, pp. 380–401.

170   The writer Joshua Wolf Shenk has pointed out the truly astounding num-
       ber of pairs . . . Joshua Wolf Shenk, *Powers of Two: Finding the Essence
       of Innovation in Creative Pairs* (Houghton Mifflin Harcourt, 2014).

171   "What I saw . . . in creative pairs was trust . . ." Ibid., p. 33.

171   Even Sartre and de Beauvoir . . . Ibid., p. 119.

171   An acclaimed book at the dawn of the Internet age . . . Frances Cairn-
       cross, *The Death of Distance: How the Communications Revolution Is
       Changing Our Lives* (Texere Publishing, 1997).

172   It isn't just the simple explanation that more people would produce more
       ideas . . . Luís M. A. Bettencourt, Geoffrey B. West, "Bigger Cities
       Do More with Less," *Creativity*, published by Scientific American
       Mind, 2013.

172   Some researchers have said it's because with so many people in one
       place . . . These proposed explanations, as well as the explanation
       based on social ties, are in Wei Pan, Gourab Shoshal, Coco Krumme,
       Manuel Cebrian, Alex Pentland, "Urban Characteristics Attribut-
       able to Density-Driven Tie Information," paper presented at the
       NetSci Conference, Evanston, Illinois, 20 June 2012.

173   You might expect that it would cause people to make fewer phone calls . . .
       As shown in ibid.

173   But patterns of communication between companies within these clus-
       ters . . . Thomas J. Allen, Ornit Raz, Peter Gloor, "Does Geographic
       Clustering Still Benefit High Tech New Ventures? The Case of the
       Cambridge/Boston Biotech Cluster," MIT Engineering Systems Di-
       vision Working Paper Series, ESD-WP-2009-01, April 2009.

174   Research has shown that communication between engineers about tech-
       nical matters . . . T. J. Allen, G. W. Henn, *Organization and Architec-
       ture for Innovative Product Development* (Elsevier, 2006). Cited in
       Thomas J. Allen et al., op. cit.

175   Adam Grant of the University of Pennsylvania and James Berry of the
       University of North Carolina . . . Grant and Berry, op. cit.

176   It also requires buzz, interest, excitement . . . Peter A. Gloor, Jonas
       S. Krauss, Stefan Nann, "Coolfarming–How Cool People Create

Cool Trends," MIT Center for Collective Intelligence, USA & galaxyadvisors AG, Switzerland (2009).

CHAPTER TEN

178 You'll recall that teams have an intelligence all their own . . . The research was in Woolley et al., op. cit. (chap. 7, n. 7).

179 You look at thirty-six black-and-white photos of just the eye region . . . You can take the RME test at http://kgajos.eecs.harvard.edu/mite/.

179 In the new experiments, group members were separated . . . David Engel, Anita Woolley, Lisa X. Jing, Christopher F. Chabris, Thomas Malone, "Theory of Mind Predicts Collective Intelligence," *Proceedings of Collective Intelligence 2014*, Cambridge, Massachusetts, http://humancom putation.com/ci2014/papers/Active%20Papers%5CPaper%20106.pdf.

181 When researchers studied one-year-olds . . . Svetlana Lutchmaya, Simon Baron-Cohen, "Human Sex Differences in Social and Non-Social Looking Preferences at 12 Months of Age," *Infant Behavior and Development*, vol. 25, no. 3, 2002, pp. 319–325.

181 But in fact researchers had previously studied one-day-old babies . . . Jennifer Connellan, Simon Baron-Cohen, Sally Wheelwright, Anna Batki, Jag Ahluwalia, "Sex Differences in Human Neonatal Social Perception," *Infant Behavior and Development*, vol. 23, no. 1, 2000, pp. 113–118.

181 For that matter, it's possible to measure the testosterone in a baby's system before it's even born . . . Svetlana Lutchmaya, Simon Baron-Cohen, Peter Raggatt, "Foetal Testosterone and Eye Contact in 12-Month-Old Human Infants," *Infant Behavior and Development*, vol. 25, no. 3, 2002, pp. 327–335.

182 The deep distinction between men's and women's brains . . . Simon Baron-Cohen, "The Extreme Male Brain Theory of Autism," *Trends in Cognitive Science*, vol. 6, no. 6, 2002, pp. 248–254.

183 Of course, a number of computer pioneers were unsung women . . . Many of their stories are told particularly well in Walter Isaacson's *The Innovators* (Simon and Schuster, 2014).

184 An important one was articulated by Sally Helgesen . . . Sally Helgesen, *The Female Advantage: Women's Ways of Leadership* (Currency Doubleday, 1990).

184 Based on her study of women CEOs, and on earlier studies of men CEOs . . . The studies of male executives prominently included Henry Mintzberg's highly influential book, *The Nature of Managerial Work* (HarperCollins College Division, 1973).

185 Women's peripheral vision is wider than men's . . . Katharine McLennan, "The Neuroscience of Leadership and Culture," Mettle Group, pp. 15–16.

185   Brain imaging shows that in general, women's attention is engaged by
       many different things . . . "Intelligence in Men and Women Is a Gray
       and White Matter," *Science Daily*, 22 January 2005, http://www.sci
       encedaily.com/releases/2005/01/050121100142.htm.

185   Meredith Whitney, a financial analyst, predicted deep trouble . . .
       "The Analyst Who Rocked Citi," *Bloomberg Businessweek*, 26
       November 2007.

185   Sheila Bair, who chaired the Federal Deposit Insurance Corporation . . .
       Ryan Lizza, "The Contrarian," *New Yorker*, 6 July 2009.

186   Yet women seem to handle it easily . . . Helgesen, op. cit., pp. 58–59.

187   A quick and easy way to wipe out women's powers . . . Jack van Honk,
       Dennis J. Schutter, Peter A. Bos, Anne-Wil Kruijt, Eef G. Lentjes,
       Simon Baron-Cohen, "Testosterone Administration Impairs Cogni-
       tive Empathy in Women Depending on Second-to-Fourth Digit
       Ratio," *PNAS*, 7 February 2011, doi: /10.1073/pnas.1011891108.

188   Yet women's superior social abilities can also be negated in a different
       way . . . Anna T. Mayo, Jin Wook Chang, Rosalind M. Chow, Anita
       W. Woolley, "Do Women Make Groups Smarter? Understanding the
       Effects of Gender and Status Competition on Collective Intelli-
       gence," manuscript in preparation.

190   People who grow up in larger families tend to be more "prosocial" as
       adults . . . Paul A. M. Van Lange, Wilma Otten, Ellen M. N. De
       Bruin, Jeffrey A. Joireman, "Development of Prosocial, Individual-
       istic, and Competitive Orientations: Theory and Preliminary Evi-
       dence," *Journal of Personality and Social Psychology*, vol. 73, no. 4,
       1997, pp. 733–746.

190   We see that bigger families produce offspring who are more prosocial . . .
       Family size is declining worldwide in large part because average fam-
       ily size declines as average life expectancy and income increase.

190   Similarly, much research has shown that children raised in settings . . .
       Van Lange et al., op. cit.

191   Baron-Cohen, who proposed the distinction between the systemizing
       male brain and the empathizing female brain . . . Baron-Cohen, op. cit.

CHAPTER ELEVEN

195   Children whose "parents are very attentive to their elementary needs . . ."
       Van Lange et al., op. cit. (chap. 10, n. 18).

196   "We're changing how students interact . . ." Personal interview with
       Garth Saloner, 19 February 2013.

196   The Harvard Business School similarly puts all first-year students . . .
       The program is called Field Immersion Experiences in Leadership

Development (FIELD). For a detailed description, see http://www
.hbs.edu/mba/academic-experience/FIELD/Pages/default.aspx.

197 **Most important, as dean Nitin Nohria noted** ... From Nohria's January 2014 update to alumni and others associated with Harvard Business School.

197 **For example, DARPA developed software for the U.S. Navy** ... Robert R. Hoffman, Paul Ward, Paul J. Feltovich, Lia DiBello, Stephen M. Fiore, Dee H. Andrews, *Accelerated Expertise: Training for High Proficiency in a Complex World* (Psychology Press, 2014), pp. 102–103.

197 **Or consider what happened after Stanford professor Sebastian Thrun launched the era of massive open online courses** ... Presentation by Sebastian Thrun, Kiawah Island, South Carolina, 21 March 2013.

198 **As Sherry Turkle has written** ... Turkle, op. cit. (chap. 4, n. 16), p. 14.

199 **An important task on which certain teams of soldiers and Marines are trained** ... The task and the digital training are described in Chatham, "Toward a Second Training Revolution."

200 **Software created for the army as a demonstration project called Think Like a Commander** ... Scott B. Shadrick, James W. Lussier, "Training Complex Cognitive Skills: A Theme-Based Approach to the Development of Battlefield Skills," in *Development of Professional Expertise: Toward Measurement of Expert Performance and Design of Optimal Learning Environments* (Cambridge University Press, 2009).

201 **That came along in a program called Darwars Ambush** ... Chatham, "Toward a Second Training Revolution."

201 **One response was software called the Tactical Iraqi Language and Culture Trainer** ... Ibid.

202 **Soon the software could understand soldiers speaking in their beginner's Arabic or Pashto** ... W. Lewis Johnson, LeeEllen Friedland, Peter J. Schrider, Andre Valente, Sean Sheridan, "The Virtual Cultural Awareness Trainer (VCAT): Joint Knowledge Online's (JKO's) Solution to the Individual Operational Culture and Language Training Gap," updated version of a paper presented at ModSIM 2010.

202 **How much difference such software made to soldiers on the ground** ... Chatham, "Toward a Second Training Revolution."

202 **Then, in 2011, DARPA aimed to go far beyond all that** ... For DARPA's official description of SSIM, see http://www.darpa.mil/Our_Work/BTO/Programs/Strategic_Social_Interaction_Modules_SSIM.aspx.

203 **In job interviews, applicants have been asked how much they should charge to wash all the windows in Seattle** ... See, for example, this list of Google job interview questions at *Business Insider*: http://www.businessinsider.com/15-google-interview-questions-that-will-make-you-feel-stupid-2009-11?op=1.

203   **But, in fact, skills of human interaction are key even at Google** . . . The
      description and quotations are from Eric Schmidt and Jonathan
      Rosenberg, *How Google Works* (Grand Central Publishing, 2014).
204   **Google developed a cloud-based mobile game for helping team members
      work together** . . . Julie Clow, David Metcalf, "Mobile Gaming Mod-
      els: A Google Case Study and More," presentation at DevLearn
      2009, San Jose, California, 10–13 November 2009.

INDEX

Also by Geoff Colvin

"A profoundly important book."
—Dan Pink, author of *A Whole New Mind* and *To Sell Is Human*

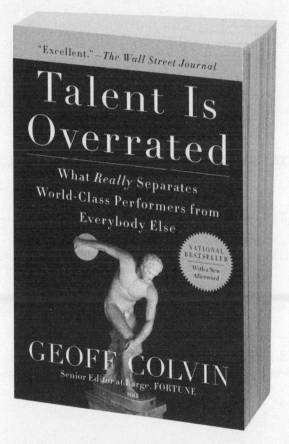

"A fascinating book." —Charlie Rose

"Provocative." —TIME

PORTFOLIO
PENGUIN